MURIEL SPARK:
An Odd Capacity for Vision

MURIEL SPARK:
An Odd Capacity for Vision

edited by
Alan Bold

VISION
and
BARNES & NOBLE

Vision Press Limited
Fulham Wharf
Townmead Road
London SW6 2SB

and

Barnes & Noble Books
81 Adams Drive
Totowa, NJ 07512

ISBN (UK) 0 85478 475 6
ISBN (US) 0 389 20482 X

Printed and bound in Great Britain by
Unwin Brothers Ltd.,
Old Woking, Surrey.
Phototypeset by Galleon Photosetting,
Ipswich, Suffolk.
MCMLXXXIV

Contents

Introduction

by ALAN BOLD

By imparting a metaphysical element of mystery to the facts of her fiction—for example Elsa's shadow that falls 'in the wrong direction' in *The Hothouse by the East River* (1973)—Muriel Spark has become well-known as one of the most enigmatic writers of her time. She has never been satisfied with photographic naturalism and even her realistic descriptions have an atmosphere of illusion. A self-conscious stylist, she always seems to sense a spiritual presence behind a physical substance. Her poem 'Elementary' considers the matter in the first two quatrains:

> Night, the wet, the onyx-faced
> Over the street was shining where
> I saw an object all displaced
> In black water and black air.
>
> Was it myself? If so I found
> An odd capacity for vision.
> Capacity, I understand
> Is limited by fixed precision. . . .

It is this 'odd capacity for vision' that is under investigation in the following pages.

Mrs. Spark's life has been an absorbing experience. She was born in Edinburgh in 1918 and educated at James Gillespie's School for Girls, fictionalized as Marcia Blaine School in *The Prime of Miss Jean Brodie* (1961). Growing up in Edinburgh, a city whose elegant appearance often conceals a squalid reality, she was aware of psychological as well as physical divisions since she was both Scottish and Jewish. In a letter of 22 April 1979 to the present writer, she said:

> I am certainly a writer of Scottish formation and of course think of myself as such. I think to describe myself as a 'Scottish

7

Writer' might be ambiguous as one wouldn't know if 'Scottish' applied to the writer or the writing. Then there is the complicated question of whether people of mixed inheritance, like myself, can call themselves Scottish. Some Scots deny it. But Edinburgh where I was born and my father was born has definitely had an affect on my mind, my prose style and my ways of thought. I wrote poetry from the age of nine. I spent most of my free hours in the Morningside Public Library between the ages of ten and sixteen.

After Edinburgh she lived for some time in Central Africa; during World War II she worked, in London, for the Political Intelligence Department of the Foreign Office. Her literary career began in post-war London where she edited, from 1947–49, the *Poetry Review* and wrote *Child of Light: A Reassessment of Mary Wollstonecraft Shelley* which was published in 1951, the year she won an *Observer* short-story competition. Her verse-collection *The Fanfarlo* appeared in 1952 but it was only after her conversion to Roman Catholicism, in 1954, that she began to publish novels, beginning with *The Comforters* (1957). By the time this first novel materialized Mrs. Spark was a mature woman of 39 whose 'odd capacity for vision' was firmly established in her own mind. Life, according to her outlook, was to be treated as a spectacle that must be scrutinized for evidence of spiritual, or supernatural, signs. Appearance was not to be accepted empirically but penetrated by the artist's vision.

The magnificent opening paragraph of *The Girls of Slender Means* (1963) shows how Mrs. Spark can peel back layer after layer of significance when she observes with her 'odd capacity for vision'. Ingeniously, she begins with a fairytale format ('Long ago') and ends on a metaphysical assumption:

> Long ago in 1945 all the nice people in England were poor, allowing for exceptions. The streets of the cities were lined with buildings in bad repair or in no repair at all, bomb-sites piled with stony rubble, houses like giant teeth in which decay had been drilled out, leaving only the cavity. Some bomb-ripped buildings looked like the ruins of ancient castles until, at a closer view, the wallpapers of various quite normal rooms would be visible, room above room, exposed, as on a stage, with one wall missing; sometimes a lavatory chain would dangle

8

over nothing from a fourth- or fifth-floor ceiling; most of all the staircases survived, like a new art-form, leading up and up to an unspecified destination that made unusual demands on the mind's eye. All the nice people were poor; at least, that was a general axiom, the best of the rich being poor in spirit.

As that passage shows, Mrs. Spark is an artist who imposes herself on her material. The scene is not simply depicted, it is transformed by linguistic means. There are striking similes— 'like giant teeth . . . like the ruins of ancient castles . . . like a new art-form'—and authorial opinions. It is apparent, indeed, that Mrs. Spark herself is making 'unusual demands on the mind's eye'. The straightforward rendering of so-called reality is not challenging enough for Mrs. Spark, so her work confronts realistic detail with surrealistic tension, invests natural incidents with supernatural overtones. Her fiction is not contained by a rigid narrative framework; it unfolds in a visionary dimension.

'I didn't go in for motives, I never have', says the partly-autobiographical narrator of Mrs. Spark's *Loitering With Intent* (1981). Fleur Talbot also says, speaking for Mrs. Spark,

> Without a mythology, a novel is nothing. The true novelist, one who understands the work as a continuous poem, is a myth-maker, and the wonder of the art resides in the endless different ways of telling a story, and the methods are mythological by nature.

Mrs. Spark's perception of the novel as a sustained prose-poem deserves to be taken seriously as it accounts for the extreme compression of her language, the elusive attitude to plot, the ostentatious artistry that often reminds the reader that a fictional character is actually an imaginative invention. Only Jean Brodie, among Mrs. Spark's creations, seems to exist independently of the novel that defined her; so much so, of course, that Miss Brodie has been remade in (successively) theatrical, cinematic and televisual images. Mrs. Spark's other characters are an integral part of an elaborate textual structure.

The most obvious early application of Mrs. Spark's poetic method of construction occurs in her fourth novel *The Ballad of Peckham Rye* (1960). Metrically we expect a ballad to unfold in

couplets or, more often, in quatrains such as those employed
by Mrs. Spark in 'The Ballad of the Fanfarlo':

> 'Oh I am Samuel Cramer,' he said,
> 'Born of a German father
> Who was as pale as my naked bone,
> And a brown Chilean mother.'

But the ballad techniques can also be recast in prose by
writers who plunge rapidly into the action, who use con-
versational contrasts to advance the narrative, and who
habitually allude to other-worldly phenomena. *The Ballad of
Peckham Rye* uses these methods, and Mrs. Spark draws the
reader into her design by opening on an exchange that could
be read as a quatrain with identical rhymes:

> 'Get away from here, you dirty swine,' she said.
> 'There's a dirty swine in every man,' he said.
> 'Showing your face round here again,' she said.
> 'Now, Mavis, now, Mavis,' he said.

Like some of the greatest verse-ballads, Mrs. Spark's prose-
Ballad has a supernatural participant. After discussing the
devil, Dougal Douglas asks Humphrey Place to feel the little
bumps on his head and explains he had them removed by a
plastic surgeon who 'did an operation and took away the two
horns'. In closing, the book restates the ballad motif by
indicating that the world we see is not all there is, for
Humphrey is aware of Peckham Rye 'for an instant looking
like a cloud of green and gold, the people seeming to ride upon
it, as you might say there was another world than this.'

As a satirist Mrs. Spark also uses poetic precedents ranging
from Dryden to Eliot. Not for her the hyperbolic savagery, the
verbal overkill, of Swift or Wyndham Lewis. Instead, in *The
Abbess of Crewe* (1974) she does as Dryden, in *Absalom and
Achitophel*, did before her; she establishes religious parallels for
the politically powerful and presents them in an exquisitely
textured work. Mrs. Spark's satire sets in an English abbey the
scandal that eventually forced Richard Nixon to resign as
President of the United States in 1974. The Nixonian figure in
Mrs. Spark's book, Alexandra, rises from Sub-Prioress to
Abbess in an election campaign she orchestrates expertly. She
puts electronic surveillance on her rival Sister Felicity who—

like Nixon's opponent George McGovern—'wants everyone to be liberated'. Aided by the trouble-shooting, globe-trotting Sister Gertrude, as Nixon's Secretary of State Henry Kissinger, and abetted by Sisters Mildred and Warburga, as Nixon's closest advisers John Ehrlichman and Bob Haldeman, Alexandra encourages a Nixonian dirty trick and two Jesuit novices break into the Abbey to steal love-letters from Felicity's work-box. When Alexandra is compelled to release her tapes she finds, as did Nixon, that 'some passages are missing'.

Like Dryden, Mrs. Spark sustains the satire through an intelligent attention to details. But *The Abbess of Crewe* is not only poetic in its satiric tone for the entire text is organized like a modernist sequence. Ecclesiastical allusions are juxtaposed against poetic quotations, discursive sections are set against lyrical interludes, fantasy is counterpointed with farce. After a factual passage about systems of recorded sound the nuns incongruously utter 'Amen', then Mrs. Spark lifts her prose to another level:

> The Abbess of Crewe's parlour glows with bright ornaments and brightest of all is a two-foot statue of the Infant of Prague. The Infant is adorned with its traditional robes, the episcopal crown and vestments embedded with such large and so many rich and gleaming jewels it would seem they could not possibly be real.

The glow and the jewels were perhaps prompted by 'A Game of Chess' in *The Waste Land*. Certainly Mrs. Spark's abrupt changes of narrative mood, her swift transitions between everyday and exalted modes of language, her combination of ritual and romance are all reminiscent of Eliot's great poem. The constructional principles of *The Waste Land* have not been lost on Mrs. Spark. She has been able to assemble *The Abbess of Crewe* as a modernist work of satire. As an amalgam of special compositional effects it is a highly effective scenario and, as the Abbess of Crewe says of scenarios:

> They are an art form based on facts. A good scenario is a garble. A bad one is a bungle. They need not be plausible, only hypnotic, like all good art.

At the end of *The Abbess of Crewe*, Alexandra gives instructions for the preparation of selective transcripts of her tape-recordings. Instead of the Nixonian euphemism 'Expletive deleted' she opts for the phrase 'Poetry deleted'. Were the poetry to be deleted from Mrs. Spark's novels there would be little point reading them. As it is, a poetic consciousness informs the novels. In approaching Mrs. Spark's novels as prose-poems the reader is not, of course, looking for a series of purple passages; poetry for Mrs. Spark is the formal arrangement of her imaginative impulses, not a synonym for emotional over-indulgence. She brings to prose the literary repertoire of a poet. Even such a seemingly conventional novel as *The Mandelbaum Gate* (1965) is rich in poetic devices, and not simply because Freddy Hamilton, the diplomat, composes 'rondeux, redeoubles, villanelles, rondels or Sicilian octaves' or discusses with Barbara Vaughan, the heroine, 'the dear subject of formal English lyrical verse'. The novel has a characteristic set of contrasts—for example Barbara's personal predicament versus the Eichmann trial—as well as a highly poetic use of imagery. Thus we learn that 'the Israelis treated facts like antibiotic shots, injecting them into the visitor'; that Barbara searched 'her own motives like a murder squad'; and that Freddy

> experienced the sensation of one who has had a disturbing dream, the culmination of which was the ringing of a telephone, and wakes with relief to discover the telephone is in fact ringing beside his bed, and answers it, only to hear disturbing news.

Mrs. Spark's ability to make her novels read like 'disturbing news' is, I submit, a poetic gift since it depends on subtle linguistic methods. In his stimulating essay 'Is Verse a Dying Technique?' Edmund Wilson distinguishes between verse and poetry by regarding the former as a prosodic matter and the latter as a visionary manner, and he cites Flaubert's desire (expressed in a letter of 27 March 1853 to Louise Colet) 'to give verse-rhythm to prose, yet to leave it prose and very much prose'. While the epics of Neruda, Pound, Williams, Zukovsky, MacDiarmid and others refute his general contention that the long poem is a thing of the past, Wilson's conclusions have a particular application to the works of Mrs. Spark:

> the technique of prose is inevitably tending more and more to take over the material which had formerly provided the subjects for composition in verse. . . . The technique of prose today seems thus to be absorbing the technique of verse.

Modernist prose, as initiated by Flaubert and evolved by Joyce, does not use language as a means to an end but as a ritual defining a religion of art. Roman Catholic by conversion and poetic by inclination, Mrs. Spark subscribes to the aesthetic religion of modernism, and so uses her verbal material ritualistically to create an ambiance in which events do not occur according to a conventional narrative logic but appear to satisfy the author's imaginative needs. She produces a sacramental aura, a 'Transfiguration of the Commonplace', to use the title of Sandy Stranger's psychological treatise in *The Prime of Miss Jean Brodie*.

It is worth observing Mrs. Spark's poetic muse in action in two distinct ways as seen, first, in *The Prime of Miss Jean Brodie*; and, second, in three stylistically similar novels that virtually amount to a macabre trilogy. These examples confirm, I think, that what Mrs. Spark brought to the novel was a poetic sensibility and an aesthetic obsession with ritual. *The Prime of Miss Jean Brodie* is a persuasive study of the closed mind, the élitist mentality that powers the body of the heroine. Jean believes in the principle of leadership and the Calvinist doctrine of the elect. When Sandy Stranger, member of the Brodie set, muses on Edinburgh she realizes that Calvinism is built into the city and she aches for its influence:

> In fact, it was the religion of Calvin of which Sandy felt deprived, or rather a specified recognition of it. She desired this birthright; something definite to reject. It pervaded the place in proportion as it was unacknowledged. . . . Sandy was unable to formulate these exciting propositions; nevertheless she experienced them in the air she breathed, she sensed them in the curiously defiant way in which the people she knew broke the Sabbath, and she smelt them in the excesses of Miss Brodie in her prime. . . . In this oblique way, she began to sense what went to the makings of Miss Brodie who had elected herself to grace in so particular a way and with more exotic suicidal enchantment than if she had simply taken to drink like other spinsters who couldn't stand it any more.

Miss Brodie's heroes are Mussolini, Franco and Hitler, and she believes women should be dedicated. Although 'in many ways Miss Brodie was an Edinburgh spinster of the deepest dye' her closed mind contains fascinating fantasies. She

13

intends to live vicariously through her set of selected disciples, her élite and her elect: 'all my pupils are the *crème de la crème*', she says; 'Give me a girl at an impressionable age, and she is mine for life.' Sandy Stranger, the most reflective of the disciples, realizes the truth about the self-styled leader: 'it occurred to Sandy, there at the end of the Middle Meadow Walk, that the Brodie set was Miss Brodie's *fascisti*.'

Like many other Scots, Miss Brodie has a divided self. She idolizes the fascists yet deplores the team spirit; she speaks of love and freedom yet sleeps with the dreary Mr. Lowther and denies herself to one-armed Mr. Lloyd because he is married; she loves Rome and the Italians yet opposes the Church of Rome:

> Her disapproval of the Church of Rome was based on her assertions that it was a church of superstition, and that only people who did not want to think for themselves were Roman Catholics.

With frequent time-shifts the novel closes in on the action, usually seen through Sandy Stranger's eyes. Sandy is a schemer who becomes Miss Brodie's Judas, but also a dreamer who has imaginary conversations with fictional characters like Alan Breck and great artists like Pavlova. With her friend Jenny Gray she concocts a romantic tale around Jean Brodie's love affair with Hugh Carruthers (who died at Flanders). Sandy's fantasies are flattened by the arbitrary facts of life and she retreats from Miss Brodie who is suddenly seen as ridiculous rather than sublime. After ruining Miss Brodie's teaching career, Sandy becomes Sister Helena of the Catholic Church 'in whose ranks she had found quite a number of Fascists much less agreeable than Miss Brodie'.

The novel creates its own claustrophobically closed world in which the characters move with ritualistic deliberation. It is an uncertain world whose ethical ideals are destroyed by internal division and external threat. Mrs. Spark enters into this world as a poetic explorer and is acute enough to record contradictions native to Edinburgh. For example, the privileged girls who attend Marcia Blaine School are out walking when they are confronted by a sight that shows them their less fortunate fellow citizens:

They had come to the end of Lauriston Place, past the fire
station, where they were to get on a tram-car to go to tea with
Miss Brodie in her flat at Churchhill. A very long queue lined
this part of the street. They were without collars, in shabby
suits. They were talking and spitting and smoking little bits of
cigarette held between middle finger and thumb.

'We shall cross here,' said Miss Brodie and herded the set
across the road.

Monica Douglas whispered, 'They are the Idle.'

'In England they are called the Unemployed. They are
waiting to get their dole from the labour bureau,' said Miss
Brodie. 'You must all pray for the Unemployed, I will write you
out the special prayer for them. . . . Sometimes they go and
spend their dole on drink before they go home, and their
children starve. They are our brothers, Sandy, stop staring at
once. In Italy the unemployment problem has been solved.'

The incident has touches reminiscent of Eliot who watched
'lonely men in shirt sleeves' (in 'The Love Song of J. Alfred
Prufrock'), noted 'a city block . . . And short square fingers
stuffing pipes' ('Preludes'), observed 'Twisted faces from the
bottom of the street' ('Morning at the Window'). Thus the
passage represents a real scene transfigured by an outlook
shaped by modernist poetry. At such moments Spark comes
across as a virtuoso who can imply a universal truth from a few
particular juxtapositions. Indeed, her physically small novel
expands imaginatively to contain religious tension, class
conflict, international politics, civil war and unemployment.
Such concision is rare, but this densely packed prose is Mrs.
Spark's way of expressing poetic insights in a fiction formed by
her own vision.

Mrs. Spark excels at evoking the enigmatic overtones of
modern life. In three thematically related novels—*The Driver's
Seat* (1970), *Not To Disturb* (1971), *The Hothouse by the East River*
(1973)—she makes a prolonged raid on the bizarre. All three
novels are written in the present tense and Mrs. Spark must
have kept both senses of the word 'tense' in her mind, for the
books are as full of tension as they are of immediacy. They
suggest the coexistence of fact and fantasy, exhibit a
surrealistic ambiguity, and allow dreams to dissolve into
nightmares. In the traditional novel the author knows all; in

the first of Mrs. Spark's quintessentially poetic novels the author keeps her distance from her heroine, for 'Who knows her thoughts? Who can tell?'

The Driver's Seat is the study of a willing sacrificial victim. Lise, a 34-year-old office worker, flies south to organize her own murder. In order to attract the maximum attention she dresses in an outrageous outfit—red and white striped coat; purple, orange and blue skirt; yellow top—which provokes the hilarity of onlookers who, when the events of the novel are over, will become witnesses with good cause to remember this particular victim. Lise is conspicuous by her colourful presence. She is obsessively in search for a man who is, to use her favourite expression, her type. To drive home the macabre nature of the situation Mrs. Spark elevates prolepsis to a stylistic principle. Chapter Three begins by giving the game away, so depriving the reader of a major element of surprise:

> She will be found tomorrow morning dead from multiple stab-wounds, her wrists bound with a silk scarf and her ankles bound with a man's necktie in the grounds of an empty villa, in a park of the foreign city to which she is travelling on the flight now boarding at Gate 14.

Lise chooses for her murderer a rosy-faced young businessman who conforms to her type. For much of the book he is conspicuous by his absence then reappears for the bloody climax the book has been inexorably reaching for. At first the man avoids Lise's attentions; when she sits near him on the plane he moves away. Lise talks instead to Bill, a food faddist about to set up a macrobiotic establishment in Naples. Explaining to Lise that her macrobiotic régime demands an orgasm a day, he wonders if she will oblige him that evening. As he takes her to her hotel in a taxi he makes a pass at her and spills his macrobiotic seed on the floor. This sexual metaphor is at once comic and revealing. Lise, it seems, is not interested in sustaining life through sex.

All the symbols are substantiated in this way. Lise assumes the driver's seat, literally and figuratively, to proclaim that in a deterministic universe she will nevertheless choose her own destiny. Eventually her dream comes true when she finds her perfect homicidal type—the man from the plane. Lise presents him with a knife, although she knows, intuitively, he is a sex maniac recently charged with attempted murder. She persuades him to come with her in the car and, once more in the driver's seat, takes him to a park. She instructs him exactly how to kill her and he carries out every instruction but one. Readers aware of Mrs. Spark's meticulous attention to language will realize that her pun on 'plunges' makes it plain that the murderer ignores Lise's request to desist from sexual penetration:

> 'I don't want any sex,' she shouts. 'You can have it afterwards. Tie my feet and kill, that's all. They will come and sweep it up in the morning.'
> All the same, he plunges into her, with the knife poised high.
> 'Kill me,' she says, and repeats it in four languages.

Not To Disturb, the second book in the macabre poetic trilogy, portrays people who exist without recognizably human emotions. Like *The Driver's Seat*, it relies on prolepsis. Lister, butler to the Baron and Baroness Klopstock, stage-manages the aftermath of a violent event—the suicide of the Baron after he has murdered the Baroness and her lover Victor Passerat. Lister has arranged a press conference, sold the movie rights of the sensational story, and has a cinematographer and soundtrack man on hand. Mr. Samuel, the cinematographer, thinks the whole plot a 'first-rate movie script' as there is a Gothic mood of menace, a symbolic storm and a cast of eccentrics including the Baron's imbecile brother who is kept in the attic. Mrs. Spark is, again, making a verbal assault on the idea of a deterministic universe; in her life and her art she insists on free will. Lister, for example, explains that his own plot is a foregone conclusion: 'To all intents and purposes, they're already dead although as a matter of banal fact, the night's business has still to accomplish itself.' As a matter of equally banal fact, a novel is normally narrated in a deterministic manner. Mrs. Spark's poetic approach rejects the rôle of the novelist as surrogate God and solipsistic creator. By playing conceptual games with the reader Mrs. Spark suggests that life, like art, should never be treated as a foregone conclusion. The title of her novel is appropriately ironic. The Baron has given orders that the servants are not to disturb him. Yet they

are more than disturbing, they are determined to com-
mercialize his death while he is still alive. Mrs. Spark is
compressing the novel into an overwhelming image that
projects her vision of an infernal world whose citizens seem
more dead than alive.

'One should live first, then die, not die then live; everything
to its own time.' That sentence poignantly informs the fantasy
The Hothouse by the East River which is told, like the other two
powerfully poetic novels, in the present tense. It concerns a
group of ghosts who have been brought into collective consciousness by the restlessness of one of them—Paul Hazlett, a
reluctant corpse whose 'heart knocks on the sides of the coffin'.
Paul lives in a posh New York apartment with his wife Elsa
whose shadow falls in the wrong direction. Mrs. Spark
introduces a suspenseful element into the novel by bringing
Elsa in contact with Helmut Kiel, a double agent she last
glimpsed in 1944. Paul would be alarmed unless he could
rationalize on the impossibility of it all, for he knows that he
and Elsa were killed in 1944, at St. Pancras station, when a
V-2 bomb fell directly on the train in which they were sitting.
The novel thus explores the life Paul and Elsa might have had
if they had settled in New York after the war, if they had had
two children, if they had acquired enough money to live in
comfort. They have a life, nevertheless, as literary creations
that hover between the reality the reader invests them with
and the illusion the author attributes to them. Mrs. Spark is
alive to the way so many people—in life and in art—accept a
death-in-life. When Paul and Elsa watch the ghosts of friends
who died with them in 1944, she says 'You would think they
were alive' and he adds 'One can't tell the difference.'

Even as she teases the reader with fantasies and tricks them
with poetic ploys that disrupt the narrative, Mrs. Spark has a
serious purpose. Her novels do not evade what governments
recognize as reality, as witness her catalogue in *The Hothouse by
the East River*:

> We already have the youth problem, the racist problem, the
> distribution problem, the political problem, the economic
> problem, the crime problem, the matrimonial problem, the
> ecological problem, the divorce problem, the domiciliary
> problem, the consumer problem, the birth-rate problem, the

middle-age problem, the health problem, the sex problem, the incarceration problem, the educational problem, the fiscal problem, the unemployment problem, the physiopsychodynamics problem, the homosexual problem, the traffic problem, the obesity problem, the heterosexual problem . . .

and so on. Her poetic aesthetic insists that this level of reality is itself an illusion and that those who are aware of it alone are as good as dead, since they refuse to recognize that art offers access to a more intense form of existence. The road to this richly spiritual life is paved with poetic intentions, and Mrs. Spark encourages her readers to accept the life-enhancing rewards of literature. As Fleur Talbot says, in *Loitering With Intent*, 'you must understand that everything happens to an artist; time is always redeemed, nothing is lost and wonders never cease.'

Like Gerard Manley Hopkins, Mrs. Spark is possessed by the grandeur of the world and correspondingly distressed by the everyday evidence of negativity. In her fiction the grandeur is simulated by a language that draws attention to its own creative qualities; the negativity is expressed through sinister or diabolic interventions. This struggle between good and evil, always present in Mrs. Spark's work, has a moralistic point. Still, by saturating her prose in poetic qualities she draws an entirely aesthetic moral. Accepting Eliot's assurance that there is . 'a lifetime burning in every moment' ('East Coker'), Mrs. Spark creates characters who are perpetually in search of their own salvation. Miss Brodie, Barbara Vaughan, Elsa Hazlett and others command the reader's attention because of their immense energy and constant search for a destiny. For Mrs. Spark the world is forever made anew, through imaginative involvement, and she opposes the defeatism of determinism. In her poem 'Canaan' she issues her artistic credo in a succinct quatrain:

> No year is twice the same, nor has occurred
> Before. We bandy by the name of grief,
> Grief which is like no other. Not a leaf
> Repeats itself, we only repeat the word.

'I have never', says Fleur Talbot in *Loitering With Intent*, 'known an artist who at some time in his life has not come into contact with pure evil.' Mrs. Spark frequently indicates the existence of evil in the world, but she is equally anxious to deliver an optimistic message. As she says, again through Fleur Talbot, 'I conceive everything poetically' and this accounts for the edifying endings, the final flourishes that bring her books to a triumphant conclusion. There is the 'cloud of green and gold' (*The Ballad of Peckham Rye*), the 'harking image of former and former seas' (*The Public Image*), the 'sunlight . . . laughing on the walls' (*Not To Disturb*), the 'lithe cloud of unknowing' (*The Hothouse by the East River*), the 'cornfield of sublimity' (*The Abbess of Crewe*), the 'kindly fruits of the earth' (*The Takeover*), the 'grace of God' (*Loitering With Intent*). It is, finally, the poetic quality that shines through and makes Mrs. Spark such an affirmative writer. Indeed, the only problem is in recognizing the place of the visionary in a world short on values.

Acknowledgements: extracts from the works of Muriel Spark are reprinted by permission of Harold Ober Associates Inc., copyright © 1984 by Copyright Administration Ltd.

Note: as this book went to press before the publication of Muriel Spark's novel *The Only Problem* (London: The Bodley Head, 1984), contributors have throughout referred to *Loitering With Intent* as Mrs. Spark's latest novel—which it was at the time of writing.

Part One:
THE FLESH MADE WORD

1

Ridiculous Demons

by FRANCIS RUSSELL HART

'What are you writing about these days?' Baron Willi asks the heroine-novelist of Muriel Spark's first novel.[1] Caroline is, she replies, still at her book on 'Form in the Modern Novel', but is having difficulty 'with the chapter on realism'. One always does. Likewise, with a chapter on 'supernaturalism'. For the term, like 'realism', is notoriously relative and variable. Like 'realism', it may refer to a metaphysical belief, or to an aesthetic mode, or to one of numerous kinds of rhetorical or symbolic relation between belief and mode. The nature of reality and of realism in Spark's fiction partakes of both. The relations between the real and the supernatural are not mere problems of aesthetic mode or affiliation, but problems of meaning and belief.

The Sophisticated Reader comes, as usual, armed with generic expectations; and as usual, the armour may become a trap. Shall we 'place' Muriel Spark in the 'Gothic' tradition deriving from the late enlightenment, or in its romantic aftergrowth, Natural Supernaturalism?[2] Her early literary interests might suggest as much; she has, after all, written at length about Mary Shelley and Emily Brontë. Shall we associate her instead with the mock-Gothic—originating, in fact, at the same time and in the same fiction (see Walpole's *Castle of Otranto*), but commonly linked with Jane Austen? One critic has called Spark 'Jane Austen of the Surrealists', and another amends the phrase to 'Jane Austen; nevertheless, the grotesque'.[3] Is she affiliated with the later nineteenth-century development, the psychological 'ghost story', as done by Aiken, Harvey, Blackwood, the two Jameses (M.R. and Henry), and sketched by Peter Penzoldt?[4] Her books are amply supplied with apparitions and demons, with preternatural interventions. However, that tradition of the 'supernatural', as Penzoldt observes, represents an attack on rationalism, a counter-rationalistic motive; Spark's motive is radically otherwise.

It may be that—in the puzzling cliché of literary historians— her fiction has grown out of such traditions. It may be possible to misread her as a late romantic seduced by the occult. But for the people of her novels such a seduction is a great spiritual danger, and a surrender to it results in demonic absurdity. The novelist too is subject to that danger; the process of fiction itself becomes a struggle against that surrender. And so, the reader must also be vulnerable to such a misunderstanding, for demonology and the ridiculous, often joined in folklore, mix uneasily in the novel. It is not the worst of plights that the reader should discover his vulnerability.

Spark's latest novel offers striking clues to the danger and the struggle. *Loitering With Intent* (1981) is a novel about autobiography, and—that most ambiguous of fictions—an autobiographical novel. It is as the heroine-writer says in *Robinson* (1958):

> I am as near the mark as myth is to history, the apocrypha to the canon. I seek no justification for this habit, it is one of the things I do.[5]

One of the things Muriel Spark does best is to play teasingly with the veridical rôle of the novelist. But in this case it is difficult not to catch two reliable clues.

The heroine Fleur has a clerical-editorial job working for a blackmailer, Sir Quentin Oliver, who presides over an Autobiographical Association. After a long contest of blackmail and counter-blackmail, theft and counter-theft, Fleur escapes and has this to say about it:

> Although in reality I wasn't yet rid of Sir Quentin and his little sect, they were morally outside of myself, they were objectified. I would write about them one day. In fact, under one form or another, whether I have liked it or not, I have written about

them ever since, the straws of which I have made my bricks.
(196)

The same might easily be said by and about Muriel Spark. It
is the text of this essay.

The other clue has to do with two opposing models Fleur
brings to her reflections on autobiography. She urges members
of the Autobiographical Association to read Newman's
Apologia pro vita sua, only to find that Newman is dangerously
misunderstood, only to reject 'the whole Newman idea which
up to now I had thought enchanting' (95), and to prefer the
Life of Cellini, 'a far better model . . . robust and full-blooded
as it was' (104–5). The 'Newman idea' for which she now feels
'a revulsion against an awful madness' is the belief Newman
ascribes to his evangelical youth: 'my mistrust of the reality of
material phenomena . . . the thought of two and two only
supreme and luminously self-evident beings, myself and my
Creator' (94–5). Fleur protests, 'You can't live with an I-and-
thou relationship to God and doubt the reality of the rest of
life' (96). The long imaginative struggle of Fleur-Muriel with
the Sir Quentins and their sects is, in fact, a struggle for the
'reality of the rest of life' against those who would deny it.

It is a struggle to affirm what Matthew Finch says in *The
Bachelors* (1960):

> What do you expect of a spiritualist? His mind's attuned to the
> ghouls of the air all day long. How can he be expected to
> consider the moral obligations of the flesh? The man's a dualist.
> No sacramental sense. . . . You've got to affirm the oneness of
> reality in some form or another. (87)

To affirm what Barbara says in *The Mandelbaum Gate* (1965):

> either religious faith penetrates everything in life or it doesn't.
> There are some experiences that seem to make nonsense of all
> separations of sacred from profane—they seem childish. Either
> the whole of life is unified under God or everything falls apart.
> (283)

And to demonstrate what Muriel Spark observes in an essay
on Proust (quoted by Peter Kemp as the genesis of *The
Bachelors*,[6] but equally basic to the other struggles with Sir
Quentin and his sect):

25

present-day Christian creative writing, that which is most
involved in an attempt to combat materialism, reflects a
materialism of its own; this takes the form of a dualistic attitude
towards matter and spirit. They are seen too much in moral
conflict, where the spirit triumphs by virtue of disembodiment.
This is really an amoral conception of spirit.

Such amoral disembodiments of spirit provide Spark's fiction
with its ghosts and demons. The struggle is between two
materialisms and two kinds of materializers.

The trick is that the two have much in common. Like the
spiritualist's, the artist's mind is 'attuned to the ghouls of the
air all day long'. Both traffic in demons, and both practise
exorcism. Confusion may result from the fact that the
antagonists can possess a single person—Dougal in *The Ballad
of Peckham Rye* (1960) and Ronald in *The Bachelors*, to mention
only two. Artist and diabolist may seem hard to distinguish,
for the fiction-maker is of the devil's party even when serving
God's ends. Demonology occasionally takes its revenge, even
on unsuspecting readers who miss the admonition: 'Our revels
now are ended. Be still, be watchful.'[7] Reader-critics who seek
High Seriousness, who demand simple coherences, who dislike
the mingling of terror and absurdity and distrust parodic
play—such readers have been puzzled, put off, even (with
Patricia Stubbs) dismayed to find Spark pulling the carpet out
from under her characters, 'hampering her reader's willing
suspension of disbelief', leaving him 'baulked of his normal
reaction to a story'.[8] The language exposes the critic here. A
Coleridgian suspension of disbelief has little to do with the
problem of belief in Spark. Many an artist in satire has
operated by baulking 'normal reactions'. And yet, the 'problem', as Elsa might say, gazing out at Nothing over the East
River, is Real.

We must not use our time belabouring the difficulties of
Spark's critics, and yet the assumptions of two are instructive
when it comes to her 'supernaturalism'. Stubbs expects Spark
to allow her religious belief to 'harmonize' life's 'disparate
entities'. A truly 'religious' novel, she insists, must not only
sustain a 'perspective . . . larger than that of the ordinary
novel', but also have 'the effect of lifting up her narrative onto
another plane, giving a sense of the human spirit reaching up

and outwards with all the grandeur and sublimity of which it is capable'. Such a perspective, such an effect, cannot be sustained in an art of satiric or parodic play, where 'delight and amusement' undercut 'logic and reason', and where the novel is seen as an 'odd, irresponsible' thing to write, inspired by the Father of Lies.[9]

There are several revealing fallacies in the Stubbs position, not least in the conviction that *The Mandelbaum Gate* is (as of 1973) Spark's 'most successful novel' and at the same time 'quite different in kind' from all the rest. (I have no idea which of the novels is 'most successful', nor does the question interest me.) Which of the fallacies is most interesting? Is it the mistaking of the nature of satire and parody? (Eminent critics of *Don Quixote* still struggle with this problem, after all.) Is it the mistaking of Spark's intent, which, as *Loitering With Intent* best reminds us, is the aim of the comic exorcist? Is it the misunderstanding (or rejection) of Spark's religious perspective? Perhaps so. The insistence that a religious novel be removed from the 'ordinary' onto 'another plane' reveals the problem. The taste for 'grandeur and sublimity' sounds perilously close to the very romantic 'spirituality' that Spark is consistently ridiculing. The taste is for a spiritual joy and transcendence that humanity (Spark believes[10]) is incapable of achieving for long, if ever. The taste is for harmony and balance, and these can have little force in a world where, amid an elegant, secular city, there arises a black primitive crag proclaiming Nevertheless. The attitude toward such 'supernaturalism' in the novels is, in fact, that of a satiric demonologist for whom 'harmony' and 'balance' are signals of ridiculously Slender spiritual Means.

Appropriately, Stubbs quotes Frank Baldanza's article (1965) on the supernatural in Spark:

> What she is in fact doing, over the trajectory of her entire career, is experimenting with a series of solutions to the aesthetic problem of accommodating both the supernatural and the naturalistic in her works, with the result that the naturalistic point of view has, at least for the present [as of *The Girls of Slender Means*], gradually gained ground over the occult, and has greatly subordinated the supernatural.[11]

Now, in the blessed light of hindsight this statement is worth scrutiny for what it reveals. There is the assumption that

27

'accommodation' of the supernatural to the natural is an *aesthetic problem*, and that 'accommodation' is what is sought. There is the term 'naturalistic', which is quite alien to Spark's Catholic Realism, a realism not of aesthetic mode but of metaphysical belief. Finally, the 'supernatural' is virtually equated with the 'occult'. On the contrary, Spark's imaginative struggle with the Sir Quentins and their sects is the battle of that Realism against the occult, for the occult is a spurious spiritualism. Her Realism insists on the reality of the commonplace (recall the title of Sandy Stranger's odd treatise[12]) and holds that the commonplace may be transfigured. Indeed, if it is not transfigured it may turn demonic. 'You've got to affirm the oneness of reality in some form or other', and Spark's form is the novel. 'Either the whole of life is unified under God or everything falls apart', and Spark shows it falling apart into ridiculous and demonic unrealities. When gods are gone, said Novalis (more or less), ghosts are everywhere. When you believe in God, Spark wrote, you can believe in everything.

Ronald, the priestly epileptic of *The Bachelors*, is often afflicted with the thought that the people of his world are all 'a company of ridiculous demons' (111). He gets up from his bed at midnight and goes out to 'walk off his demons', to 'send these figures away like the demons of the air until he could think of them again with indifference or amusement or wonder'. But 'it is all demonology and to do with creatures of the air', he thinks (218–19). What does he mean?

Demonology, according to conventional definitions, has two meanings. It is the study of demons and of demonic possession; it is also a belief in the reality and the activity of demons. The question of belief is the one that concerns us. Does Spark believe—do her characters believe—would she have the reader believe—in demons? If we accept the naturalistic definition of Martin Ebon, it is not difficult to do so (and in fact his will suffice for the 'Gothic' novel's demonology):

> The demons among us have many psychological, sociological, political, and even economic names. We are each other's demons. We are, above all, our own demons. The person who feels possessed by a demon is simply a few steps beyond the many irrational acts of compulsion and taboo that most of us practise almost automatically and unknowingly.[13]

28

We see the people of *The Takeover* (1976) taken over by such demons. For them, the nature of reality undergoes a radical change, and all they can do, we are told, is to personalize and demonologize the abstractions of their lives, believing them to be real. They are not, of course. They are mere apparitions; they come to seem real, material, hence demonic. A demon is an unreality reified, given spurious materiality, and believed in as reality.

What permits the takeover by demons? Ebon's kind of naturalistic explanation will not suffice. For Spark, it is the denial of reality, which is the denial of God and of the substantial manifestations of grace. Demonology is unreality and disunity. The only corrective is a discipline that is from God; other disciplines are from the self, hence unreal. The countervision to demonology is sacramentalism, which affirms the oneness of spiritual and material, of sacred and profane. Sacramentalism mediates by the power or grace of transfiguration. Such is the positive corrective. The negative way is by ridicule, satiric exposure, whereby demonic apparitions are shown to be unreal and are made to disappear. The negative way—the way of the satiric artist—is complex. The novelist places Sir Quentin and his sect 'morally outside of myself', where she can think of them 'with indifference or amusement or wonder'. They are turned, that is, into the demonic apparitions of story, of art. To be denied the reality they pretend to, they must be accorded a reality they do not warrant, must be materialized. Thus, the novelist must traffic in 'ghouls of the air', practise a kind of demonology, summon up apparitions to fight apparitions. The novelist's creative process is a demonological battle with her subject.

The preternatural elements of Spark's fiction are best understood as parts of this process, however remote they may seem from what is conventionally labelled 'supernatural'. Some are mysterious intervenients that have no worldly source or origin. Others are commonplace in origin, but in function and impact they have the same effect. The mysterious shadow that trails after Elsa in *The Hothouse by the East River* (1973) can hardly be confused ontologically with the grotesque 'apparition' of a toy balloon that hovers outside Annabel's window in *The Public Image* (1968) and terrifies the blackmailer Billy, but the

29

effect of terror and disorientation is the same. Georgina Hogg in *The Comforters* (1957) is not a conventional ghost, nor is Lise of *The Driver's Seat* (1970) a spectral demon. But they have given up reality and so their effect is spectral or demonic. The telephones of *Memento Mori* (1959), the typewriters of *The Comforters*, the 'bugs' in the cloistral trees of Crewe, the body in the pensione garden of *Territorial Rights* (1979), the dormant bomb in the garden of *The Girls of Slender Means* (1963) and the Schiaparelli dress upstairs—all are 'real' enough. But when characters engage with them in mysterious encounters, they imply powers of another world; they loiter with revelatory intent. Abruptly, sometimes catastrophically, they intervene in commonplace lives to admonish. They are what writers on ghostlore call 'veridical', truth-speaking; like ghosts, they harbour or disinter powerful secrets.[14]

The servant Pablo in *Not To Disturb* (1971) claims that ghosts and fantasies arise from sex repression.[15] And most of the people of the novels 'see' such interventions in the same way, the way they see the shadow of *Hothouse*, the way Baron Willi treats Caroline's ghostly typewriter in *The Comforters*. They deny such manifestations reality, believe them figments of psychic allegory (as some critics treat Spark's books), treat them as 'problems' to be exorcized by secular therapies or specious spiritualisms. A few—including the heroines— believe them real, as Barbara in *The Mandelbaum Gate* believes that the Transfiguration really happened. The question is not whether they are real, but rather Hamlet's question: where do they come from, Heaven or Hell? are they for good or evil?

The answer is not simple. For even the demons, properly understood, may serve a divine purpose. Even the 'bugs' of Crewe evoke a sense of the eyes of God. But 'properly understood' implies a true system of belief, and it is a nagging hermeneutic question whether Spark can be understood without it. (As a believer, I cannot get outside to seek an answer.) At any rate, the effects of such interventions are profoundly ambivalent. They convey dangerous power, cause disorder, lead some to spiritual anarchy and others to flight or withdrawal. They transfigure the commonplace—there is Sandy Stranger's odd treatise again—hinting at another world, transforming the reality of this one.

Literally, transfiguration means a change in 'figura', appearance. For Catholic doctrine, it is a change in the appearance of the material world, a change wherein the glory of the divine shines through the natural. It is a sign or event that declares in the voice of God that Christ the incarnate is God's Word. Its effect ·is tremendous awe or fear. Other experiences have similar effects. Seeing an apparition is one, an apparition being the apparent materialization of something believed unreal, invisible, or purely spiritual. The crucial distinction between transfiguration and materialization pervades the novels. Materialization is a false transfiguration, a fictional one, but on occasion a necessary one in the economy of Christian art. Their perilous similarity is the problem. They may seem to come by way of the same doubtful agency and reveal the same demonic truth. The Schiaparelli dress is a false sacrament that effects a true transfiguration.

To materialize apparitions is to practise demonology. We see the people of *The Takeover* engaged in it at dinner as they discuss changes in the meanings of money and property:

> They talked of hedges against inflation, as if mathematics could contain actual air and some row of hawthorn could stop an army of numbers from marching over it. They spoke of the mood of the stock-market, the health of the economy as if these were living creatures with moods and blood. And thus they personalized and demonologized the abstractions of their lives, believing them to be fundamentally real, indeed changeless. (127)

The benign but indifferent old sociologist of *Memento Mori*, Alec Warner, practises the same kind of ghostly reification in his file of cards. He is not called a demonologist, but the destruction of his files is an apocalyptic event that declares otherwise. The trickster-diabolist of Peckham Rye, Dougal Douglas, is a very modern materializer who also reifies the abstractions of social science into apparitions of human behaviour. Still, the final impact of his materialization includes (for one observer at least) a true transfiguration. As Humphrey drove

> swiftly past the Rye, he saw the children playing there and the women coming home from work with their shopping-bags, the

31

Rye for an instant looking like a cloud of green and gold, the people seeming to ride upon it, as you might say there was another world than this. (202)

The commonplace transfigured is really seen.

What follows the bomb blast and fire at the May of Teck Club in *The Girls of Slender Means* is transfiguration. The physical slenderness of 'means', the commonplace elegances summed up in the Schiaparelli dress, are transfigured for the poet Nicholas, take on transcendent meaning, become a vision of Hell (even the commonplace Jane calls it so). That vision is accompanied by the vision of selfless sanctity in the martyred Joanna, she whose voices have floated down from the top floor largely unheeded. Nicholas's life is transfigured.

Recall the hellishly contrary voice that floats down from the maniac in the attic in *Not To Disturb*, one of the three novellas that followed on *The Mandelbaum Gate*. All three portray efforts at false transfiguration, which is to transform reality into pure appearance or apparition. The agents of the process are those who believe, as do Willi in *The Comforters* and Hubert in *The Takeover*, that reality *is* an apparition, that appearances *are* reality. Her husband and others seek to transform Annabel, the film star of *The Public Image*, into mere appearance. Lise, the enigmatic *nouveau roman* heroine of *The Driver's Seat*, does the same for herself. In a parodic ritual of suicide, she finds the right dress, garbs herself in sheer spectacle, fabricates a non-identity, throws away all evidence of a real self. And the Klopstock tragic triangle of *Not To Disturb*, locked out of sight in their library, carry out their invisible bloody catastrophe, while the servants led by Lister the butler—he who believes reality is scandal—transfigure their reality into pseudo-event, film scenario, profitable public image.

By contrast the transfigurations of *The Mandelbaum Gate*, no less awesome, are true. We first see Barbara on Mount Tabor by the Basilica of the Transfiguration. She believes in what happened there. Or happened somewhere:

> Wherever it did take place, she thought, I believe it did take place all right. Transfigured, and in a radiant time of metamorphosis, was seen white and dazzling, to converse with Moses and Elias. (48)

But it is Freddy, the timid bachelor embassy officer, whose life is transfigured.

When Barbara crosses over to Jordan and disappears, he goes after her and loses all memory of three days. (No explicit allegory is forced here: the days are 12–15 August; the Feast of the Transfiguration is 6 August.) Slowly his memory returns, and 'looking back at the experience in later years Freddy was amazed. It had seemed to transfigure his life, without any disastrous change in the appearance of things' (165). But appearances do change for him at the time. Reality becomes real. Freddy sees himself 'in a physical way', sees the realities of the room he sits in, acquires a 'sense of his appearance'.

> Freddy felt Alexandros's eyes upon him and experienced that sense of his own physical qualities, and the qualities of the room, and, most of all, the carpet glowing on the far wall. And he, in turn, perceived large Alexandros in his physical presence . . . and was perfectly at ease with his own self-awareness. (143)

True transfiguration is a revelation of the real, not a materialization of apparitions, not a denial of the real in favour of image or psychic projection.

Barbara's pilgrimage is aimed at a real shrine, but what makes a shrine real? It is real if one really prays at it. Why take the trouble to go there?

> 'It's an act of presence,' Barbara said, 'as when you visit a bereaved friend and there's nothing to say. The whole point is, that a meeting has materialised.' They stood on the cliff-edge outside the Church of St. Peter in Gallicantu and looked across the valley into Israel, where men were working in the fields. (283)

As at the end of *Peckham Rye*, the commonplace is truly seen. Reality is gained in the only way possible. 'Either the whole of life is unified under God, or everything falls apart.' Either reality is transfigured or it becomes demonic.

But the transfigurations that come upon Ronald in *The Bachelors* appear demonic enough, and the effort to make them otherwise is his. The party at Isobel's

> stormed upon him like a play in which the actors had begun to jump off the stage, so that he was no longer simply the witness of a comfortable satire, but was suddenly surrounded by a company of ridiculous demons. (111)

At times, he repels the figures, sends them back to 'comfortable satire'. At other times, however, when the 'company of demons' is 'passing through his thoughts', he performs a painful act of will. He attempts to transcend the 'truth-machine, under which his friends took on the aspect of demon-hypocrites' (16), and to transfigure them positively, to force upon their characters 'what attributes of vulnerable grace he [can] bring to mind' (115). But after he has made such an 'effort of will toward graciousness', he becomes ill, suffers a seizure, 'as if a devil in his body was taking its revenge' (116). It is the demonological struggle of artist with subject. It is the same struggle Caroline carries on against the thought of Georgina Hogg, first of the 'demon-hypocrites'. She fears that Hogg may become an obsession and undertakes the novelist's process, objectifies, places the obsession outside of herself. It is the same for Fleur with Sir Quentin and his sect, the intent of her loitering. The novelist plays medium, exorcizes by materializing, summons up apparitions to fight apparitions.

Her chief antagonist in the game is the spiritualist forger-blackmailer, the false priest. Her antagonist demonologizes reality while she exorcizes the demons. He wields the power of secrecy while she publicizes the secrets. She must fight him on his turf with his weapons.

The power of secrecy is a central motif of Spark's plots, as indeed it has been in the 'Gothic' tradition from Radcliffe and Godwin through Dickens to Henry James and beyond. Her novels are as filled with fearful secrets as ghost stories, where the function of a preternatural apparition is to declare the presence of a powerful secret. Some writers on the folklore of ghosts connect ghosts definitively with repression, haunting with the idea of secrecy. If there is a ghost, there is a secret, and the ghost is a threat of revelation, a veridical potentiality.[16] What Tzvetan Todorov writes of the ghostly tales of Henry James applies remarkably well to the ghostly secrets of Spark:

> The Jamesian narrative is always based on *the quest for an absolute and absent cause.* . . . It is absolute: for everything in this narrative ultimately owes its presence to this cause. . . . Thus the secret of Jamesian narrative is precisely the existence of an essential secret, of something not named, of an absent and superpowerful force which sets the whole present machinery

of the narrative in motion. . . . On the one hand he deploys all his forces to attain the hidden essence, to reveal the secret object; on the other, he constantly postpones, protects the revelation.[17]

The significant difference is that in Spark the secret essence is normally available, but some characters harbour it, for the power secrecy gives them, while others misunderstand it or deny its existence. The power of secrecy is demonic (as in the 'Gothic') and must somehow be overthrown if 'all' is not to be 'mere demonology'.

The dormant bomb buried in the garden is a terrible secret. So is the body divided and buried in the pensione garden (in *Territorial Rights*, everyone has something to hide and everyone is blackmailed or blackmailer). There are the secret past of Charmian (and that of her husband) in *Memento Mori*, the secret crimes of Patrick in *The Bachelors*, the secret death pact of *Not To Disturb*, the secret corruption of Hubert in *The Takeover*, and of the publisher in *Slender Means*, the secret identity of Lise with her secret thoughts, the secret of Robinson's whereabouts, the secret of Annabel's husband's suicide. There are his lying secret letters, the secret files of *Loitering*, and Alec Warner's files. There is the secret anarchic power of the Abbess of Crewe, and that of Jean Brodie, and the secret of the secretive one who betrayed her.

Mere enumeration reveals the point of the secrecy. Those who keep the secrets and live by their power are the blackmailers. The blackmailers are false priests, the same ones who deny reality to others and themselves, deny the oneness of reality. They demonologize reality by dividing it. They divide it, we have seen, into matter and spirit, deny sacramental unity. They also divide it into private and public, and in so doing make both private and public unreal. Either they seek to live by a 'private morality'—which, as January tells Robinson, is unreal. Or they seek to turn reality into mere 'public image', as do Lister the butler and Annabel's husband.

The division is sharply drawn in *The Prime of Miss Jean Brodie* (1961). The other teachers at Marcia Blaine's preach the team spirit, preach loyalty only to the school, have no thought of personality outside of public rôle. The opposite extreme is

Miss Brodie, whose only morality is her own romantic anarchism, whose only loyalty is to herself and to her subjective vision of her girls' vocations, mere projections of herself. Elsewhere, the first extreme is seen in Georgina Hogg, who has no 'private existence'; in *Public Image*, where Annabel fights to achieve private reality; in *The Driver's Seat*, where Lise destroys all vestiges of private identity. The second is found in the suicidal privacy of the triangle in *Not To Disturb*; in the Newmanite solipsism of *Loitering With Intent*; in the radical subjectivity of those who profess to live by a private morality, believe in psychic projections, and, like Robinson, are 'constitutionally afraid of any material manifestation of Grace' (100). They are the ones who demonologize reality by dividing it. Those who oppose them seek to recover reality by reconciling private and public through exposure and revelation, ending the power of blackmail, of secrecy. They are the artists, the betrayers. We cannot understand Spark's demonological struggle without understanding her betrayers.

Betrayal is the climax of *Memento Mori*. Here as elsewhere it is the obligatory action of one who has been intensely loyal. Jean Taylor, retired companion to Charmian, finally sees that the long entrapment of blackmail can be broken only by betrayal:

> I don't want to, but I will. . . . I see it is necessary that Godfrey Colston should stop being morally afraid of Charmian—at least it is worth trying. I think, if he knows of Charmian's infidelity, he won't fear any disclosures about his. . . . There is a time for loyalty and a time when loyalty comes to an end. (148–49)

It is precisely what Sandy learns in *The Prime of Miss Jean Brodie*.

When Derek Stanford wrote that 'truth, for Muriel Spark, implies rejection', he was surely thinking of Sandy's betrayal.[18] Sandy needs 'something to react against', 'something definite to reject' (52, 159). Rejection means betrayal. Rejection for her is a visionary, a mental act. She screws up her little piggish eyes, her untrustable eyes, even smaller 'in the effort of seeing with her mind' (26), in order to see the wholeness of Miss Brodie's influence, and the resulting transfiguration leads her to betray. Elsewhere I called her action the 'most complex moral action' of Spark's fiction,[19] but it occurs in many other novels, and is manifestly linked to their creative process.

In *Not To Disturb*, only the gatekeeper Theo and his wife are disturbed, and Theo tries to resist. It is he who suggests breaking down the doors; he opens gates where others would keep them closed. The vocation places him in a difficult position of alienation. It makes him the one who would betray the secrecy of the power in control, who threatens Lister and his crew, yet another version of Sir Quentin and his sect. The act and its consequences are basically the same for Caroline in *The Comforters*, for Robert in *Territorial Rights*, for Fleur in *Loitering With Intent*. In publishing her novel, Fleur publicizes and fictionalizes Sir Quentin. When her friend Dottie accuses her of betrayal, she freely confesses. 'You are a fiend', says Sir Quentin (190), and from his viewpoint he is right. She betrays him and departs for Paris, much as, after her betrayal of the blackmailer, Annabel (*Public Image*) departs for Greece. To place the Sir Quentins and their sects morally outside the self, the intent of the artist, is also, for the Christian, to accept spiritual exile. 'A constitutional exile', Muriel Spark has called herself, one for whom exile is not a fate but a calling.[20] Fleur manages in her exile to 'go on my way rejoicing'. For the poor Sandys and Ronalds, there is no rejoicing but only a shaking of the bars; like the pilgrim Barbara, they are free and not free.

Likewise, Freddy Hamilton. The initial act of the three 'lost days' that transfigure his life is to free himself from the spiritual tyranny, the moral fear, of his mother—a tyranny inseparable from her lies—and thus to free himself from life as a mere disorderly feeling. Only by betrayal can he do this. He has refused to protect her any longer, and like Sandy he must carry the burden of betrayal through life. The menacing last letters from her and from the fanatical companion Benny, who will murder her, are flushed down a toilet.

Letters destroyed, letters revealed, are a recurrent motif of betrayal. Nicholas of *Slender Means*, the poet hanger-on whose life is transfigured into missionary martyrdom, inspires betrayal. To him, Jane betrays the secrets of her crooked publisher, and in his final worldly act he stuffs his forged letter down a murderous seaman's blouse on V.J. Night. Ronald the 'truth-machine' wins back Seton's false letter and, resisting all

37

persuasions to keep the secret, is key witness and betrayer at Seton's trial. Annabel ends her blackmailer's power when, at the inquest, she publicizes her husband's suicide notes. Betrayal is an act against the moral tyranny of blackmail, the tyranny of private morality, the demonic power of secrecy. Lies and secrets published are exorcized for the ridiculous demons that they are. There is a time when loyalty comes to an end.

Betrayal must, to many readers, seem an uncomfortable ethic; the acts of betrayal cast an odd light on the betrayers. Sometimes, as with Fleur, the betrayer uses the methods of her antagonist, and in such a case as Dougal Douglas's, they are hard to distinguish. In the peculiarly complex spy-thriller world of *Territorial Rights*, Robert in hiding writes his blackmailing novel to publish the truth about a long-buried crime and end the power of blackmail. In one of Spark's most macabre scenes—the midnight dance on the burial places of the pensione garden—the ghostly secret is exorcized, and from his unseen gondola Robert's 'convulsed' laughter fills the night. The odd light is often ludicrous. Pauline Thin, Sandy-like disciple of Brodie-like Hubert in *The Takeover*, finally feels she must speak out, testify, and at the great gathering of his pseudo-Diana cult, she betrays him with ludicrous results. Sister Felicity, rival and betrayer of the Abbess of Crewe, brings down her superior with scandalous publicity. And in a more grotesque but similar climax, Elsa of *Hothouse* betrays her theatrical son at the opening of his obscene geriatric production of *Peter Pan*, ending the performance in a barrage of rotten tomatoes.

It may seem a long way from the conscientious betrayals of Jean Taylor, Freddy, Ronald, Sandy, to the farcical betrayals of Elsa and Robert, but the act is the same. Its intent is exorcism, its means is exposure, and its mode is satiric, sometimes wildly, savagely so. The mixture of a struggle with demons and a savagery of satire has, understandably, left some readers feeling betrayed. But, while it would be simplistic to force a 'Gothic' classification on Spark, it is worth recalling that ever since Horace Walpole, the Gothic tale of demons and ghosts has occasionally mingled terror and farce, as if, as one critic has said, 'Harpo Marx were God's stage

manager'. Satiric extravagance and the play of demons have
been brought into uncomfortable proximity, in order to
'repudiate the encounter with the unknown and feared', to
'laugh out of consciousness' the very darkness the artist would
reveal and explore.[21] However 'comfortable' it may seem,
however elegant its stylistic surfaces, satire is a savage and
primitive act, rooted, as Robert Elliott has shown us,[22] in
archaic rituals of sorcery, exorcism, the expulsion of evil. Even
the elegant ridicule of Jane Austen has been persuasively
described as 'regulated hatred'.[23] Such satire is hardly
'comfortable'.

Sandy asks Teddy Lloyd à *propos* of Jean Brodie, 'Why are
you obsessed with that woman? Can't you see she's ridiculous?'
He says, yes, he can see that she is (179). But of course for
many readers it is *not* easy to see Jean Brodie as a fool, and the
difficulty is essential to Spark's satire. To exorcize demons as
ridiculous is not easy. Caroline says of the Black Mass, 'I don't
say there isn't great evil in it. I only say it's a lot of tomfoolery.'
And when her lover Ernest protests, 'I wouldn't dismiss it so
lightly as that', she replies, 'It depends on how you regard evil'
(98). Muriel Spark regards evil as a demonic force that is
somehow contained within the providence of God and the
economy of salvation, but also as a 'lot of tomfoolery', a play of
demons to be belittled and exorcized. The cure for an
obsession with evil is ridicule.

The fools are of certain kinds. Some are unpleasant fanatics,
some are pathetic solipsists, some are elegant or lyric dancers
in the choreography of manners, their manners a mere parody
of real order, a slender means of grace in the face of Last
Things such as bombs. All act out of absurd compulsions, even
(as with Georgina Hogg) 'primitive manias'.

Their liturgies are mock. They are figures of parody.
Parody, as Todorov and others have observed,[24] is a delicate
and slippery mode. It undercuts by mimic repetition, yet as
repetition it comes close to stylization; stylization affirms what
it mimics, while parody invalidates what it mimics, and their
closeness may mislead. A parody of true liturgy may seem
lovely but it is false. Spark has said that her Catholic belief
provided the norm for her satire, which means, I take it, that
her belief provided the touchstone by which parodic imitations,

specious orders, are found unreal. The true touchstone remains after the fraud has been betrayed, sent away like the lovely loot of *The Takeover*, eternal life remaining behind. The norm is evident when we look at the fools who parodize it.

Their behaviour is ritualized by false orders, whether on the elegant highways of modern Nemi or the vulgar byways of modern Peckham. They are obsessed with 'plans', but their 'plans' are, like the obsessive wills of *Memento Mori*, parodies of genuine disciplines. Maggie, the false Diana of *The Takeover*, is obsessed with plans, we are told, but is incapable of understanding the rules of anything (83). She is a variation of Jean Brodie, who has planned her entire cycle of life according to her own design (her idea of 'prime'), but for whom there is no true design outside of her own ego. Robinson with his antinomian private morality (Prospero on his enchanted island) is such another, reminding January of her Brodie relative.

Akin are those who surrender themselves to 'the realm of predestination': the romantic triangle of *Not To Disturb*; Lise of *The Driver's Seat* (Who is the Driver?); Freddie's mother and her maniacal servant. Such fools believe with Lister the butler that 'there is no armour against fate.' The abbess of Crewe believes herself the central player in a drama governed by some fatal agency and sails proudly off to her excommunication. Curran flees the blackmail of *Territorial Rights* to India and his guru. Some of them may seem protagonists in romantic tragedy, for so they see themselves. Some carry still the spurious grandeur, the haughty anarchism, that Spark recalled with ambivalent nostalgia from her Edinburgh childhood.[25]

The surrender to fatality produces not romantic tragedy but parodic satire. The surrender may have the effect of awe, as at the 'takeover' of one's life by some demonic power, as if one were doomed to a rôle in archaic ritual. But the ritualistic quality, the most evocative stylization, hangs always on the edge of self-parody. The rôle-play may quickly slip into ridiculous mechanism, the tragedy into grotesque satire. When it does, such a takeover may well seem to the incautious reader, the unstill, unwatchful reader, as if Spark has indeed 'pulled the rug out from under her characters', for this is what parodic satire does. The fools play out their scenes, denying their own reality, and are treated accordingly.

They are treated as Caroline treats Georgina Hogg, 'not a real-life character . . . only a gargoyle', thus lapsing, says the author, 'into the Catholic habit of belittling what was secretly feared' (194). The habit, of course, is not exclusively Catholic. Ridiculous demons are familiar in folklore, notably in Scottish tradition, where ridicule by belittlement is also familiar.

The ultimate form of satiric belittlement must surely be that which exposes the offender as unreal. We are accustomed to the mode of satiric exposure in neoclassic tradition—Molière, Fielding, Sheridan—where the pretender is shown, as it were, with his moral pants down, poor naked thing he really is. There is another kind, that of the romantic ironist, the exposure of what Lionel Trilling called inauthenticity. It is found in Austen and Carlyle. It is found in Byron's *Don Juan*, when Juan suspects there is no real self at all beneath the crystalline surface of Adeline and prefers the real ghost of the Duchess of Fitzfulke. It is the revelation that behind the pretence or at the centre of the pretender is no reality; what seems real is only an apparition. Spark's parodic satire works this way.

When Fleur believes that Sir Quentin and his sect have been placed 'morally outside' of herself, then, she is hinting at a complex view of the process of satiric fiction and at a key to the difficulties some readers have felt. To objectify is to give independent reality to figures who are unreal, not just in the sense that they are fiction, 'ghouls of the air', but also in the sense that they have denied reality to 'the rest of life', denied materiality and the material manifestations of grace, and thus are themselves demonologized into unreality, into mere apparitions, ridiculous demons. And yet, like Ronald Bridges, Spark would try to 'force upon' such ridiculous demons 'what attributes of vulnerable grace' she can bring to mind, and thus to include them within the Christian economy they have denied themselves. For the unwary reader, this forcing of vulnerable grace may well be mistaken for moral affirmation, as in the supreme case of Jean Brodie, or in the similar case of the lovely lyrical Abbess of Crewe.

Yet the warning is sounded at the end of *The Abbess*, as it is sounded in the seizures of Ronald. Do not be misled by the ridiculous play, the comic exorcism. These demons are real, and the play of the artist will not 'get rid of them'. Only the

sacramental sense can do that, only the faith that unifies the whole of life under God. The mimic graces of the artist are vulnerable indeed. Novels are odd things to write.
Our revels now are ended. Be still, be watchful.

NOTES

1. *The Comforters* (1957; New York: Avon, 1965), p. 62. Other texts cited in my essay are as follows, in the order of first publication (in some cases paperback printings alone are available to me): *Robinson* (1958; New York: Avon, 1964); *Memento Mori* (1959; New York: Avon, 1966); *The Ballad of Peckham Rye* (1960; New York: Putnam Perigee, 1982); *The Bachelors* (1960; Philadelphia: Lippincott, 1961); *The Prime of Miss Jean Brodie* (1961; Philadelphia: Lippincott, 1962); *The Girls of Slender Means* (1963; London: Macmillan, 1963); *The Mandelbaum Gate* (1965; New York; Penguin, 1967); *The Public Image* (1968; New York: Penguin, 1970); *The Driver's Seat* (1970; Harmondsworth: Penguin, 1974); *Not To Disturb* (1971; New York: Penguin, 1974); *The Hothouse by the East River* (1973; New York: Penguin, 1975); *The Abbess of Crewe* (1974; New York: Viking, 1974); *The Takeover* (1976; London: Macmillan, 1976); *Territorial Rights* (1979; New York: Coward McCann & Geoghegan, 1979); *Loitering With Intent* (1981; New York: Coward McCann & Geoghegan, 1981).
2. See M. H. Abrams, *Natural Supernaturalism* (New York: Norton, 1973). Interpretations of 'gothic' are legion. My own approach is set forth in 'The Experience of Character in the English Gothic Novel', in *Experience in the Novel*, ed. R. H. Pearce (New York: Columbia, 1968), pp. 83–105.
3. C. A. Hoyt, 'Muriel Spark: The Surrealist Jane Austen', *Contemporary British Novelists*, ed. C. Shapiro (Carbondale: S. Illinois University Press, 1965), p. 126; F. R. Hart, *The Scottish Novel: From Smollett to Spark* (Cambridge: Harvard, 1978), p. 300.
4. Peter Penzoldt, *The Supernatural in Fiction* (London: Peter Nevill, 1952), especially pp. 56–7.
5. *Robinson*, p. 138.
6. Kemp, *Muriel Spark* (London: Paul Elek, 1974), p. 59. It is impossible to document specifically how much I have learned from this elegant, insightful book over the years.
7. *The Abbess of Crewe*, p. 116.
8. Stubbs, *Muriel Spark* (London: Longman's for the British Council, 1973), p. 6.
9. Stubbs, pp. 15, 22, 25, 31.
10. See 'What Images Return', reprinted in *Memoirs of a Modern Scotland*, ed. K. Miller (London: Faber & Faber, 1970), pp. 151–53.
11. Quoted by Stubbs, p. 14.
12. *Prime of Miss Jean Brodie*, pp. 52–3. Karl Malkoff, in *Muriel Spark* (New

York: Columbia, 1968), p. 3, sees Sandy's title as 'an appropriate description of the fictive method of Muriel Spark' throughout the earlier novels and stories.

13. Martin Ebon, *The Devil's Bride* (New York: Harper & Row, 1974), p. 5. I apply the same naturalistic meaning in 'Experience of Character', above, Note 2.

14. Claire Russell, 'The Environment of Ghosts', in *The Folklore of Ghosts*, ed. H. R. E. Davidson and W. M. S. Russell (Cambridge: Folklore Society, 1981), p. 126.

15. *Not To Disturb*, p. 92.

16. Russell (Note 14), p. 126.

17. *The Poetics of Prose*, trans. R. Howard (Ithaca: Cornell, 1977), p. 145.

18. *Muriel Spark* (Fontwell: Centaur, 1963), p. 45.

19. *The Scottish Novel*, p. 295.

20. 'What Images Return' (Note 10).

21. Paul Lewis, 'Mysterious Laughter: Humor and Fear in Gothic Fiction', *Genre*, XIV (Fall, 1981), 313–20 *passim*.

22. *The Power of Satire: Magic, Ritual, Art* (Princeton: Princeton University Press, 1960).

23. D. W. Harding, 'Regulated Hatred: An Aspect of the Work of Jane Austen', *Scrutiny*, VIII (1940), 346–62.

24. Todorov quotes Yuri Tynianov in *Poetics of Prose*, p. 245.

25. 'What Images Return' (Note 10).

2

Fun and Games with Life-stories

by VALERIE SHAW

In her poem 'Against the Transcendentalists' Muriel Spark makes a resolute and somewhat disdainful attack on writers who offer grand abstractions in their work and see themselves as visionaries. 'There are', Spark reckons, 'more visionaries/ Than poets and less/ Poets than missionaries'; as a result, the kind of art that does not suffer from 'Delphic insanity' has become a rare and precious commodity which needs vigilant protection. Presenting herself as one of the few, a member of that 'meagre species' poets are, Spark dissociates herself from every writer who claims to show us Everyman in a poem, or whose flights into 'Empyreal vacuity' she suspects are made with 'an eye to/ Publication', and not because of any personal conviction. Instead of vague mysticism or giddying, and often pretentious, philosophies, so the speaker in 'Against the Transcendentalists' proposes, art should deal with lived experience; it should not try to 'Fulfil the wilderness' or tantalize us with images of irretrievable perfection, but reflect the immediacy of life in a particular place, at a particular time:

> for what am I to
> Byzantium or Byzantium
> To me? I live in Kensington
> And walk about, and work in Kensington
> And do not foresee departing from Kensington.
> So if there's no law in Kensington

44

Adaptable to verse without contravening
The letter to prove
The law, I'll make one.

The insistence on empirical reality here is characteristic of Spark in all of her writing, whether in verse or prose, and so too is the almost swaggering note of self-confidence. The tone is assured and defiant, buoyed up on the certainty that although 'Poets are few' they are far better equipped 'to love and animate the letter' than even the angels in heaven; no doubt angels 'make sweet moan' high above us, but unlike men and women they 'never write a stanza down'.[1]

If visions do come to this poet, then they will be revelations that depend upon, rather than wish away, material realities. Speaking of her religious conversion, Spark has said that one of the things she found particularly interesting about the Church was 'its acceptance of matter', and the same concern is discernible when the speaker in 'Against the Transcendentalists' takes a patient stand in her own limited earthly condition,

Hoping that if Byzantium
Should appear in Kensington
The city will fit the size
Of the perimeter of my eyes
And of the span of my hand.[2]

The stance is patient, since the poet may have the luck to be granted a vision, but it is not passive: she must be ready for the gift, and readiness means teaching her hands and eyes to understand the law framed by her intellect—the law of which a central text is 'the thing defined,/ the flesh made word'.[3]

To make the 'perimeter' of her eyes define the limits of her material while holding what she has called 'a sacramental view of life which is nothing more than a balanced regard for matter and spirit', has been a constant aim in Spark's work.[4] For her, as for Proust, whose method of gaining redemption from time by means of memory she admires, eternity can be apprehended 'through our senses' in a way that is 'analogous to our sacramental understanding of eternity by faith'.[5] What this has always involved with regard to her art is the belief, so clearly evident in 'Against the Transcendentalists', that the

45

true poet is endowed with special perceptiveness. There may be nothing special, indeed plenty of ordinariness, about living, walking around, and working in Kensington, but only the true poet can capture ordinary, daily events and communicate them in such a way that they seem wonderful. We can see the process at work in 'Daybreak Composition', the first of a sequence of poems called 'A Tour of London'; the view from the speaker's 'top-floor flat' is spread out for 'Anyone' to see, but it is her own selection and disposition of particular visual elements (the leaning houses, or the glimpse of sky, 'the colour of threadbare dungarees') which frame the scene, making it Spark's, not just 'Anyone's'. She has created a word-picture which she playfully suggests is her very own Picasso (unsigned, of course), hanging there in the window, 'an oblong canvas of Kensington/ Almost ready for looking at'.[6] What we are offered here is precisely 'the thing defined', a picture evoked and given meaning by the artist's shaping of disparate sense impressions into a pleasing whole.

The kind of shaping for which Spark has become famous is of course story-telling and not the writing of poetry. Although she herself finds 'writer' a more accurate term than 'novelist' to describe her profession, it is for her novels, where her ability to devise fast-moving plots full of bizarre events is most apparent, that she has been widely and enthusiastically recognized.[7] But her own description of the essential nature of poetry, 'the poet's experience perpetuated in a poem', applies equally well to her methods as a novelist; in her fiction, as in the poems she was writing when she offered that description in a *Poetry Review* editorial, she resolutely opposes 'transcendentalism', and maintains a steady, though also joyful, attention to the contingencies of place, time and personality.[8]

This is not to suggest that Spark is a realist in any simple sense. There is clearly a strong case to be made for her work as being actually subversive of realism; it would be misguided to ignore the experimental, post-modernist qualities of her fiction, and it is hard to disagree with the comment, from one Spark critic, that, 'although some of her novels are very evocative of the period they describe . . . realistic events are always subordinated to the demands of the plot.'[9] But perhaps it is not on the level of 'event' that we should ever look for realism in Spark, but rather in her use of setting, which has attracted less critical notice than it deserves. It is notable, for example, how persistent (and precise) are Spark's references to Kensington, the area of London in which she herself lived when she returned from Africa in 1944. While living in Kensington, it seems, Spark gathered impressions and experiences which she chose to 'perpetuate', not just in poems but in novels, and which have kept all their piquancy through several decades and many travels.

The vistas and corners of Kensington do feature a lot in Spark's poetry, as can be seen from even the brief extracts already quoted, and there is a sense in which the speaker in 'Against the Transcendentalists' is accurate when she foresees that she will not depart from Kensington. Metaphorically at least, and despite the cosmopolitanism of her later career, Spark has never left Kensington or relinquished what she discovered there about human nature—the dominant concern of her fiction, whatever its setting. It is highly significant that for her most recent novel, *Loitering With Intent* (1981), she should return to Kensington as a location, basing her heroine there and charting many journeys across West London, and that she should make this heroine discover in the London of the late 1940s and the early 1950s material to last a lifetime of novel-writing.

What this suggests at the outset is that it is wrong to talk of a 'London period' in Spark's writing, or to suggest that her interest in the city as a setting for fiction ended with *The Girls of Slender Means* (1963). There was plainly a definite purpose in Spark's choice of the post-war London she herself knew so well, and at a decisive stage in her life, as the setting for *Loitering With Intent*, her first novel in autobiographical form since *Robinson* (1958). The exact nature of that purpose can only be a matter of conjecture, in so far as it involves profoundly personal motives and impulses, and it is important to remember the emphasis Spark always places on the instinctual and mysterious aspects of being an artist. But we also have her authority for believing that any fine work of art is 'polygonal', constantly yielding to fresh analysis and reassessment; 'whatever section of time' a work of art faces, so Spark argued in 1948, 'a fresh type of excellence may become apparent which

47

in no way detracts from the value of those facets which have been recognized and celebrated in the past'.[10] *Loitering With Intent* is one such 'polygonal' work; it offers us a new vantage point from which to assess the excellence of Spark's entire career and to recognize the skill with which she weaves autobiographical strands into her fiction. Kensington plays an interesting part in all of this, and it is with a reminder of some of its appearances in early Spark novels that we must begin.

References to Kensington pervade the fiction Spark wrote in the 1950s and 1960s. Sometimes, admittedly, the mention of her familiar territory is fleeting and inessential to narrative action, as it is in *The Public Image* (1968). This novel is set principally in the glamorous section of Rome, and we are given no more than a retrospective glance into Annabel's previous life in her Kensington flat. In other works, however, West London is taken to epitomize an entire way of life; in *The Bachelors* (1960), we are taken into an urban landscape which is characterized by a combination of dreary sameness and nervous restlessness, totally devoid of the colour and serenity displayed in the poem 'Daybreak Composition'. *The Bachelors* opens:

> Daylight was appearing over London, the great city of bachelors. Half-pint bottles began to be stood on the doorsteps of houses containing single apartments from Hampstead Heath to Greenwich Park, and from Wanstead Flats to Putney Heath; but especially in Hampstead, especially in Kensington.

Here, the bachelors emerge from their 'single apartments' and on Saturday mornings sally forth on shopping expeditions, stopping to chat with one another in the Old Brompton Road, the street to which Muriel Spark moved in July 1950—a crucial date in the chronology of her later novel *Loitering*, for it is on 'the last day of June 1950' that the heroine feels her life to have changed irrevocably. In *The Bachelors* the emphasis is rather on triviality; the men old-maidishly discuss the dreadful price of frozen peas, exchange cookery tips (how to make cod taste like halibut, for example), and in a variety of ways demonstrate that, outside their professional City lives, they are banal and rootless. These men are uncommitted in a potentially sinister way, ready to fall into the service of a malign authority, and Spark uses their wanderings to and fro within their narrow ambit as a way of suggesting their spiritual emptiness and aimlessness. The journeys they make are, like all journeys in Spark, meticulously charted, frequent use being made of South Kensington Station, which is something of a landmark in the early novels. As a point of transit, the station is a place where characters can show that they know exactly where they are going and how they will get there or, more probably, that they are quite incapable of making any decisive move. In Spark's first novel, *The Comforters* (1957), South Kensington Station is the scene of a typically spasmodic telephone conversation between Helena Manders and her brother-in-law Ernest:

> 'Can you come right over, Ernest? You could take a taxi.'
> 'It would cost ten bob.'
> 'Where are you speaking from?'
> 'South Kensington Underground.'
> 'Oh well, come by tube if you like. But take a taxi *if* you like.'
> 'I'll be with you presently.'[11]

Such moments illustrate exactly what Spark was getting at when she observed that 'We're not happy with things. We want machines to handle them'—a situation from which she sees religion as rescuing us.[12]

Religion is a central theme in *The Comforters*, and in the course of the novel we are taken inside Brompton Oratory along with the convert heroine Caroline. Although Spark has stated that the novel is not about her own breakdown and illness, there are clearly affinities between herself and her protagonist. Caroline has a tiny flat with a balcony from which she can see the whole of Queen's Gate, a view which must have been familiar to Spark while she was living in Queen's Gate Terrace and studying to become a Catholic. To girls who, like Caroline or the young Muriel Spark, have 'rooms in Kensington' (p. 50), the area is virtually a world in itself, within easy reach of other similarly small worlds, notably Soho where literary coteries gather in pubs. This point is emphasized in *The Comforters* when we are told that Caroline's friends find it very peculiar that she should 'go so far out of London' for Catholic instruction; 'Why don't you go to Farm

Street?' (p. 60) they ask, as perhaps Spark's own friends asked while she was taking instruction from Father Agius of Ealing Priory. Spark's actual reception into the Catholic Church did take place in the Jesuit Church, Farm Street, but during her conversion help and support (like Caroline's) came from a Benedictine Father. Fact and fiction come extremely close together here, even down to small details; in the novel, Caroline sits in the little parlour at the Priory and is served milk and biscuits, a courtesy which Spark too received: according to Derek Stanford, Father Agius 'sensed she was half-starving herself, and used to have her served with warm milk and biscuits in a little parlour'.[13] For Caroline, the parlour is a refuge warmed by Father Jerome's friendly under-standing and by memories of 'the early dark evenings' (p. 61) throughout the previous winter when she made weekly visits to the Priory. In comparison, even Kensington seems frenetic and ultra modern. It is significant that when Caroline returns to her flat after visiting Father Jerome it is to find her boyfriend Laurence 'fiddling about' (p. 63) with a new gadget—a machine on which he vainly hopes to record what he calls her 'spook-voices' (p. 64). The juxtaposing of atmospheres—the Priory is all calm and reflective, the flat is hilarious but full of anxiety—sets a timeless, monastic way of life alongside a worldly one; we are not asked to praise one and reject the other, but only to acknowledge that *sub speciae eternitas* all our choices as human beings are choices between different kinds and degrees of limitation.

Spark's fascination with enclosed communities is well known, and the principle observed at work in *The Comforters* can be seen again in the later novel *The Girls of Slender Means* (1963) where, within the small world of Kensington, we find the even smaller world of the May of Teck Club. The club is based on the Helena Club in Lancaster Gate, where Muriel Spark lived for a while, and it is characteristic of her way of working that she should alter the location sufficiently to avoid straight realism but still manage to preserve the atmosphere of the institution and its surroundings. In *Girls*, not only is the hostel firmly located in Kensington, but care is taken to establish various perspectives from the interior. Girls look out of windows which have been three times shattered between

1940 and 1945, the year in which the novel is set. Standing 'obliquely opposite the site of the [Albert] Memorial', the club offers from its upper bedrooms a view of 'the dip and rise of treetops in Kensington Gardens'.[14] At this distance, people walking on the opposite pavement look 'tiny' and insignificant, 'carrying little dots of shopping bags' (p. 8) as everyone in 1945 did, 'in case they should be lucky enough to pass a shop that had a sudden stock of something off the rations' (p. 9). From the lower dormitories, however, the people 'looked larger, and the paths of the park were visible' (p. 9), suggesting that the importance of human beings and their worldly environment depends very much on the observer's point of view. Like the speaker in 'Daybreak Composition', the hostel residents look out of the windows from a secure position, though in the novel the emphasis is more on youthful expectancy than it is in the poem—and as the climax of the novel demonstrates, the May of Teck Club is not as safe as it seems to be. Even while these 'nice' (and therefore poor) girls—'and few were nicer, as nice people come, than these girls at Kensington'—are glancing 'out of the windows in the early mornings to see what the day looked like', or gazing out on the 'green summer evenings' (p. 9), there is an unexploded bomb in the garden. The girls, with their eyes full of 'an eager spirited light that resembled near-genius, but was youth merely' are dreamier than the poet of 'Daybreak Composition', seeming to be 'reflecting on the months ahead, on love and the relations of love' (p. 9). Deftly, at the very beginning of her story, Spark has created an authentic Kensington setting and at the same time established a mood epitomizing post-war optimism and buoyancy.

In *The Girls of Slender Means*, then, Spark uses Kensington, and in particular Kensington Road, as a setting which will highlight the 'delightful', the 'movingly lovely' qualities she attributes to the girls, but which is yet not so softly pastoral as to exclude the 'savage' (p. 9) aspects of human life; it is the savagery hinted at in the first chapter of the novel that emerges in the final tragedy when the May of Teck sinks into its centre, 'a high heap of rubble' (p. 130), taking Joanna with it. Violence is an undercurrent too in the V.J. celebrations with which the novel ends, and 'general pandemonium'

51

(p. 141)—including a stabbing and a fight between British and American servicemen—is the context in which Nicholas sees Jane, standing 'sturdy and bare-legged on the dark grass' (p. 142), pinning up her hair. He marvels at her stamina and preserves until his death the image of her, 'as if this was an image of all the May of Teck establishment in its meek, unselfconscious attitudes of poverty, long ago in 1945' (p. 142). The effect is to put the events of the novel at a great distance from us, not just historically but emotionally, as though what we have been shown is something precious but irretrievable. There is pathos here, and it is increased by our knowledge that Nicholas will be martyred in Haiti, but the dominant feeling left is one of admiration for Jane's resilience, her sheer indestructibility. Jane exemplifies the power of survival which Spark always admires, and which she celebrates again in *Loitering With Intent*, though Fleur Talbot represents something of an advance on Jane, whose 'normal state' is one of 'unhappiness and hope' (p. 139). Fleur certainly has lots of hope, but she is less constitutionally unhappy than her fictional predecessor; she remembers how in her young days she 'preferred to be interested as I was than happy as I might be'.[15] But then, she is actively involved in becoming a writer, and conventional happiness means nothing to her.

Yet already in Jane we can see Spark's interest in the female character who is prepared to be an individual. Although Jane in many ways typifies the May of Teck way of life, in others— and most notably in her involvement with the literary world— she is exceptional. From Kensington she makes her way to the area of Red Lion Square and the publisher's office where she works. In this vicinity was the Parton Press, which gave its name to a group of poets (the Parton Street Poets) and was associated in the 1940s with 'a motley band of younger poets . . . who were gipsy and bohemian in their behaviour'.[16] With figures on the fringes of such groups, Jane goes to poetry readings at a hired meeting-house in the Fulham Road, or to parties where she will

> meet the people she longed to meet, young male poets in corduroy trousers and young female poets with waist-length

hair, or at least females who typed the poetry and slept with the poets, it was nearly the same thing. (p. 61)

But thrilled as Jane is to keep such company, Spark leaves us in no doubt as to its ephemeral and restricted nature. The London literary scene which she and Derek Stanford knew in the 1940s is exposed as full of bogus sentiments and empty aspirations; like members of 'a resistance movement against the world' (p. 61), capable of understanding nobody outside their own circle, and communicating with one another by means of 'a kind of secret instinct' (p. 62), most of these young bohemians (many of them were unfit for active war service) are destined to 'fail and fade into a no-man's land of Soho public houses in a few years' time and become the familiar messes of literary life' (p. 62). Others, more talented to begin with, will falter 'from lack of stamina' (the quality Jane possesses in abundance) and will take jobs 'in advertising or publishing, detesting literary people above all' (p. 62); and if others actually succeed, they become 'paradoxes', like the dark-eyed Ernest Claymore, one of 'the Cosmic school of poets', who by the 1960s will have become a 'mystical stockbroker' (p. 63), dividing his life between the City, his country cottage and a monastery. In Jane's eagerness to cultivate such people Spark is evidently laughing at her own younger self, and in the way she depicts the literary set her distinctive talent for parody is fully apparent. She conveys exactly the situation which was to lead Cyril Connolly in 1947 to observe that 'the English Renaissance, whose false dawn we have so enthusiastically greeted, is further away than ever.'[17] Two years after the Labour election victory which plays a prominent part in the narrative of *Girls*, Connolly gloomily noted that the literary scene was dominated by a clique of

> literary 'Best People', who somewhat resemble a galaxy of important prima dònnas, while round them rotate tired businessmen, publishers, broadcasters, and civil servants who were once poets, novelists, and revolutionary thinkers.[18]

In *Girls*, disillusionment still lies ahead of the young men— 'poets by virtue of the fact that the composition of poetry was the only consistent thing they had so far done'—who sit 'in their corduroy trousers in a café in Bayswater with their silent listening admirers', impressing the girls as they talk about 'the new future' and flick 'the page-proofs of an absent friend's novel' (p. 19).

What this generation of poets saw itself creating was a neo-Romantic revival, specifically directed against the intellectualism embodied in Auden's work of the 1930s. Its heroes were poets with romantic flair, men like Roy Campbell, an eye-catching enough figure on the Kensington landscape, or Dylan Thomas, whose name is often mentioned in Spark's fiction. Indeed Stanford, who could well have been one of those recently demobbed young men in *Girls*, credits Spark with converting him to a liking for Thomas's work by reading 'Fern Hill' aloud; 'Somewhere about 1949 Muriel Spark made me see sense', he recalls, having admitted that he was at first 'not much interested' in 'the modern Celt'.[19] But in *Girls* it is not the excitement of anticipating social and cultural changes that is registered; when Nicholas Farringdon smiles 'boredlike' (p. 19) at a friend's allusive quotation, we recognize the self-congratulation of someone who belongs to a clique. More than explaining the lines to Jane, or even answering her when she asks who wrote them, it matters to him that he can be proudly 'conscious that very few in all the great metropolis and its tributary provinces were as yet privy to [their] source' (pp. 19–20).

The reference here to 'the great metropolis' echoes the final words of *The Bachelors*, where there is a similarly ironic edge to the words, 'London, the metropolitan city'. The irony arises from the clarity with which Spark exposes parochial attitudes in so many of her early characters. Her novels do not show us people inhabiting a vast metropolis; rather, London is seen as a collection of villages, the most popular with her characters being Hampstead and Kensington. Between the two goes Godfrey Colston in *Memento Mori* (1959), another novel in which Spark uses her intimate knowledge of Kensington topography. Godfrey and his novelist wife Charmian live in Vicarage Gardens, a stone's throw from Vicarage Gate, where Spark was living in the latter part of 1949—the time during which Fleur, in *Loitering*, takes a secretarial job. It was from No. 1 Vicarage Gate that Spark edited her own magazine *Forum*, and in the same street lived Charles Wrey Gardiner, who ran the Grey Walls Press (for which Muriel Spark later did editorial work), edited *Poetry Quarterly* (where some of Spark's work was published) and was also literary editor of the *Daily Mirror*'s weekly *Opinion*, which had a short run but which included in one of its numbers Spark's poem about the Round Pond in Kensington Gardens.

Vicarage Gate and Vicarage Gardens both run off Kensington Church Street, where Jane Wright takes a furnished room after the May of Teck has burned down in *Girls*. Kensington Church Street is a long steep street joining Kensington with Notting Hill in the north, and in it is the sharp bend where Spark in *Memento Mori* to all intents and purposes kills off poor Godfrey. As the final strands of the novel are tied up and the characters' subsequent careers summarized, we are told that Godfrey died

> as a result of a motor accident, his car having collided with another at a bend in Kensington Church Street. He was not killed outright, but died a few days later of pneumonia which had set in from the shock. It was the couple in the other car who were killed outright.[20]

The occurrence, though not the setting, is repeated in very similar words in *Loitering With Intent*, where Dottie informs the heroine Fleur that ' "Sir Quentin's been killed in a car accident. A head-on collision" ' (p. 208). Fleur's first thoughts are for the others involved: ' "What about the other car?",' she asks, ' "Anyone hurt?" ' Dottie says that ' "they were killed too",' but Fleur insists on knowing ' "How many in the other car?" ' The answer is, ' "Two, I think" ' (p. 208). The purpose of this circumstantial detail in both novels seems to be partly to remind us of the way violence suddenly and 'accidentally' intrudes itself on human affairs, but mainly to emphasize that egotists like Sir Quentin and Godfrey cannot be disposed of without the innocent being caught up and destroyed—and not just singly, either. Sir Quentin is a far more sinful man than Godfrey, and perhaps that is why he is killed outright; it is certainly worth noting that despite Fleur's quick concern for the innocent parties in the crash her principal feeling is one of relief: ' "Thank God he's dead",' she says, ' "the man was pure evil" ' (p. 208). It is almost as though the lives of the two others have been sacrificed in a just cause.

Locally, Sir Quentin's death is 'justified' in a more personal way—personal to Fleur as a would-be novelist. The accident proves to her that the theme of the novel she has written, *Warrender Chase*, is 'valid'. She is now fully convinced of the authenticity of her imaginings: 'Such events as I'd portrayed, even in a different way from the reality, could happen' (p. 208). This certainty fulfils and completes a process which has already reached an important stage at the end of the previous chapter; out of work, and without a publisher for her novel, Fleur is aware of new strength and freedom as an artist:

> Although in reality I wasn't yet rid of Sir Quentin and his little sect, they were morally outside of myself, they were objectified. I would write about them one day. In fact, under one form or another, whether I have liked it or not, I have written about them ever since, the straws from which I have made my bricks. (p. 199)

The realization, both in Fleur's present and in the long view taken by her as autobiographer, is momentous; she is discovering her power as a moral judge and, looking back, she is seeing herself as an artist who has been compelled to write again and again about the same subject. 'Vocation' is not too strong a word for what Fleur finds in the course of *Loitering With Intent*. Her own word is 'changing-point', and she can place it exactly in time and place as well in her own mental landscape: 'It was right in the middle of the twentieth century, the last day of June 1950, warm and sunny, a Friday, that I mark as a changing-point in my life' (p. 200). The place where this 'changing-point' occurs is no less precisely located; it is 'an old disused Kensington graveyard' where Fleur has gone, taking a sandwich lunch with her, to write a poem. Evoking this scene at the start of the final chapter, Spark offers a reprise (with variations) of the novel's opening paragraph, for it is in the churchyard that Fleur's story begins, the storyteller's manner being instantly given a 'once upon a time and far away' flavour:

> One day in the middle of the twentieth century I sat in an old graveyard which had not yet been demolished, in the Kensington area of London, when a young policeman stepped off the path and came over to me.

Hints of fantasy mingle with suggestions of realism here, and indeed the novel as a whole offers a blend of the wonderful and the prosaic. As she does elsewhere in her work, Spark documents an era, and the phrase 'in those days', which also recurred throughout *Girls*, is frequently repeated in *Loitering With Intent* to remind us that once again we are being given glimpses of social history, and not just what Fleur calls 'a whole chunk of my life' (p. 7). The events which affect Fleur so decisively in the ten months between the autumn of 1949 and the summer of 1950 are included in a wider picture of the period; there are references to Utility clothes, the New Look, food, clothes and petrol rationing, early morning postal deliveries, money-grubbing landlords. And of course the policeman who steps up to Fleur would have the right to demand that she produce an Identity Card. Another sign of the times is the existence of little groups of literary people reading their work to one another, not all that changed since the days of *Girls*, it seems—still an 'intellectual fringe' (p. 65), and, as Fleur remarks, comparable to Eastern Europe today. All of these details, which might strike the reader as no more than the paraphernalia of realism, have a special edge to them, however, when seen in terms of Spark's own experience; Fleur Talbot's memories are in many respects Spark's own, though sifted and arranged so as to chart a progress, really a destiny, that is mythic in quality.

The very first moments of *Loitering* contain a striking piece of accurate recollection. Spark's fictional persona Fleur Talbot does not name the 'old disused Kensington graveyard' where she sits 'on the stone slab of some Victorian grave writing my poem as long as the sun lasted', but there seems no doubt that it is the small area tucked behind Sir Gilbert Scott's famous neo-gothic church St. Mary Abbots. The steeple of St. Mary Abbots (which is probably one of the 'discrepant churches' making up the picture in 'Daybreak Composition') could be seen from the front door of Spark's place in Vicarage Gate, and in the 1940s there were apparently many occasions on which she had an even closer view of this grand building. In his personal memoir of Spark, Derek Stanford recalls:

> In those days, behind St. Mary Abbots, all unfenced from Church Walk, Kensington, there lay a small graveyard containing old tombs. Here Muriel would sometimes sit, obedient to the Muses, with notebook in hand, writing or re-writing her

verses 'among the hundred-and-fifty-year-old dead'. The stones have now been planted against a high wall, and the little graveyard with its tussocks of grass, is today a small public garden with trellises of roses, benches and borders.[21]

Stanford remembers too how one hot day, when he and Spark 'had been working seated on the grass of St. Mary Abbots graveyard', the ice-cream-man's bell suddenly rang: 'all of the child in Muriel Spark, for me, is enfolded in the memory of her running towards me carrying an ice-cream cone in either hand.'[22] Sunshine, ancient tombs, and the grassiness of the place are the common factors between the setting as described by Stanford and as evoked in *Loitering* by Fleur Talbot, who has plenty of the 'determination' noted in Spark throughout Stanford's reminiscences. If anything, Fleur is surer of herself, firmer in a sense of personal identity than her creator appears to have been in this period; Stanford presents Spark in the 1940s as a compound creature, unable to 'locate her own image' and therefore mercurially adopting 'rôles which were sometimes contradictory'.[23] Among the 'self-images' enumerated by Stanford were 'the editorial professional woman'; the impractical 'inspired writer . . . very much a feminine Shelley'; the smart 'young-woman-about-town', resplendent in green New Look costume and looking like 'an Edwardian belle of the hunting-field'; and of course the little girl who likes ice-cream.[24] But paramount seems to be Stanford's impression of Spark as 'a figure of the Muse', or, as he puts it more plainly, 'very much the poet'.[25] While Stanford presents his subject in the rôle of poet as distinct from novelist, however, her fictional counterpart is all set for a career as a prose storyteller; she has already finished one novel, is 'well ahead' with her second, and has her third planned by the time the narrative of *Loitering* closes. Yet although Spark's own first novel was not even started until the 1950s were well under way, she had already in 1949 expressed the view that prose was a 'freer medium' than poetry.[26] Indeed, one of her aims as the editor of *Forum* was to stimulate experimentation with prose and to invigorate the English short story, which she felt was falling into neglect. This suggests that, while 'it was natural', as Stanford recalls, for 'the company' in which he and Spark chiefly found themselves in the 1940s to comprise 'poets rather than novelists', Spark was already moving towards the inclusive view of poetry and fiction which she attributes to Fleur.[27] It is also worth bearing in mind Spark's lasting interest in narrative poetry of all kinds, since this alone brings her close to Fleur, who believes that novels are continuous poems, and the novelist a mythmaker: ' "I've started a novel which requires a lot of poetic concentration",' she tells Dottie, ' "because, you see, I conceive everything poetically" ' (p. 28).

The issue here is that of artistic vision, the topic with which I began this essay. For Fleur, as for Spark, conveying her individual vision does not mean repudiating technique for the sake of inspiration. On the contrary, the more 'poetically' everything is conceived, the greater the artist's responsibility in the search for the best form in which to 'concentrate' ideas. That is why Fleur, perched on the tombstone, is shown, not waiting for some muse to descend, but working hard to develop the skills of her chosen trade. Looking back, she can't remember what the particular poem she was working on was about, but she is fairly sure that it was

> an exercise in a fixed form, such as a rondeau, triolet or villanelle; also I was practising Alexandrines for narrative verse about that time, so it might have been one of those; I always found the practice of metre and form for their own sake very absorbing and often, all at once, inspiring. (p. 200)

Significantly, inspiration is said here to flare 'all at once' in the midst of technical practice—it is not what the writer starts with, but a sudden reward, a gift.

Fleur's attitudes towards writing are recognizably similar to those expressed by Spark in 1961 when she exclaimed, 'Oh, I could go on forever about technique', and described her realization that after her breakdown she could control her ideas as having been 'like getting a new gift'.[28] Technique has always fascinated Spark, and there is no doubt that she approved of the views expressed by Father Agius in an essay entitled 'The Psychology of Poetry'. Agius's piece was published in the *Poetry Review* while Spark was editor and in it he argues that although the poet is a seer, a visionary, with special gifts, these are gifts that must be worked upon.

'Inspiration', Agius contends, 'should be spontaneous. And it will react spontaneously to external stimulus. But the stimulus must be self-chosen.'[29] It is easy to see the appeal this balanced approach, blending conscious and unconscious elements, would have held for Spark—and, if one can imagine her taking the *Poetry Review*, Fleur Talbot.

Loitering With Intent may not tell us that Fleur ever belonged to the Poetry Society, but it does make clear that she shares Spark's admiration for Cardinal Newman's writing. *Apologia pro vita sua* plays an important part in the novel's plot, and also in its theme. It is well known that Newman was a major influence in Spark's conversion to Roman Catholicism, and Stanford recalls how she once copied out for him Newman's statement that a Christian view of the universe is almost by necessity a poetic one.[30] A liking for Newman is only one of many affinities between Spark and her heroine Fleur which contribute to an impression that *Loitering* is autobiographical in more than its fictional form. But if it is a kind of memoir, then it is not the memoir of a self-satisfied author who surveys a full and varied career in its entirety; rather, its mood is one of elation at still being in the business of writing entertainingly and profoundly at one and the same time, of being a moralist *and* a comedienne—in sum, of fulfilling a destiny. The achievement is there to be recorded, celebrated, and now added to, which is why only the beginning of the story, as it were, can be told. And what is more, it can only be told from one point of view, the protagonist's; it is perhaps worth bearing in mind that Newman, who was every bit as obsessively anxious about the safety of his papers as Fleur is shown to be (and as Stanford remembers Spark being), once wrote in a note, 'Had I my will no Memoir should be written of me.'[31]

Not that Newman is the sole figure from the literary past to haunt and animate the experience of reading *Loitering With Intent*. Ostensibly so utterly different from Newman, but akin to him in having an introspective as well as an egotistical side to his make-up, Benvenuto Cellini plays an equally important part as one of Fleur's mentors. In the penultimate chapter of the novel, Fleur actually sets alongside one another an extract from the Preface to Newman's *Apologia* and the opening sentence of Cellini's *Life*. From Newman, apparently, she derives the impulse to be her own truth-teller, however reluctant she may be to put herself on display. Misconceptions must be scotched, as Newman rather histrionically declares in the passage Fleur reads:

> . . . I recognized what I had to do, though I shrank from both the task and the exposure it would entail. I must, I said, give the true key to my whole life; I must show what I am that it may be seen what I am not, and that the phantom may be extinguished which gibbers instead of me. I wish to be known as a living man, and not as a scarecrow which is dressed up in my clothes. . . .

The melodramatic tone is congenial to Fleur, and her practice as a writer follows exactly the principle enunciated by Newman when he replied to critics who blamed him for being 'satirical': 'What they think exaggeration', Newman wrote, 'I think truth.'[32] And Fleur is not without traces of the 'poetic paranoia' (p. 98) which she is quick to detect in Newman. Still, Newman's solemnity reflects only one aspect of the kind of autobiography Fleur envisages writing, 'one day when the months between the autumn of 1949 and the summer of 1950 should become long ago' (p. 199). For a more exuberant and uninhibited model of autobiographical writing, she turns to Cellini; and as her selections from his *Life* make plain, it is as a fellow artist as well as for his personality that she prizes him:

> . . . All men, whatever be their condition, who have done anything of merit, or which verily has a semblance of merit, if so be they are men of truth and good repute, should write the tale of their life with their own hand. (pp. 198–99)

Fleur does not need to choose between Newman and Cellini— she can 'look from one to another, admiring both' (p. 199). And so can Muriel Spark, if we are right to suggest that *Loitering* is at least partly 'the tale' of her own life. In her early 60s, having written fifteen novels, several volumes of criticism, numerous short stories, poems and dramatic pieces, and having indisputably established herself as an artist of 'good repute', Spark had every reason to feel justified in including herself among those 'who have done anything of merit' and whose own truth should be told.

Truth is a priority for Newman and Cellini, both of whom offer self-justifications in their autobiographies, and both of whom are aware that they have enemies. Cellini's combative attitude; his delight when he sees anyone who has plotted against him destroyed (as he is confident they will be, thanks to divine justice); his ability to use language as if it were spoken, and to digress while all the time shaping his material into a strongly plotted narrative rich in characterization and varied in mood; his preoccupation with his own defeats and triumphs rather than with the political events of his time; above all, his essentially heroic view of himself as a single-minded artist following his destiny: all of these are marked features of his *Life*, and all have equivalents in *Loitering With Intent*. Newman's *Apologia*, Cellini's *Life* and Spark's novel are alike too in that they do not purport to tell the whole story, but only significant parts, though no doubt Cellini's sense of growing old adds urgency to his account. In Spark's case, fiction is perfectly suited to the purpose of 'giving the true key' to her life as a writer (and it is as a writer that she claims 'merit') because of its oblique manner. She is not one to put raw personality on show, preferring the neo-classical restraint and detachment associated with T. S. Eliot to the confessional mode favoured by some neo-Romantics in the 1940s. The warning Fleur gives Dottie against making true revelations is apposite to Spark's method in this novel; in fiction, the desire to conceal and disguise, to keep secrets and guard privacy can be fulfilled while autobiographical, maybe self-justifying, elements can be included in the form of clues which may or may not be picked up by readers. The immense verve of *Loitering* does not depend on the clues being spotted, and Spark knows perfectly well that when we read her marvellous opening sentence our attention will be caught by the encounter between the girl and the young policeman, and that we will be intrigued by the bland way Fleur introduces herself as some-one who frequents old graveyards, and for whom the approach of a policeman is not in the least intimidating. So accustomed is she to taking the initiative, that she simply tells him about her poem and then offers him a sandwich. We are expected to feel dislocated, puzzled, and surely not to be thinking about where Muriel Spark herself was living and writing in the summer of 1950.

It might seem that what is being observed here is no more than Spark's liking for private jokes, something that has irritated some readers. Peter Kemp, for example, objects to the 'self-conscious doodling' that goes on in *Robinson* and criticizes Spark for casually allowing 'barely transmuted bits of personal material' to 'break jarringly through the fictive covering'.[33] But with *Loitering* there is no question of what Kemp, referring to early Spark, describes as 'content' not being 'fully subdued to an imaginative pattern'; the centrality of the allusions to Newman and Cellini, whose work inhabits the very public realm of literature, ensures that no 'private code' is being used.[34] Both these writers saw their lives as destined and providentially arranged, as Fleur does, and allusions to their work add to the tautness with which Spark designs her narrative and thematic patterns. These allusions are far more closely integrated with plot and style than happens in other Spark novels; although she has always included references to literary works when she writes (the use of stanzas from 'The Wreck of the Deutschland' as a leitmotif in *Girls* is just one example), she has never before made them so relevant to the form she is using. The vital change is that it is part of the heroine's experience to realize the full weight and marvel of her inheritance as a writer. She rejoices in knowing exactly what Spark herself knew when she wrote, in her first *Poetry Review* editorial: 'The poet of to-day is rich in heritage and cannot but count his new idiom a compound of what has gone before.'[35]

On one level, then, *Loitering With Intent* is a suspense story, told by someone who, like Spark, 'dearly love[s] a turn of events' (p. 202), but it is also a contemplation on the nature of fiction and the nature of all 'life-stories'; and it is a tribute to literary tradition. Writing biography is sometimes compared to criminal detective work, and within the novel Fleur acts a kind of sleuth, or even a spy. When she takes her 'top-secret' job with the name-dropping snob Sir Quentin Oliver she enters a sphere where questions about the relationship between memoirs and truth are paramount. Sir Quentin's weird group the 'Autobiographical Association' is a kind of literary Alcoholics Anonymous; the members are supposed to write candid memoirs which will be hidden away for seventy years in case of libel action, but as time goes on Fleur realizes that Sir Quentin has a sinister hold over his neurotic, 'more or less illiterate' (p. 40) acolytes, and that in order to further his own evil plans he is actually stealing from her first novel *Warrender Chase*.

The idea of a novel about someone writing a novel is not exactly new, and of course Spark had herself used this device in *The Comforters* (her own 'first novel'). A good deal of the fun in *Loitering* comes from the way Spark plays around with the idea that the boundaries between reality and fiction are unstable. At one point Fleur feels as though it is Sir Quentin who is the unreal invention while her fictional character Warrender Chase is a real man—the original, so to speak, of Sir Quentin. And as was earlier noted in connection with the incident of the car crash, life sometimes satisfies the dictates of her art after the fact of creation. Readers don't need to be post-modernist theorists to recognize that these games are all being played within a novel; there are constant reminders that Fleur herself is made up of words, that the novel *Warrender Chase* does not exist, and that exactly in the same way as Fleur sees the people she meets as 'sheets of paper on which I could write short stories, poems, anything I cared' (p. 99), Spark is free to write exactly what she chooses, even if the sheet is not entirely blank to start with, marked as it is with her own memories of the mid-twentieth century.

What actually deepens *Loitering With Intent*, making it far more than just another clever game with fiction and reality, is the persistence of its concern with the notion of freedom. Spark manages to combine humour of a broad, sometimes farcical, nature with a searching examination of the artist's freedoms—and responsibilities. By making her narrator a blithe, untroubled character (quite the reverse of what might be expected of the poetess among the tombstones), Spark makes the novel simultaneously funny and marvellously open, in a moral sense. The book is full of ambiguities which Fleur sees but refuses to find disturbing or in any sense disabling; in her own way, she is every bit as much of a manipulator, and as secretive, as Sir

Quentin, and if it were asked what makes her kind of manipulation benign while Sir Quentin's is baleful, then the answer seems to lie in the way the manipulating is done and in the view of life it promotes. Fleur exploits life joyfully, emulating Cellini's 'delight in every aspect of his craft' (p. 125) and exulting in the way life keeps satisfying her hunger as an artist. She goes about like a kind of merry spy (even when she is depressed she knows that the mood will pass) on the listen-in for telling phrases, and looking out for those little gestures that reveal fundamental human traits; and she is perpetually exhilarated by the feeling that she is a magnet for the experiences she needs as a writer. She strongly resembles Cellini in the mood where he proclaims, 'I was born free and meant to remain free.'[36]

There are other resemblances too. Fleur's dedication to her art and her untiring watchfulness for promising material are very reminiscent of Henry James, whose style Fleur at one point fears is influencing her rather too much. And to think of James, particularly in his 'artist stories' of the 1890s, in connection with *Loitering* is to acknowledge that the questions raised in the novel have their sombre side. If it is true that the only real difference between Fleur and Sir Quentin is that she manipulates through enjoyment while he manipulates through guilt, then on what basis can the novelist be said to be morally responsible, capable of affecting people's lives and attitudes? Sir Quentin's methods actually result in a suicide, but it is not certain that Fleur's art constitutes a strong enough affirmation to nullify what he stands for. Touching Spark's fiction is the question that so preoccupied James in his later work, namely, is the artist, in his infinite freedom to invent and create, merely exerting his own power, justifying himself by egotistically manipulating fictional characters, but all the time really evading responsibility in life? An early Spark story 'Bang-bang You're Dead' seems to hint at a similar worry; having kept her cool poise while a group of conventional people watch films of her stay in Africa, and concealed the truth about the passion and violence beneath the film's images, the central character wonders calmly, 'Am I a woman . . . or an intellectual monster?'[37] Here, as in *Loitering*, it is emphasized that truth is not equivalent to fact, and that the only way out of the

Jamesian problem is not to try to resolve it morally, but to see that truth is something felt, identifiable by the amount of wonder it arouses. In this sense, Fleur is right to claim that the novelist can enhance life by making it more interesting, though not necessarily any better, and to act accordingly in her dealings with the Autobiographical Association. Dreary and banal stereotypes in themselves, these people have done nothing of 'merit' to warrant the writing of memoirs, and Fleur comments:

> I could have realized these people with my fun and games with their life-stories, while Sir Quentin was destroying them with his needling after frankness. (p. 117)

And from the reader's point of view, how right she is; her idea of putting Sir Eric's nanny and the butler on the nursery rocking-horse while little Eric is locked in the pantry to clean the silver is zany, but far more interesting (and actually truer) than the maundering recollections of a happy childhood which the grown-up Sir Eric wants to put in his memoir. Fleur *is* 'justified', though not in any absolute sense, a situation which, with Newman and his influence on Spark in mind, takes on a religious dimension; one of the reasons Newman gives for adopting Catholicism and rejecting Calvinism is the Catholic notion of different degrees of justification. No one can be certain that he is in a state of grace, and this applies equally to Fleur and to those she knows she could 'realize' with her fanciful imagination.

What makes Fleur superior to the 'unrealized' members of the Autobiographical Association is her understanding of what I take to be the central paradox on which Spark has constructed this novel. By choosing self-revelation as their vehicle, the members of the club are actually denying themselves existence—taken to an extreme, frankness produces despair and self-destruction, as Bernice Gilbert's suicide proves. Fleur knows that complete frankness spoils art as well as friendships, and from this she derives her personal aesthetic, which consists in a belief that, 'the wonder of the [novelist's] art resides in the endless different ways of telling a story, and the methods are mythological by nature' (p. 141). As a mythmaker, the novelist is a committed opportunist who is always loitering with the intent of catching someone out in an act that is typical. Fleur can be simultaneously repelled by Dottie's English Rose perfume and thrilled to be confirmed in her artistic certainty that there is such a thing as the English Rose type of character.

Narrowed down a bit farther, and applied to Spark's own position as a woman writer beginning her career in the post-war period, *Loitering* appears to be a very special kind of *apologia*; partly, it is a warning against self-indulgent confessional writing of the kind which enjoyed a vogue in the late 1940s, and which has still not disappeared completely. Against the odds, Fleur feels wonderful to be an artist and a woman in the twentieth century, and she is strikingly independent; she seems to have no family, no ties, and she can adjust easily to life without her lover since for her, writing is 'like being in love and better' (p. 60). The novel ends happily, in the festive mood of romantic comedy, but there is not a man in sight; Fleur, like Cellini, goes on her way rejoicing. Perhaps Spark is making her own retort to all those women writers who keep telling us how awful it is to be—or even try to be—a woman and an artist in the twentieth century.

Loitering With Intent certainly lends itself to a reading of it as a parable which offers comic optimism as an alternative to existential anguish, and which demonstrates that, as Newman expressed it, material phenomena are both the types and instruments of real things unseen: 'how little one needs, in the art of writing', Fleur observes in her characteristically colloquial way, 'to convey the lot' (p. 84). Connected with this is an attempt to make clear the distinction between wit and callousness, and to meet the objections sometimes made by people who find Spark's penchant for exaggerated and violent events cruel. Alan Massie, for example, feels that Spark's work lacks warmth, and that she shrinks from human love in her books: 'The appeal is to the mind and the imagination rather than to the heart.'[38] But although Fleur seems to fit this mould (she treats her story with a 'light and heartless hand' as is her way, so she tells us, when she has to give 'a perfectly serious account of things' (p. 82)), she is actually more warm-hearted than perhaps any other Spark heroine. She is far from heartless in her treatment of the dotty old Lady Edwina, and her grief for her dear friend Solly is intense and passionate. In fact the entire novel is more genial than other Spark novels, as though instinct were triumphing over intellect more completely than ever before.

What we are offered in *Loitering With Intent* is, as we expect from Spark, a highly wrought work of art, with every name carefully chosen, every historical detail meticulously accurate, and at the same time a kind of song in praise of the casual and inadvertent. Fleur's digressive, easy-going style is sustained within a tightly patterned and carefully plotted narrative; the casual and the informal co-exist, and if there is any risk of egotism about Spark looking back and reliving in fiction ten months which gave her the subject for a lifetime's writing, then it is avoided by the way she emphasizes that the artist is as much at the mercy of luck as anyone else. Luck, or God's grace: the difference between the two depends entirely on one's religious position, and there is something very modest as well as proud about the mature novelist's identification with Cellini, who realizes 'with terror and wonder' as he begins his autobiography that he has come to 'this age of fifty-eight, from which, by God's grace, I am now going on my way rejoicing'. *Loitering With Intent* ends with the same words, and the last action we see is Fleur kicking a football back to some small boys who are playing; as every man knows, no woman can kick a ball properly, but Fleur kicks this one with 'a chance grace' which she would probably never have managed had she been trying too hard. The moment is like an epiphany—a moment when the commonplace is made radiant and the mystery of life seems far more important than anything we can know or describe.

Any desire to use the writing of *Loitering With Intent* as a way of measuring her own worth or to give her own account of herself has been harmonized by Muriel Spark with a sense of mystery in the profoundest sense. There is no pretence that any worthwhile achievement comes purely from effort and self-determination—that is the corrupt egotist's belief, the making of oneself into one's own absolute that we see in Sir Quentin. Against such evil, Fleur Talbot asserts an eager willingness to discover and then to follow her destiny, knowing well that chance will always play its part—and knowing too that precisely because she is human her vision must be limited. In her wisdom as well as in her singleminded devotion to 'the thing defined/ The flesh made word', she is a reincarnation of the speaker in 'Against the Transcendentalists', who asks:

> Who is Everyman, what is he
> That she should stand in lieu of
> A poem? What is Truth true of?
> And what good's a God's-eye view of
> Anyone to anyone
> But God?

NOTES

1. 'Against the Transcendentalists', *Collected Poems* I (London, 1967), pp. 10–11.
2. 'My Conversion', *Twentieth Century*, CLXIX (Autumn 1961), 63; *Collected Poems* I, p. 11.
3. *Collected Poems* I, p. 11.
4. 'The Religion of an Agnostic', *Church of England Newspaper*, 27 November 1953, p. 1.
5. Ibid.
6. 'Daybreak Composition', *Collected Poems* I, p. 39.
7. 'How I became a Novelist', *John O'London's Weekly*, III, No. 61 (1 December 1960), 683.
8. *The Poetry Review*, XXXIX, No. 1 (April–May 1948), 4.
9. Ruth Whittaker, ' "Angels Dining at the Ritz": The Faith and Fiction of Muriel Spark', *The Contemporary English Novel*, Stratford-Upon-Avon Studies 18 (London, 1979), p. 168.
10. Editorial, *The Poetry Review*, XXXIX, No. 2 (June–July 1948), 103.
11. *The Comforters*, Penguin paperback edition (Harmondsworth, Middlesex, 1963), p. 136. Subsequent page references to this edition follow quotations in the text.
12. 'My Conversion', p. 63.
13. *Inside the Forties* (London, 1977), pp. 190–91.
14. *The Girls of Slender Means*, Penguin paperback edition (Harmondsworth, Middlesex, 1966), p. 8. Subsequent page references to this edition follow quotations in the text.
15. *Loitering With Intent* (London, 1981), p. 111. All subsequent page references follow quotations in the text.
16. Stanford, *Inside the Forties*, p. 137.
17. *Horizon*, XVI, No. 90 (July 1947), 1.
18. Ibid., XV, No. 87 (April 1947), 154.
19. *Inside the Forties*, p. 135.

20. *Memento Mori*, Penguin paperback edition (Harmondsworth, Middlesex, 1961), pp. 218–19.
21. *Muriel Spark* (London, 1963), p. 52.
22. Ibid., p. 69.
23. *Inside the Forties*, p. 151.
24. Ibid.; *Muriel Spark*, p. 22.
25. *Muriel Spark*, p. 22; *Inside the Forties*, p. 176.
26. Editorial introduction, *Forum*, No. 1 (Summer 1949).
27. *Inside the Forties*, p. 176.
28. 'My Conversion', p. 62, p. 60.
29. 'The Psychology of Poetry', *The Poetry Review*, XXXVIII, No. 6 (November–December 1947), 496.
30. *Muriel Spark*, p. 58.
31. *Autobiographical Writings*, ed. Henry Tristram (London, 1956), p. 23.
32. *Apologia pro vita sua*, ed. Martin J. Svaglic (Oxford, 1967), p. 296. Cf. *Loitering*, pp. 89–90.
33. *Muriel Spark* (London, 1974), p. 37.
34. Ibid.
35. Editorial ('The Catholic View'), *The Poetry Review*, XXXVIII, No. 6 (November–December 1947), 405.
36. *Autobiography*, translated George Bull, Penguin paperback edition (Harmondsworth, Middlesex, 1956), p. 34.
37. *Bang-bang You're Dead and other stories*, Granada paperback edition (London, 1982), p. 40.
38. *Muriel Spark* (Edinburgh, 1979), p. 91.

3

Autonomy and Fabulation in the Fiction of Muriel Spark

by FAITH PULLIN

> But it was a sunny day for November, and, as he drove swiftly past the Rye, he saw the children playing there and the women coming home from work with their shopping bags, the Rye for an instant looking like a cloud of green and gold, the people seeming to ride upon it, as you might say there was another world than this. (*The Ballad of Peckham Rye*)[1]

> It then came to me again . . . what a wonderful thing it was to be a woman and an artist in the twentieth century.[2]

The nature of Muriel Spark's fiction is its duplicity; she specializes in the subverting of expectations. As she herself claims, in the well-known *House of Fiction* interview, 'what I write is not true—it is a pack of lies.'[3] She is a juggler rather, with various kinds of truth—metaphorical, moral, anagogical—but behind it all is the absolute truth of her religious belief. In the eye of eternity, all human activity is comic, even trivial. In fact, the question often arises, as it does explicitly in *Memento Mori*, 'Do . . . other people exist?'[4] The problem as to whether or not other people are 'real or illusory' has particular relevance to *The Public Image* in which the heroine's character and nature are dissolved and a pleasing fiction substituted—one which will ensure a moneyed and successful life style.

71

Off the screen Annabel Christopher looked a puny little thing. . . . To those who had not first seen her in the new films, or in publicity pictures, she still looked puny, an English girl from Wakefield, with a peaky face and mousey hair.[5]

Annabel has become so identified with her rôle as 'English Lady Tiger' that 'reality' no longer exists. She has become a well-produced, self-created artifact, falsifying her memories in the manner of her own popular films. Here, Billy O'Brien is the reality tester who functions to explode her romantic script:

Once, when he came home late with Billy—towards two o'clock in the morning—she said sentimentally, 'It was lovely in the old days when I used to write one letter sometimes and go out and put it in the box; just one letter. And then—'

'Oh, stop posing,' Billy said. She was standing on the carpet, one hand on a side-table, gazing back into her youth, as if playing a middle-aged part.[6]

Annabel's success resides in her ability to imitate the appearances of things; she is a picker-up of other people's phrases and mannerisms. Frederick is 'infuriated' by this triumphant deception:

He was firm in his opinion that an actor should be sincere in the part he played, and should emotionally experience whatever he was to portray, from the soul outward. Even in her acting, he thought, Annabel is a sort of cheat, she acts from a sense of manners only.[7]

Eventually, Frederick out-acts Annabel, stage-managing his own suicide in a final, competitive attempt to destroy her image. However, so inventive has Annabel become that she is able to subsume this secondary material into her rapidly developing myth and use it to effect her surprising, but inevitable, escape. She, the woman, has proved the greater 'artist' of the two. Nevertheless, Frederick's contribution is a hard act to follow. His dexterous manipulation of an Italian newspaper convention reveals a fine eye for detail and a sound understanding of local mores:

Every week, every day sometimes, letters from sons to Mammas appeared in the Italian papers—in letters from sons in prison, sons on trial, from students who had killed themselves in a nervous crisis, from sons who had seduced their neighbours' daughters, or run away with their wives, from priests who had got married in France. 'Mamma. It is I, your son who writes to you. . . .'

> 'His mother died three or four years ago. Why does he write "Mamma?" He never called her "Mamma".'
> 'He was thinking of his public image.'[8]

Annabel develops greater control of her fictional image as her career progresses; initially, she is the product of Luigi Leopardi's publicity machine:

> Before I made you the Tiger-Lady, you didn't even look like a lady in public, never mind a tiger in private. It's what I began to make of you that you've partly become.[9]

However, acting the Tiger-Lady rôle in her characteristically passionless style, galvanizes Annabel into self-protective action at the time of Frederick's suicide. In the scene with the neighbours, Muriel Spark uses the satirical device of the child commentator in order to keep the reader in touch with the actual situation:

> 'It is what Frederick would have wanted,' Annabel said. 'I know he would have wanted me to carry on with my career.' . . .
> 'If that's what he wanted why did he commit suicide and make a scandal for you?'[10]

But in the world of Muriel Spark's fiction, nothing is simple; the naïve child here is as unattractive as the truth itself but is protected by the national tenderness for children. Annabel recognizes her as a worthy adversary ('Get out, you beast!') and one impossible to dislodge. Nevertheless, the child is reduced to the status of a little girl on a level with all the other non-speaking girls and boys in the scene and Annabel is free to arrange herself and her neighbours in attitudes of grief and sympathy for the benefit of the press 'just as successfully as if the scene had been studied and rehearsed for weeks'. Annabel does not forget to tie up any loose ends connected with that tableau. The doctor will have to be pressurized to admit that his daughter suffers from an over-active imagination, or a neighbour will be asked to give a verdict that the child is highly-strung. All this to safeguard the Lady-Tiger image and to modify and develop it in more subtle and sophisticated ways, so that a new image need not be manufactured—'It's the widowed Lady-Tiger or nothing.' Thus Annabel's fictional self can continue to perform in the usual way, making a new marriage, producing the same kinds of films—a new wild woman, supporting Frederick's fictional theory, need not be born.

Finally, Annabel's control over events seems to be about to be dissipated by the punitive action of Billy O'Brien. However, Muriel Spark's sleight-of-hand operates to the very last lines of this economical and witty fable. Billy proves duplicitous but Annabel simply removes herself from the scene, 'appearing' not at the inquest but at the airport, thereby making her greatest effect. She has finally stepped out of her rôle, or rather, in Spark's typical manner, one complex effect is contained within another. Earlier in the narrative, the reader has been told that 'the baby, Carl, was the only reality of her life'. Although the baby is notoriously good for her image in himself, her situation as 'mother' is the only one in which she feels an almost superstitious horror of acting, as if any falsification of the relationship might, in this case only, destroy it:

> She felt a curious fear of display where the baby was concerned, as if this deep and complete satisfaction might be disfigured or melted away by some public image.[11]

As obtains at the end of *The Ballad of Peckham Rye*, the concluding image moves the narrative mode into a different register, the tone of which measures a permanent and disturbing truth:

> She was pale as a shell. She did not wear her dark glasses. Nobody recognized her as she stood, having moved the baby in a sense weightlessly and perpetually within her, as an empty shell contains, by its very structure, the echo and harking image of former and former seas.[12]

The Public Image, though functioning in terms of intense, revelatory mockery of contemporary European mores, nevertheless remains within the mode of ironic parody. *The Driver's Seat*, on the other hand, manifests the coldness of a mathematical equation. This metaphysical fable edits out, or evades, emotion to an even greater extent than is customary in Spark's work, so that the reader is forced into the collusive enterprise of providing the heroine's psychological motivation. This bleak and elegant fable carries Spark's later, highly stylized manner to extremes. Like Annabel, Lise is a typical Muriel Spark heroine, dull and undistinguished, until she takes charge as the author of her own fate.

The Driver's Seat begins with an ominous insistence on the present tense and with a strong undertone of emotional violence; the salesgirl shouts, the customer, Lise, shrieks. The sense of pressure is intensified by Lise's rapid, almost frenzied, movements. The functional, diagrammatic appearance of Lise's room (paralleled by the similar nature of the text itself) is a container for this violence. Spark's deliberately one-dimensional description of Lise's preparation for her departure (a departure which in itself has been accruing disturbing detail in the preliminary pages of the novel) is subverted by the one image of derision with which the first chapter ends: 'The woman comes to the street door emitting noise like a brown container of laughing-gas until the taxi is out of her scope.'[13]

Having established the emotional atmosphere of the novel, Spark proceeds to lay a trail of clues embedded in the consciously naïve narrative style:

> Lise's eyes are widely spaced, blue-grey and dull. Her lips are a straight line. She is neither good-looking nor bad-looking. Her nose is short and wider than it will look in the likeness constructed partly by the method of identikit, partly by actual photography, soon to be published in the newspapers of four languages.[14]

It is during the scene at the airport that Spark begins to involve the reader more closely in a collaborative contribution to the action. This consists largely in the extensive use of the celebrated, anticinematic flash forward. This type of narrative mode means that the present collapses into the future; the woman from Jo'burg, in establishing a 'transient intimacy' with Lise, has already predetermined her coming forward and repeating 'all she remembers and all she does not remember' to the police. Again, Lise's remarks about her boyfriend project a future, not a present, reality—'I'm going to find him.' The subversion of a normal time-sequence is paralleled by the defeat of (apparently) normal, logical expectations, as in Lise's nonsensical indignation at being offered a stainless dress, 'as if I would want a dress that doesn't show the stains!' It is the certainty of this remark (*the* stains) which creates tension; but the reverse technique produces similar unease in the expectation of the arrival of the murderer. It is certain that he will come, but the time and place are unknown. At this point, the reader begins to gather that the nephew of Mrs. Fiedke is to play the destined rôle: 'My poor nephew has been unwell, we had to send him to a clinic. It was either that or the other, they gave us no choice.'[15]

Much of the macabre humour of this section arises from the reversal of predictable ideas; Lise weeps at the non-appearance of her murderer and Mrs. Fiedke indulges in a mild diatribe against the male sex:

> They are demanding equal rights with us. . . . There was a time when they would stand up and open the door for you. They would take their hat off. But they want their equality today. All I say is that if God had intended them to be as good as us he wouldn't have made them different from us to the naked eye. They don't want to be all dressed alike any more. Which is only a move against us. You couldn't run an army like that, let alone the male sex. With all due respects to Mr. Fiedke, may he rest in peace, the male sex is getting out of hand. Of course, Mr. Fiedke knew his place as a man, give him his due.[16]

The dénouement involves Lise directing her own murder, even to the final scream, thus becoming the author of her own fate. Her dramatic instinct had been acute from the beginning, for it is revealed that Mrs. Fiedke's nephew is the original projected victim on the plane. But it is the author, not Lise, who in the last lines of the book, relates her creation to the more significant world of Greek tragedy in her comment on the trappings of the policemen's uniforms 'devised to protect them from the indecent exposure of fear and pity, pity and fear'.

The Driver's Seat is an illustration of Robert Scholes' dictum, 'we do not imitate the world, we construct versions of it.' Muriel Spark's severe editing of her text encourages the reader to suspend his belief, not his disbelief. The world she presents in this novel is a version of hell, of meaningless contingency, made meaningful by Lise's autonomous act of seeking her own death.

Death, as many critics have remarked, is Muriel Spark's subject, not for its own sake but because it reveals a pattern in life. This pattern is in itself aesthetically pleasing and involves a high degree of intricate lexical play. Charmian, the novelist in *Memento Mori*, seems to voice Spark's own distinction between art and life, or rather, between fictional and spiritual truth: 'the art of fiction is very like the practice of deception . . .', whereas 'in life everything is different. Everything is in the Providence of God.'[17]

Muriel Spark's first book, *The Comforters*, is explicitly 'a novel about writing a novel'.[18] Only an interest in fictional technique as its own *raison-d'être* can rescue the novel from its status of inferiority to poetry; and, in fact, Spark consistently domesticates typical poetic strategies for novelistic purposes. This is especially true of the latest novel, *Loitering With Intent* (1981) in which the quotation from the *Life* of Benvenuto Cellini—'I am now going on my way rejoicing'—figures as a recurrent motif. In many respects, *Loitering With Intent* is a more polished, witty and sophisticated variant of the first novel.

To Caroline, the protagonist of *The Comforters*, the religious dedication of both Catholics and Jews is the product of repellent narcissism.[19] Although she has recently become a convert herself, she feels a fastidious distaste for certain aspects of the faith. Her own vocation, as it develops through the book, is to be that of a creative writer. Having finished her book about novels, she is to embark on a novel herself. She escapes from being a trapped character enclosed in a novel to the freedom of autonomous creativity; she leaves her notes behind her since she has outgrown them. Religion has changed her, but so has the process of learning to write.

The comic device of the unseen typewriter, with its disturbing echoes of the voices that torment Waugh's Gilbert Pinfold, functions to bring together the novel's twin themes, those of religion and fictional inventiveness. From one point of view, of course, the writer, with his ability to create plot and character, is imitating God. So it is natural that Baron Stock should immediately assume that Caroline is haunted, that she has gone through a traumatic religious experience (in his terms, a delusion). Significantly, Caroline is having difficulty with the chapter on realism in the critical work on *Form in the Modern Novel* on which she is currently engaged. Spark would probably concur with the critical theory that realism has failed, but that, as readers and writers, we also have to deal with the failure of fantasy:

> No man has succeeded in imagining a world free of connection to our experiential world, with characters and situations that cannot be seen as mere inversions or distortions of that all too recognizable cosmos. Thus, if we must acknowledge that reality inevitably eludes our human languages, we must admit as well that these languages can never conduct the human imagination to a point beyond this reality. If we cannot reach it, neither can we escape it.[20]

Significantly, also, Caroline feels at ease only with the priest, Father Jerome, 'he never treated her as someone far different from what she was' and it is in his presence that she realizes the truth: 'it is as if a writer on another plane of existence was writing a story about us.' Having found this out, her religion requires her to resist it: 'The Mass is a proper obligation. But to acquiesce in the requirements of someone's novel would have been ignoble.'[21] And again:

> 'I won't be involved in this fictional plot if I can help it. In fact, I'd like to spoil it. If I had my way I'd hold up the action of the novel. It's a duty.'[22]

Paradoxically, Laurence's very irritation with Caroline's scruples about the 'artificial plot' causes it to be enacted; and Caroline's enforced absence from that plot in hospital induces in her a yet more intense consideration of the problems of fictional strategy:

> Caroline among the sleepers turned her mind to the art of the novel, wondering and cogitating, those long hours, and exerting an undue, unreckoned, influence on the narrative from which she is supposed to be absent for a time.[23]

Supporting Spark's own contention that novelists are liars, the typing ghost continues to arrange overlapping plots and random events. Indeed, novel-writing seems at times equated not just with lying, but with insanity: 'is the world a lunatic asylum then? Are we all courteous maniacs discreetly making allowances for everyone else's derangement?'[24] The answer to this question seems to be that we are merely dabbling in different kinds of relative truths, unless we have a clear grasp of essential reality. In any case, Caroline determines to exercise free will and invades the plot, trying to change it. But the issues are resolved on the level of myth. Caroline engages in a deathly struggle by water with Mrs. Hogg and re-emerges triumphant. After this, she is able to enter into the creative life herself:

> 'That dreadful experience with poor Georgina in the river hasn't had any harmful effects on Caroline,' Helena said. 'She must have a strong constitution. In fact, since then she's been much more lighthearted. She seems to be amused by something.'[25]

Caroline has succeeded in taking over the rôle of the typing ghost. Laurence has become a character in her novel; although in life he throws away his letter to Caroline, in fiction nothing is lost: 'and he did not then foresee his later wonder, with a curious rejoicing, how the letter had got into the book.'[26]

The amusement Caroline feels reappears in the delight felt by the protagonist of *Loitering With Intent* in the exercise of her observational powers, 'this process of artistic apprehension', as she herself calls it. Fleur Talbot's response to character creates a kind of exhilaration as life provides, not just the raw, but the finished material, for her fiction:

> I was finding it extraordinary how, throughout all the period I had been working on the novel, right from Chapter One, characters and situations, images and phrases that I absolutely needed for the book simply appeared as if from nowhere into my range of perception. I was a magnet for experiences that I needed. Not that I reproduced them photographically and literally. I didn't for a moment think of portraying Sir Quentin as he was. What gave me great happiness was his gift to me of the finger-tips of his hands touching each other, and, nestling among the words, as he waved towards his cabinet, 'In there are secrets,' the pulsating notion of how much he wanted to impress, how greatly he desired to believe in himself.[27]

Loitering With Intent is rich with a sense of the possibilities, complexities and surprises of life. Fleur Talbot rejoices in the potentiality of fiction. Thus:

> The process by which I created my characters was instinctive, the sum of my whole experience of others and of my own potential self; and so it has always been. Sometimes I don't actually meet a character I have created in a novel until some time after the novel has been written and published.[28]

Writing not only excites and satisfies her, it provides a rôle in life. Fleur's casual attitude, to love, sex and marriage, unnerves the more conventionally minded Beryl Tims:

> a type of woman whom I had come to identify in my mind as the English Rose. . . . The type sickened me and I was fascinated, such being the capacity of my imagination and my need to know the utmost.[29]

Fleur explains that marriage would interfere with writing. Her kind of writing 'requires a lot of poetic concentration', consequently, she is only prepared to love Leslie, Dottie's husband, 'off and on, when he doesn't interfere with my poetry and so forth'. This conflicts with traditional expectations of the woman's rôle as well as disturbing certain categories of value and behaviour; consequently Fleur, a disruptive influence, is considered unnatural. For Beryl, writing is an occupation akin to knitting, a hobby only to be embarked on for relaxation when the children have gone to bed. Dottie, on the other hand, resists Fleur's taking on a 'masculine' rôle in her attitude to Leslie. He will fit into the spaces of her life not occupied by more important things—she is decidedly not dying of romantic love.

Fleur's novelist's appreciation of character is fully satisfied by her encounters with the consciously grotesque Lady Edwina:

> As to her bizarre appearance, I liked it. I liked to see her shaking, withered hand with its talons pointed accusingly, I liked the four greenish teeth through which she hissed and cackled. She cheered up my job with her wild eyes and her pre-war tea-gowns of black lace or draped, patterned silk always hung with glittering beads.[30]

A further refinement is that she is playing a part to express in an oblique way, her detestation for Sir Quentin and Beryl.

In any case, as Fleur is perfectly well aware, 'contradictions in human character are one of its most consistent notes'.

It has often been said that what is lacking in Muriel Spark's fictive work is emotion; critics accuse her of evasiveness, even deviousness, on this issue and it is particularly noticeable in the Anglo-Saxon novel whose subject has always been considered to be romantic love. Spark possibly has more in common with continental writers in this respect, in the 'hardness' of her style and in her characteristic concerns with moral dilemmas and spiritual ideas. Fleur, although a character in a novel, surely functions as something of an alter ego and expresses Spark's personal, playful delight at being a woman and a writer in the twentieth century. Fleur's attitude to character is completely objective, acknowledging democratically both the 'good' and the 'bad'. Dottie, not Fleur, is a moralist; Fleur selects and records the details of experience. She introduces Leslie with characteristic ambiguity: on the one hand, she is 'proud' of his physical appearance, on the other she is repelled and disillusioned by his self-absorption. He is similarly ambivalent about her work—'he often liked what I wrote but disliked my thoughts of being a published writer.' Fleur resists being defined in societal terms as Leslie's 'mistress' and insists on her 'independent liaison with poor Leslie'. Leslie is to be pitied because he can't cope with his life—he is in difficulties with his wife, his 'mistress' and his boy-friend. The power situation is defined in a way totally disturbing to Dottie; it is clear that, in every respect, Fleur is dominant, not least because her vision is not blurred by emotion and she can view the situation with triumphant rationality. In any case, her interest, concern and fascination is reserved not for any person, but for her book, 'my *Warrender Chase*'. People are only valued for the contribution, as characters, that they may be able to make to it. Fleur views her world, as does Muriel Spark, with comic detachment. Her novel is like a 'secret companion' taking up the 'sweetest part' of her mind and the 'rarest part' of her imagination.

Fleur's friendships are equally detached; friends are just there, for no apparent reason and one responds to them as one will:

I don't know why I thought of Dottie as my friend but I did. I believe she thought the same way about me although she didn't really like me. In those days, among the people I mixed with, one had friends almost by predestination. There they were, like your winter coat and your meagre luggage. You didn't think of discarding them just because you didn't altogether like them.[31]

Muriel Spark's ambiguity has perplexed many readers: this is especially so in the case of Miss Jean Brodie—is she to be approved of or not? A similar case obtains with Spark's fictional character Fleur and her fictional character, Warrender Chase. The answer, as always, seems to lie with technique. The novel, not the poem, is the verbal artifact, an arrangement of words on the page. Evelyn Waugh, a clear influence on Spark, took the same view.[32] Neither writer is interested in the psychological build-up of character, their concerns are always with construction, with plot. Dottie, in *Loitering With Intent*, voices the confusion of the layman:

'I don't know what you're getting at. Is Warrender Chase a hero or is he not?'
'He is,' I said.
'Then Marjorie is evil.'
'How can you say that? Marjorie is fiction, she doesn't exist.'
'Marjorie is a personification of evil.'
'What is a personification?' I said. 'Marjorie is only words.'
'Readers like to know where they stand,' Dottie said. 'And in this novel they don't.'[33]

Not knowing where we stand seems to be a condition of existence itself, which is random and purposeless in the extreme, and it is not the task of the writer to explain ambiguity, merely to define it.

Dottie's defence against Fleur's lack of convention, in vocation and life-style, is to make the obvious accusation of lack of womanliness. Fleur, in reaction, willingly plays the female rôle, staging an hysterical scene in an unexceptional manner after which she feels 'flooded with peace'. Dottie's own rôle as 'general reader' is totally undermined by Solly:

'Fuck the general reader,' Solly said, 'because in fact the general reader doesn't exist.'
'That's what I say,' Edwina yelled. 'Just fuck the general reader. No such person.'[34]

Spark's own tough-minded approach to fiction comes out in Fleur Talbot's contemptuous rejection of categories of 'niceness', either in her characters or in herself:

> I wasn't writing poetry and prose so that the reader would think me a nice person, but in order that my sets of words should convey ideas of truth and wonder, as indeed they did to myself as I was composing them.[35]

Precision and economy, two of Spark's own stylistic tools, are favoured by Fleur Talbot also: 'I've come to learn for myself how little one needs, in the art of writing, to convey the lot, and how a lot of words, on the other hand, can convey so little.'[36] Again:

> Warrender Chase never existed, he is only some hundreds of words, some punctuation, sentences, paragraphs, marks on the page. If I had conceived Warrender Chase's motives as a psychological study I would have said so. But I didn't go in for motives, I never have.[37]

Spark documents what exists but implies that fiction may sometimes appropriate reality. Fleur's *Warrender Chase* appears to influence behaviour and events in a startling manner. Sir Quentin crudely mistakes the nature of Fleur's interest in 'Mummy' and can construe the situation only in terms of a mercenary motive. When this explanation fails, his stereotyped response can only be: ' "You have matrimonial prospects?" I went berserk. I said, "I have written a novel that's going to be a success." '

Ironically, Sir Quentin's attempt to stop publication of *Warrender Chase* is on the grounds that 'it is too close to real life'—a typical Sparkian actuality.

Muriel Spark's method, as evidenced by this novel and by her work in general, is to approach a topic from many directions and on many levels. Her comments on the art of fiction in the interview bear many similarities with the views expressed by Fleur in *Loitering With Intent*, particularly with regard to the necessity for a mythology in the novel:

> Without a mythology, a novel is nothing. The true novelist, one who understands the work as a continuous poem, is a myth-maker, and the wonder of the art resides in the endless different ways of telling a story, and the methods are mythological by nature.[38]

She seems to mean by 'myth' a universal element in the plot; without myth, presumably, the random events displayed would be too diverse and incoherent. But fiction writing is not, in any case, a rational activity; this point is well-made with comic sententiousness, at the start of Chapter Ten: 'It is not to be supposed that the stamp and feeling of a novel can be conveyed by an intellectual summary.'

Cosmetic surgery is useless if minor faults are apparent in character or event: 'change the setting of a scene and the balance of the whole work is adversely affected.' Fleur's theory here is concerned with 'essences'. The essence of the work lies in its particular emotional atmosphere and this is to be celebrated in the same way as the essential nature of personality is to be observed and appreciated.

Loitering With Intent is constructed with the tautness and intensity of poetry. It is, of course, a comic novel as well as an incidental disquisition on the nature of reality. The essence of comedy is incongruity and one of the novel's motifs is the figure of Dottie, under stress, singing 'Auld Lang Syne' beneath Fleur's window, 'a ditty that the French fail to relish at one twenty-five in the morning'. It is the significant detail— one twenty-five—that clinches the effect. The novel ends with an action of 'chance grace', the autonomous heroine kicking a football into the hands of a small boy—an image in itself of the masterly ease with which Fleur Talbot, and Muriel Spark, conduct themselves as women and writers in the twentieth century.

If Caroline and Fleur, respective protagonists of *The Comforters* and *Loitering With Intent*, are artists in their own right, and manipulators of their own destinies, Miss Jean Brodie is a failed writer, a creator of a myth in which she involves her girls but remains personally uncommitted, paring her fingernails.

At one point in *Loitering With Intent*, Dottie tells Fleur, 'you're out of your element in our world', and, to a large extent, this is true of all Spark's autonomous heroines who imitate God in their wanton creativity. The undoubted fact that they involve other people involuntarily in their intellectual games means that they are inevitably perceived ambivalently. As David Lodge has pointed out in his analysis of *The Prime of Miss Jean Brodie*, 'the answer to the question "Should we approve or disapprove of Miss Brodie" is "Both".'³⁹

The novel opens with the Biblical question: 'O where shall I find a virtuous woman, for her price is above rubies.' The remainder of the novel is a tentative attempt to answer that question and it is a question focused on Miss Brodie herself. Is Miss Brodie virtuous or not? Again the answer is a paradox: she is virtuous in some ways but not in others. The only absolutes are to be found in God and, although Miss Brodie is eventually dismissed from school on political grounds, this is a mere ploy. Her true offence is that she is playing God, creating and practising a myth. She is the victim of a perverted Calvinism, the dark side of which is represented by the grim architecture and poverty-stricken underworld of Edinburgh. The unattractive Sandy, whose psychological treatise is named significantly 'The Transfiguration of the Commonplace', is the moral reference point for the reader, not least because, destined to become a nun, she is truly out of her element in our world. Miss Brodie has not been called, but has bestowed upon herself, an enviable vocation. Sandy is gradually brought to realize why and what that vocation is. She receives illumination through thoughtful observation of the high and the low, Morningside and Canongate, and through understanding that they are all the same; all fallen creatures in a fallen world:

> Now that she was allowed to go about alone, she walked round the certainly forbidden quarters of Edinburgh to look at the blackened monuments and hear the unbelievable curses of drunken men and women, and comparing their faces with the faces from Morningside and Merchiston with which she was familiar, she saw, with stabs of new and exciting Calvinistic guilt, that there was not much difference.
>
> In this oblique way, she began to sense what went to the makings of Miss Brodie who had elected herself to grace in so particular a way and with more exotic suicidal enchantment than if she had simply taken to drink like other spinsters who couldn't stand it any more.⁴⁰

Sandy is in possession of two kinds of knowledge at the end, that Miss Brodie had to be stopped, but in spite of, or because of, the fact that she was 'an innocent'. Miss Brodie's problem is that her sphere of operations is too small, she has no scope for her imagination in the Junior School and so it is diverted into a perverse personal fable. Miss Brodie's eccentricity is of the order of other Spark heroines (compare the Abbess of Crewe) and is the consequence of misplaced theory: ' "Where there is no vision," Miss Brodie had assured them, "the people perish. Eunice, come and do a somersault in order that we may have comic relief." '[41]

Commentators have noted that the reader's attention is focused on the Brodie set as young children as a result of the deliberately a-chronological narrative. It is only by a series of flash-forwards that we learn essential information about the future fates of the main characters; for instance, that Mary Macgregor was killed in a hotel fire during the war, that Sandy entered an enclosed order, and that Miss Brodie died of cancer in 1946. Miss Brodie's forceful, larger-than-life personality is demonstrated in the description of her physical appearance at the novel's beginning, but she is shown to rule by words. It is her verbal expertise that makes her an arch-manipulator as she is infinitely more diffident about entering the world of action:

> Miss Brodie forced her brown eyes to flash as a meaningful accompaniment to her quiet voice. She looked a mighty woman with her dark Roman profile in the sun. The Brodie set did not for a moment doubt that she would prevail. As soon expect Julius Caesar to apply for a job at a crank school as Miss Brodie. She would never resign. If the authorities wanted to get rid of her she would have to be assassinated.[42]

As we learn elsewhere in the narrative, Eunice was not allowed to do cartwheels on Sundays, 'for in many ways Miss Brodie was an Edinburgh Spinster of the deepest dye'. In spite of her talents, Miss Brodie is very much a type; what is unusual is that she is an unconventional person teaching in a conventional school. Miss Brodie (outwardly at least) is not 'unique' nor is she 'off her head':

> There were legions of her kind during the nineteen-thirties, women from the age of thirty and upward, who crowded their war-bereaved spinsterhood with voyages of discovery into new ideas and energetic practices in art or social welfare, education or religion. The progressive spinsters of Edinburgh did not teach in schools, especially in schools of traditional character

like Marcia Blaine's School for Girls. It was in this that Miss
Brodie was, as the rest of the staff spinsterhood put it, a trifle
out of place. But she was not out of place amongst her own
kind, the vigorous daughters of dead or enfeebled merchants, of
ministers of religion, University professors, doctors, big ware-
house owners of the past, or the owners of fisheries who had
endowed these daughters with shrewd wits, high-coloured
cheeks, constitutions like horses, logical educations, hearty
spirits and private means. They could be seen leaning over the
democratic counters of Edinburgh grocers' shops arguing with
the Manager at three in the afternoon on every subject from the
authenticity of the Scriptures to the question what the word
'guaranteed' on a jam-jar really meant. They went to lectures,
tried living on honey and nuts, took lessons in German and then
went walking in Germany; they bought caravans and went off
with them into the hills among the lochs; they played the guitar,
they supported all the new little theatre companies; they took
lodgings in the slums and, distributing pots of paint, taught
their neighbours the arts of simple interior decoration; they
preached the inventions of Marie Stopes; they attended the
meetings of the Oxford Group and put Spiritualism to their
hawk-eyed test. Some assisted in the Scottish Nationalist
Movement; others, like Miss Brodie, called themselves Euro-
peans and Edinburgh a European capital, the city of Hume and
Boswell. . . . those of Miss Brodie's kind were great talkers and
feminists and, like most feminists, talked to men as man-to-man.[43]

Perhaps Miss Brodie *does* differ from all these in the quality of
her imagination. Her myth-making proclivities are revealed
early on in the text in the romantic story of her lost love, Hugh,
who fell like an autumn leaf on Flanders field: 'he was poor.
He came from Ayrshire, a countryman, but a hard-working
and clever scholar.' Sandy and Jenny are moved to continue
this story and their work, *The Mountain Eyrie*, provides some of
the best comedy in a book which specializes in parodic styles.
Hugh Carruthers was not killed in the war; there was a
mistake in the telegram. Wicked Miss Mackay, the headmistress who is seeking ways to remove Miss Brodie from her
post and with the help of Sandy, the betrayer, finally succeeds,
informed Hugh that Miss Brodie

> did not desire to see him, she loved another. With a bitter,
> harsh laugh, Hugh went and made his abode in a mountain

eyrie, where, wrapped in a leather jacket, he had been discovered one day by Sandy and Jenny.[44]

Perhaps the alarming, but also admirable, fact about Miss
Brodie is that she is herself, like her girls, still developing as a
personality. She is not static, not 'set in her ways'. Unlike her
colleagues who never experience a thought after the age of 20,
she continues to change and to discover new facets of life. This
is a mixed blessing for the impressionable children of her 'set'
who are good material for her influence, being 'bright' and, as
a result of her ministrations, 'precocious'. Much of the humour
of the book is a direct result of the children's misunderstand-
ings, or elaborations, of Miss Brodie's current enthusiasms. As
in her passion for Pavlova, this creates in Sandy a daydream in
which dedication to one's art is the key-note:

> 'Sandy,' said Anna Pavlova, 'you are the only truly dedicated
> dancer, next to me. Your dying Swan is perfect, such a sensi-
> tive, final tap of the claw upon the floor of the stage. . . .'[45]

The comedy is immediately undercut by a flash forward to
the time of Miss Brodie's death and her obsession with her
'betrayal'. Sandy is reported to have gone into a convent,
dedicating herself to God, and rejecting, finally, the Brodie
line. Miss Brodie, though by temperament a born Catholic,
has a Calvinistic distaste for that authoritarian church:

> What a waste. That is not the sort of dedication I meant. Do
> you think she has done this to annoy me? I begin to wonder if it
> was not Sandy who betrayed me.

Her suspicions are correct; Sandy has exchanged one
loyalty for another and this involved the insight that Miss
Bodie's hold on future girls must be broken.

The reader is shown Sandy developing beyond the limitations of Miss Brodie and her world-view. Miss Brodie the
leader, the Roman, the educational reformer still exists in her
own right, but Sandy modifies her own attitude into an almost
maternal one. And here Spark identifies Miss Brodie with the
city itself which, in its schizophrenic nature, Miss Brodie so
much resembles:

> Sandy felt warmly towards Miss Brodie at those times when
> she saw how she was misled in her idea of Rose. It was then that

Miss Brodie looked beautiful and fragile, just as dark heavy
Edinburgh itself could suddenly be changed into a floating city
when the light was a special pearly white and fell upon one of
the gracefully fashioned streets. In the same way Miss Brodie's
masterful features became clear and sweet to Sandy when
viewed in the curious light of the woman's folly, and she never
felt more affection for her in her later years than when she
thought upon Miss Brodie as silly.[46]

Miss Brodie's decisions are always couched in religious
terms; she 'renounces' Mr. Lloyd because he is married, she
'dedicates' herself to Mr. Lowther and to her girls. Her desire
is to control, rather than to participate and to risk losing
herself. Sandy and Jenny are unwilling to reveal to Miss
Brodie the episode of the man 'joyfully exposing himself
beside the Water of Leith' because of the indeterminate
nature of Miss Brodie's relationship with Mr. Lowther and
their general difficulty in seeing her as a sexual being. Again,
comedy results from the displacement of normal expectations. The girls dismiss the man and his behaviour as of no
consequence but are enchanted by the policewoman who
comes to interview them:

> The question of the policewoman was inexhaustible, and
> although Sandy never saw her, nor at that time any police-
> woman (for these were in the early days of the women police),
> she quite deserted Alan Breck and Mr. Rochester and all the
> heroes of fiction for the summer term, and fell in love with the
> unseen policewoman who had questioned Jenny; and in this
> way she managed to keep alive Jenny's enthusiasm too.[47]

The policewoman figures largely in the fantasy life of the
pre-adolescent Jenny and Sandy; Sandy becomes her right-
hand woman 'dedicated to eliminate sex from Edinburgh and
environs'.

In the last months of Miss Brodie's teaching of her set, her old
love story with Hugh becomes embroidered with new threads;
Sandy realizes that Miss Brodie is modifying it and incorporating new material in the manner of a novelist. The same
ambivalence that permeates all Muriel Spark's own fiction
features in Sandy's conflict between admiration for inventiveness and moral disapproval of behaviour:

> Sandy was fascinated by this method of making patterns with facts, and was divided between her admiration for the technique and the pressing need to prove Miss Brodie guilty of misconduct.[48]

Pattern making is Mrs. Spark's primary interest, not only in terms of plot, where the reader's expectations are constantly undermined by a sequence of trap-door effects, but also in terms of language itself. In this novel, Spark shows herself a virtuoso of style, having given herself great scope by the use of adolescents as her mouthpiece. Miss Brodie's letter of renunciation to Mr. Lowther, written by Sandy and Jenny, is an instance of her expertise:

> But I was proud of giving myself to you when you came and took me in the bracken on Arthur's Seat while the storm raged about us. If I am in a certain condition I shall place the infant in the care of a worthy shepherd and his wife, and we can discuss it calmly as platonic acquaintances. I may permit misconduct to occur again from time to time as an outlet because I am in my Prime. We can also have many a breezy day in the fishing boat at sea.[49]

The effectiveness of this letter is due to Spark's total control of diction and tone. The girls had already discussed the unsuitability of a mere bed for Miss Brodie; the drama and glamour of the occasion demanded no less than 'the lofty lion's back of Arthur's Seat' and the pathetic fallacy requires a raging storm to accompany the event. Greek tragedy is invoked in the reference to the worthy shepherd, and bathos intervenes with the descent to rational discourse ('we can discuss it calmly as platonic acquaintances'). The next sentence employs the diction of newspaper reports on sexual matters ('misconduct may occur') leading on to Miss Brodie's classic motif—'I am in my Prime'. 'The breezy day in the fishing boat' refers back to Miss Brodie's reshaping of her original love story incorporating elements of the Lowther tale— singing, painting, sailing in fishing boats—to embellish it.

Miss Brodie's 'sin' for which she has to be punished is the artist's sin of remaking the world in his own image. She refashions reality, redefining aesthetic and moral categories ('Hitler *was* rather naughty') and casting herself as author and heroine of her own myth. Sandy, however, becomes her natural enemy because she sees the importance of detail, rather than of wild artistic generalizations: 'it did not seem necessary that the world should be saved, only that the poor people in the streets and slums of Edinburgh should be relieved.' Nevertheless, what Miss Brodie represents in terms of the autonomous woman and artist manqué has an abiding value and mystery which cannot be destroyed by mere psychological or moral definitions. Sandy attempts to analyse Miss Brodie's character and behaviour in intellectual terms, but this attempt is a failure. Truth, as Spark indicates throughout her work, is not easily captured and is perhaps unknowable:

> She thinks she is Providence, thought Sandy, she thinks she is the God of Calvin, she sees the beginning and the end. And Sandy thought, too, the woman is an unconscious Lesbian. And many theories from the books of psychology categorized Miss Brodie, but failed to obliterate her image from the canvases of one-armed Teddy Lloyd.[50]

Later, when Sandy has become a nun, famous for her book on psychology, having received the gift of religion from Teddy Lloyd (with whom she has Miss Brodie's proxy love affair), she accepts the fact that Miss Brodie's influence has shaped her life and has contributed both to her vocation and to her unease, so that she clutches the bars of her grille with desperation.

The subtlety of Muriel Spark's work is nowhere more evident than in the treatment of her women characters. She practises a sleight-of-hand in manipulating the reader's view of them in the same dexterous manner she deals, insouciantly, with plot and theme. Her women are initiators, actors, magicians whose 'real' nature, like that of life itself, can never be known. 'Complete frankness is not a quality that favours art.'[51]

Muriel Spark: An Odd Capacity for Vision

NOTES

All references are to Penguin editions: *The Comforters* (1957); *Memento Mori* (1959); *The Ballad of Peckham Rye* (1960); *The Prime of Miss Jean Brodie* (1961); *The Public Image* (1968); *The Driver's Seat* (1970); *Loitering With Intent* (1981).

1. P. 143.
2. *Loitering With Intent*, p. 129.
3. In *The Novel Today*, ed. Malcolm Bradbury (1977), p. 133.
4. *Memento Mori*, p. 68.
5. *The Public Image*, p. 7.
6. Ibid., p. 14.
7. Ibid., p. 17.
8. Ibid., pp. 83, 82.
9. Ibid., p. 34.
10. Ibid., p. 64.
11. Ibid., p. 35.
12. Ibid., pp. 124–25.
13. *The Driver's Seat*, p. 17.
14. Ibid., p. 18.
15. Ibid., p. 65.
16. Ibid., p. 72.
17. *Memento Mori*, pp. 187, 188.
18. *House of Fiction* interview, p. 132.
19. *The Comforters*, p. 38, 'Catholics and Jews; the Chosen, infatuated with a tragic image of themselves.'
20. *Structural Fabulation* (Robert Scholes, 1975), p. 7.
21. *The Comforters*, p. 100.
22. Ibid., p. 105.
23. Ibid., p. 137.
24. Ibid., p. 179.
25. Ibid., p. 202.
26. Ibid., p. 204.
27. *Loitering With Intent*, p. 13.
28. Ibid., p. 19.
29. Ibid., p. 20.
30. Ibid., p. 25.
31. Ibid., p. 47.
32. In the Paris Review Interview.
33. *Loitering With Intent*, p. 53.
34. Ibid., p. 56.
35. Ibid., p. 59.
36. Ibid., p. 60.
37. Ibid., p. 61.
38. Ibid., p. 100.
39. *The Novelist At The Crossroads* (1971), p. 129.
40. *The Prime of Miss Jean Brodie*, p. 109.
41. Ibid., p. 7.

42. Ibid., p. 9.
43. Ibid., pp. 42–3.
44. Ibid., p. 18.
45. Ibid., p. 63.
46. Ibid., p. 111.
47. Ibid., p. 67.
48. Ibid., p. 72.
49. Ibid., p. 73.
50. Ibid., p. 120.
51. *Loitering With Intent*, p. 74.

4

Calvinism and Catholicism in Muriel Spark

by ALLAN MASSIE

'With the death of Henry James', Graham Greene has written,

> the religious sense was lost to the English novel, and with the
> religious sense went the sense of the importance of the human
> act. It was as if the world of fiction had lost a dimension; the
> characters of such distinguished writers as Mrs. Virginia Woolf
> and Mr. E. M. Forster wandered like cardboard symbols
> through a world that was paper-thin.

The consequence, as he saw it, was a form of solipsism; soon
even the visible world ceased to exist in its own right:

> it was only a Regent Street as seen by Mrs. Dalloway that was
> conveyed to the reader: a charming whimsical prose poem was
> what Regent Street had become: a current of air, a touch of
> scent, a sparkle of glass. But, we protest, Regent Street too has a
> right to exist; it is more real than Mrs. Dalloway. . . .

And he looked back from 'the subjective novel towards the
chop houses, the mean courts, the still Sunday streets of
Dickens. Dickens's characters', he suggested, 'were of
immortal importance, and the houses in which they damned
themselves were lent importance by their immortal presence.'
When you think of the physicality of *Bleak House*, and the
moral significance of that physicality, and compare it to the
flimsiness with which the visible world inhabited by Mr. and

Mrs. Ramsay is rendered, you can feel very strongly the truth of Greene's words.

Hence, the welcome Greene offered, and the importance he attached, to a novelist like Mauriac:

> a writer for whom the visible world has not ceased to exist, whose characters have the solidity and importance of men with souls to save or lose, and a writer who claims the traditional and essential right of the novelist, to comment, to express his views.

The difference, when you come down to it, is simply between the writer with a religious sense, who believes in the Christian God and the authority of the Church, and the writer whose only authority is that of the private conscience and a vague humanist sense of decency. 'Only connect', said Forster; but the connections were all made on the same plane.

By the time Muriel Spark came to write, Greene himself and Evelyn Waugh had redressed the balance. The religious sense had resumed its proper place in fiction. They submitted their characters to the judgement of a higher authority. Greene's words about James apply equally to his own novels: 'the violence he worked with was not accidental; it was corrupt; it came from the Pit, and had to be fully understood.' And Waugh could write his richest and most sensuous novel on the theme of 'the operation of divine grace on a group of diverse but closely connected characters'. That is a novel much misread and grossly misinterpreted which reiterates the Christian teaching that you cannot serve God and Mammon.

Something therefore had been done to restore what was lost with the death of James. Nevertheless the novelist with a religious sense now found himself working in a society where that sense was either dead or dying. Orwell justly observed that there was nothing so remarkable in our time as the decay of the belief in personal immortality. The religious novelist was therefore working against the grain.

Muriel Spark wrote no novels before her conversion to Catholicism. It is not perhaps presumptuous to suggest that this acceptance of the Faith and the Church removed certain barriers which had deterred her from writing fiction, and gave her a point of view from which to regard experience in a way that made sense. She has never believed that fiction can exactly render the real world, for it is the business of art to order that world in its own terms; but she has never denied its reality. She has written:

> I don't claim that my novels are truth—I claim that they are fiction out of which a kind of truth emerges. And I keep in mind that what I am writing is fiction because I am interested in truth—and I don't pretend that what I am writing is more than an imaginative extension of the truth—something invented. . . . There is metaphorical truth and moral truth and what they call anagogical; the different sorts of truth; and there is absolute truth, in which I believe things which are difficult to believe, but I believe them because they are absolutes.

This is an unimpeachably Catholic statement. In one sense it represents a retreat from the claim that the novel can render the full truth of human experience—it is no more than 'an imaginative extension of the truth'; on the other hand, the acceptance of authority outside personal consciousness gives the fiction a solidity it otherwise lacks.

Muriel Spark's background was different, Jewish and Protestant. Her father was Jewish, her mother Church of England, and she was brought up in Presbyterian Edinburgh where she attended James Gillespie's School for Girls. Never herself a Calvinist, she was not immune to Calvin's influence:

> Fully to savour her position Sandy would go and stand outside St. Giles Cathedral or the Tolbooth, and contemplate these emblems of a dark and terrible salvation which made the fires of the damned seem very merry to the imagination by contrast, and much preferable. . . . All that she was conscious of now was that some quality of life peculiar to Edinburgh and to nowhere else had been going on unknown to her all the time, and however undesirable it might be, she felt deprived of it; however undesirable, she desired to know what it was, and to cease to be protected from it by enlightened people. . . .

So Sandy in *The Prime of Miss Jean Brodie*, a girl who might be described as *anima naturaliter cristiana*, stands poised between the Laodicean humanism of nice people on the one hand, and this intimation of a darker, more demanding and terrifying religion on the other. Meanwhile she is in thrall to Miss Brodie whose own division of the world into her set, the *crème de la crème*, and the rest who are consigned to outer darkness, so ironically shadows the Calvinist doctrine of the Elect and the Damned, which she professes to have rejected.

The Old Testament God, the God of Israel and of Scotch Presbyterianism, is never far absent from Mrs. Spark's work. He broods over her creation. Her novels fix on the moral consequences of action. *Memento Mori* explores the condition of old age because here we can see men and women whose present state is the sum consequence of what they have been and done. They stand at the gates of eternity; judgement is ripe. They must remember—how at their age can they be so frivolous as to forget?—that they must die. In the novella *Not To Disturb* we might be living in a severely Calvinist world. The murder has not yet occurred, but it is unavoidable, predestined; the Count, Countess and the 'secretary' who has been lover to both are closeted in the library from which they cannot ever emerge. Their fate is sealed. The servants have already arranged their publicity, sold their accounts of what has not yet happened but must happen to the world's press. They exclude two visitors to the house because 'they do not belong in the plot.' All Muriel Spark has done is move what will happen back in time; but what will happen is already determined.

Calvinism, which is the way of seeing the world enjoined on her by her Jewish-Scottish inheritance and upbringing, makes her the moralist she is. When she steps back from her characters and points the finger at them and says, 'look, this is how life is arranged; this is how God is denied, these are the consequences', then the message, if not the tone, is that of an Old Testament prophet or Calvinist preacher. It is this heritage which allows her to combine a sense of the moral responsibility of action with the determinism which says that all your actions have unavoidably and unalterably fixed your life in a certain shape. This is the note that dominates the novellas of the late '60s—*The Public Image, The Driver's Seat, The Hothouse by the East River*: novellas which remarkably effect a synthesis between apparently arbitrary, wilful, undirected behaviour and the working out of a remorseless inevitable causality.

Hogg is the name of the villain of her first novel:

> Caroline began to reflect that Mrs. Hogg could easily become an obsession, the demon of that carnal hypocrisy which struck her mind whenever she came across a gathering of Catholics and Jews engaged in their morbid communal pleasures.

Caroline is herself a Catholic convert and Mrs. Hogg the housekeeper at a Retreat she goes to; primarily this is a novel about the difficulties of accepting the Christian religion, one such being the reality of your co-religionists. Principally, however, its demands

> are exorbitant. Christians who don't realize that from the start are not faithful. They are dishonest; their teachers are talking in their sleep: 'Love one another . . . brethren, beloved . . . your brother, neighbours, love, love, love—do they know what they are saying?'

Here, one theme that runs through all Muriel Spark's work is stated: there is an almost unbearable contrast between what religion demands of its adherents and what human beings are ready to give.

But of course the name Hogg is not arbitrarily chosen. It refers us to James Hogg and *The Confessions of a Justified Sinner*, that most remarkable analysis of the consequences of erecting false gods and following their teaching. For, from the beginning, Muriel Spark recognizes that it is not just a choice between indifference and true religion. There is also false religion, seductive and destroying. The name Hogg is a warning; it takes us into that world which so many of her characters will inhabit. Mrs. Hogg's 'lust for converts to the Faith was terrifying, for by the faith she meant herself'. This points the way forward to Mrs. Pettigrew and Dame Lettie Colston in *Memento Mori*, to Patrick Seton in *The Bachelors*, to Jean Brodie herself who 'thinks', in Sandy's view, 'she is Providence, she thinks she is the God of Calvin, she sees the beginning and the end. . . . Miss Brodie has elected herself to Grace.'

Most formidable and terrifying of all, there is Eichmann whose trial is the centre-point of *The Mandelbaum Gate*. Barbara, the heroine, sees that

> He was plainly not testifying for himself, but for his prewritten destiny. He was not answering for himself or for his own life at

all, but for an imperative deity named Bureau IV-B-4, of whom
he was the High Priest.

The witness, having sprung to attention, gave formal ear to
this speech from an alien cult concerning a man being dead. He
then sat down and patiently expounded, once more, the complex
theology in which not his own actions, not even Hitler's, were the
theme of his defence, but the honour of the Supreme Being, the
system, and its least tribute, Bureau IV-B-4.

The Eichmann trial and its significance permeate Muriel
Spark's fiction. He is a ghastly parody of the believer. It is false
religion, not the absence of religion, that is the vilest temptation. Bureau IV-B-4 is an idol; Eichmann has given his soul to
its adoration. It is not enough, we see, to forget self; it depends
on where you lose it. False Gods stalk through the novels. Jean
Brodie whores after them; this is her heresy, her sin, the sin
against the Holy Ghost, to say that that which is, is not, and
that which is not, is. The temptation opens a trap for the
unwary; it is possible to worship falsehood and think it truth.
Eichmann demonstrates this as he testifies to his false God,
Moloch. You can only judge actions by their fruits.

Manifestations of false religion repeat themselves, sometimes presented grimly as in *The Mandelbaum Gate*, sometimes
as matter for comedy as in *Loitering With Intent*. People wish to
remake the world in their own image, to suit their view of
things and please their vanity. Jean Brodie is one example.
Another is Sir Quentin Oliver, founder of the Autobiographical
Association, in *Loitering With Intent*. He protests, 'Did not
Cardinal Newman form under his influence a circle of devoted
spiritual followers? Am I not entitled to do the same?', and the
narrator, Fleur Talbot replies:

> you know, you're off your head. You had this desire to take
> possession of people before I came along and reminded you of
> the existence of Newman. You must see a psychiatrist and
> break up the Association. . . .

It is the result of a confusion between fiction, which is a proper
working of the imagination, and the facts of other people's
lives. 'What is truth?' asks Fleur.

> I could have realized these people with my fun and games with
> their life-stories, while Sir Quentin was destroying them with

his needling after frankness. When people say that nothing happens in their lives I believe them. But you must understand that everything happens to an artist; time is always redeemed, nothing is lost and wonders never cease.

But it is wrong to erect the sort of truth that a novel can embody as a rival to the truths religion reveals.

The heresy with which Muriel Spark peculiarly concerns herself is solipsism. The solipsist places himself at the centre of the universe; its only meaning emanates from his perception and his consciousness. Nothing indeed but that consciousness has an assured reality. So, the medium, Patrick Seton in *The Bachelors*, is correctly described by his girl-friend Alice, as 'not a materialist'. The material world is repugnant to him. Indeed it so disconcerts him that he wishes to deny its reality. When Alice becomes pregnant, he finds it easier to contemplate murdering her than to face the future as the father of her child. The birth of a child would affirm the reality of others and the existence of a material world beyond Patrick's consciousness; murder is an attempt to obliterate both. Reality is only tolerable, like Mrs. Dalloway's Regent Street, when given form and identity by his imagining or day-dreaming consciousness. But Patrick Seton is only an extreme example of the solipsistic view held by the other bachelors in the novel. For all of them reality is confined to what they can discern themselves; they decline to accept its objective existence; they are almost as ready as the spiritualists to remake the world in their own comforting image. Two of them have a conversation about marriage:

> 'It's the duty of all of us to marry,' Matthew said. 'Isn't it? There are two callings, Holy Orders and Holy Matrimony, and one must choose.'
> 'Must one?' said Ronald. 'It seems to me evident that there's no compulsion to make a choice. You are talking about life. It isn't a play.'
> 'I'm only repeating the teaching of the Church,' Matthew said.
> 'It isn't official doctrine,' Ronald said. 'There's no moral law against being a bachelor. Don't be so excessive.'
> 'One can't go on sleeping with girls and then going to confession.'

'That's a different question,' Ronald said, 'That's sex; we were talking about marriage. You want your sex and you don't want to marry. You never get all you want in life.'

That final recognition is Ronald's saving grace. It preserves him from the rank egoism of his friend Walter Press, whose refusal to accept things as they are takes the form of re-writing his own past. And it is of course only a small step from doing that to re-writing other people's pasts, as Sir Quentin Oliver will do, and then to the world of totalitarian egoism that finds its fullest expression in *Nineteen Eighty-Four* where the past is denied any authentic validity. That culmination is an expression of moral idiocy, the condition of a world without God.

Muriel Spark's problem is how to write about religion in a world that has lost faith. Mauriac was writing about Catholicism from within; his Society is still contained in the Church. It is not only Mrs. Spark's background which makes things different; it is rather that for most of her characters there is no such thing as revealed truth. Hence their inability to judge, to employ the proper scale of values; her Catholic characters exist in an alien uncomprehending world. In *Memento Mori* the old sociologist Alec Warner asks Jean Taylor, a Catholic convert, whether she thinks other people exist: 'do you consider that people—the people around us—are real or illusory?' For a moment she thinks he may be mad, then she recognizes his question is purely academic, and agrees to play his game: 'one can sometimes wonder, perhaps only half-consciously, if other people are real.' But she recovers herself. They are passing a graveyard; she suggests that it offers 'a kind of evidence that other people exist. . . . why bother to bury people if they don't exist?' The conversation is light-hearted, joky, yet a little disturbing. Only in a world that denies the reality of God is it possible to question the reality of other people. It is characteristic of Mrs. Spark's Catholic wit to puncture the idealist-solipsistic fancy by calling the dead to witness.

Two novels, *The Prime of Miss Jean Brodie* and *The Girls of*

Slender Means, turn on the act of conversion; that is to say, on the acceptance of the reality of religious truth as the only possible explanation of the mysteries of life and as the surest guard against despair. The converts, Sandy and Nicholas Farringdon, both have to reject other creeds that present themselves as possible solutions.

Jean Brodie seems at first to offer her charges, of whom Sandy is one, a life-enhancing freedom. She poses as daringly unconventional. But that first impression, as Sandy comes to realize, is false: 'she has elected herself to grace.' So the novel becomes an exposure of metaphysical evil. 'I have never known an artist,' Fleur Talbot says in *Loitering With Intent*,

> who at some time in his life has not come into conflict with pure evil, realized as it may have been under the form of disease, injustice, fear, oppression or any other element that can afflict living creatures. . . . no artist has lived who has not experienced and then recognized something, at first too incredibly evil to seem real, then so undoubtedly real as to be undoubtedly true.

So Miss Brodie turns out to be a Morningside Gilles de Rais, prepared to destroy innocence to flesh out her fantasy world, eager to incite others to acts she dare not commit herself. She is wilfully and blindly ignorant of the significance of her actions; self-absorbed, she has no conception of others. She has never come to terms with what she boasts of having rejected, for she lives only in her own mind. She would be incapable of understanding the meaning of the text: 'it is a dreadful thing to fall into the hands of the living God.'

But Sandy, who betrays and destroys her, whose conversion is the true centre of the novel, knows this. Her knowledge means she is responsible for her actions just as Miss Brodie, in her silly arrogance, is irresponsible. There is an echo here of what Julia Flyte says about Rex Mottram in *Brideshead Revisited*:

> You know Father Mowbray hit on the truth about Rex at once, that it took me a year of marriage to see. He simply wasn't all there. He wasn't a complete human being at all. He was a tiny bit of one, unnaturally developed; something in a bottle, an organ kept alive in a laboratory. I thought he was a primitive savage, but he was something absolutely modern and up-to-

date that only this ghastly age could produce. A tiny bit of a man pretending he was the whole.

Exactly the same might be said of Jean Brodie.

Sandy, on the other hand, is not easy with her own act of betrayal. She tries to excuse it in the words: 'if you did not betray us, then you could not have been betrayed by us. The word betrayal does not apply.' There is some truth in this. Jean Brodie, trying to live her own life through the members of the Brodie set, may indeed be said to have betrayed them. She has tried to rob them of their individuality, perverting the Christian teaching that you must love your neighbour as yourself; she has loved her girls as extensions of her own self. She has set out to play God with their lives. It is proper that she be put down; she has made herself an idol in her own image.

Nevertheless it is not quite so simple; there is little that is straightforward in Mrs. Spark's fictional world. The destruction of Miss Brodie has its own ambiguity. 'Give me a child of impressionable age, and she is mine for life', Miss Brodie has said, in imitation of the Jesuits; and there is something Jesuitical, in the common sense of the word, in the way Sandy deals with her. 'You'll never get her on sex,' she tells the headmistress, 'try politics.' Sandy knows that Miss Brodie's politics are absurd, while her behaviour in sexual matters is corrupt, but, as she says, 'I'm only interested in putting a stop to Miss Brodie.' This is Jesuitical casuistry—the end justifies the means—and Mrs. Spark means us to realize it.

Moreover, Sandy is acting on her own behalf too. She has used Miss Brodie to free herself of something more than Miss Brodie, of the brooding weight of Calvinism that has oppressed her childhood. She does not act ignorantly, but, though she becomes Sister Helena of the Transfiguration and writes a best-seller on 'the nature of moral perception' and becomes a celebrity visited by those in search of enlightenment, we cannot be certain that she has acted rightly. There are standards of judgement that condemn her. We are left with this disturbing image of Sandy: ' "Oh, she was quite an innocent in her way", said Sandy, clutching the bars of her grille.' There is an ambiguous and disturbing note here. Sandy sums up Miss Brodie from a position of certainty; yet her hands are 'clutching', as if she must struggle to retain that assurance. The gulf that has deepened between Sandy's self-knowledge and Miss Brodie's ignorance is pointed up by the contrast between the light tone of Sandy's new judgement on her old teacher and the desperation implicit in that act of 'clutching'. Is her life, one wonders, a penance for that airy assumption that the end can justify the means?

There can be no definite answer. Human truth and religious truth march out of step. This is made explicit in *The Girls of Slender Means*, which like *Jean Brodie* and *Brideshead*, is concerned with the operation of divine grace. This novel, with its gentle Kensington setting, is characteristically daring. It becomes a drama of religious conversion which will lead Nicholas Farringdon to a martyr's death in Haiti; the voice of God, we see, can speak as clearly where 'few were nicer, as nice people come, than those girls in Kensington' as in the sin-drenched terrors of Sandy's Calvinist Edinburgh. And, again like Waugh, Mrs. Spark points not only to the mysterious manner of which divine grace may operate but to the completely different mode of existence and perception it enjoins on those who receive it. The parable of the rich young man with many possessions who asked Christ what he must do to be saved echoes through the book.

Nicholas Farringdon is an unsuccessful poet and theoretical anarchist involved with a number of the nice girls at the May of Teck club. One of these girls, Joanna, an elocution teacher given to chanting English poetry, is to be the means of his conversion. She meets her death in a fire that destroys the club. She goes to her death chanting the Psalm for the day: 'except the Lord build the city, their labour is but lost that build it. . . .' Her last words are: 'So that they who go by say not so much as, The Lord prosper you: we wish you good luck in the Name of the Lord. Out of the deep have I called. . . .'

Nicholas tries to convey to Joanna's clergyman father something of what she has meant to him; he wishes to play him a tape-recording of her recitation of 'The Wreck of the Deutschland' (he clearly sees her as one of the nuns who went down with the ship), but it has been expunged. 'She had a sense of Hell', is all he can say, 'she told a friend of hers that she was afraid of Hell.' 'Really', her father says, embarrassed,

'I've never heard her speak morbidly. It must have been the influence of London. . . . Christianity is all in the country parishes these days', adds 'this shepherd of the best prime mutton'.

But Nicholas knows what Joanna meant; he has seen Hell gape. So, when he goes to visit the girl he has loved, Selina, who once took a course in Poise ('Poise is perfect balance, an equanimity of mind and body, complete composure whatever the social scene'), he finds that she screams at the sight of him. 'She's suffering from shock', he tells another survivor, Jane, 'I must have brought all the horrors back to her mind.' 'It was hell', says Jane. 'I know', says Nicholas, but he means something quite different. Selina cannot admit reality; she has cut herself off from the voice of God.

The paradox at the heart of Muriel Spark's picture of the conflict between the true and false religious temperament, between the religious and materialist view of life, is that it is the Catholic, affirming the reality of another world, who is capable of giving due value to this material one. He accepts a reality independent of his own being, and so he recognizes objective standards of right and wrong. The naturally religious spirit will do things for their own sake, regardless of whether advantage may accrue. So Freddy Hamilton, in *The Mandelbaum Gate*, though no more than an Anglican, accepts that you must take responsibility for your own actions. You cannot shuffle it off on some other authority; the contrast with Eichmann and Bureau IV-B-4 is marked. You need religion to keep you on the rails. When Freddy discovers that one of his diplomatic colleagues has been working for a foreign power, he reflects that the man

> had too frequently made a parade of his atheism; if a man can't hold religious convictions, well he can't, but it's a private and secret thing, and if a man can't keep his own secrets, how can he be expected to keep his country's?

It is an old-fashioned view, but Freddy's reasoning is sure: without the authority of a revealed religion a man is in thrall to his own ego.

The heroine of this novel, Barbara Vaughan, has something in common with Muriel Spark herself, as has Fleur Talbot in

Loitering With Intent, though it would be a mistake to think that either can be identified with her creator. Barbara is half-Jewish and a Catholic convert; she has 'the beautiful and dangerous gift of Faith, which, by definition of the Scriptures, is the sum of things hoped for and the evidence of things unseen'. She holds it 'as a vital principle that the human mind was bound in duty to continuous acts of definition'. Nevertheless

> one of the first attractions of her religion's moral philosophy has been its recognition of the helpless complexity of motives that prompted an action, and its consequent emphasis on actual words, thoughts and deeds; there was seldom one motive only in a grown person; the main thing was that the motives should harmonise.

The emphasis on actual words, thoughts and deeds: as Ronald Bridges put it in *The Bachelors*, 'sub-conscious tendencies, repressions, these ideas are too tenuous and simple to provide explanations.' One can only judge people by their conduct; so Eichmann, in thrall to the dead perfection of Bureau IV-B-4, must be judged by what that Bureau did, and by the surrender of his own sense of responsibility to its murderous demands.

An action can only be right if it feels right, but this by itself is not sufficient. After all, that is how the solipsist judges also. Between right action and wrong action the line may be hard to distinguish; this is part of our complexity. It also explains the need for the authority of the Church, an authority that is supported by history.

In the same novel an English priest gives a sermon at the Altar of the Nailing of the Cross. He says:

> the act of pilgrimage is an instinct of mankind. It is an act of devotion which, like a work of art, is good in itself. The questions 'what useful purpose does a pilgrimage serve? What good does it do?' are by the way. People put themselves out to visit places sacred to their religion, or the graves of poets and statesmen, or of their ancestors, or the house they themselves were born in. Why? Because this is what people do.

The importance of this passage is that it stresses that an act of piety satisfies the spirit by uniting it in harmony with others both alive and dead; it is an answer to the egoism that would deny any real or valid existence to others. We are back with Jean Taylor's question, 'why bother to bury people if they don't exist?' Acceptance of the Catholic Faith forces the recognition of others' valid existence on us, and at the same time insists on what we have in common with them.

The Catholic Church in Mrs. Spark's novels stands as the one bulwark against absurdity, mammonism and temporal provinciality of the modern world. That may be represented by New York in *The Hothouse by the East River*:

> New York, home of the vivisectors of the mind, and of the mentally vivisected still to be reassembled, of those who live intact, habitually wondering about their states of sanity, and home of those whose minds have been dead, bearing the scars of resurrection.

In this madhouse there is only one power: ' "Money," says Pierre, "is how things are done".' Or it may find expression in the world described in *The Takeover*, where, as the value of material possessions is called in question by their new insecurity, people take refuge in false religions and idol-worship. Then we see that, as Chesterton put it, 'when people cease to believe in God, they do not believe in nothing; they believe in anything.'

That is insupportable. Muriel Spark is a religious novelist because the Church offers the alternative to the absurdity and egoism of which she is so keenly aware. Like Henry James, she has, in Greene's words, a keen sense 'of the black and merciless things that are behind great possessions'. No modern novelist has a sharper sense of evil; none is more alert to the many forms it can take, of the deceptively attractive guises it assumes. It is perhaps a simplification to say that what she drew from Calvinism in her Edinburgh childhood revealed this to her, and her acceptance of the truth of the Catholic religion provided her with a defence against it; but it is the sort of simplification which can be justified because it lays bare the truth of her art. It is what makes her so formidable and important a novelist.

Part Two:
THE THING DEFINED

5

Muriel Spark: Critic into Novelist

by JANET MENZIES

How do novels come to be written? What brings novelists to spend so many hours behind their typewriters or pushing their biros, not just for the days it takes to write some six or seven thousand words but for months and years. Isolated in studies, libraries, kitchens and bed-sits they may stare at the blank window, change a ribbon or gulp lukewarm coffee—but still they press on. Word follows word until eventually a heavy stack of A4 paper indicates a novel has been written.

How does the novelist go about the task? Where does he start and how does he continue? When the moment of beginning comes how is it recognized—what happens next? Life might carry on regardless or it might lapse into abeyance. A third possibility is that life might move into a special state of heightened awareness and hyper-activity. This is the case for Muriel Spark's novelists, especially Fleur Talbot and Caroline Rose, associated by the similarity of their names—Fleur/Rose.

For Fleur and Caroline writing a first novel is bound up in a hectic phase of their lives. As Fleur is reaching the end of *Warrender Chase* she is drawn into an unpleasant and complicated scheme of emotional blackmail. Caroline's life has a background of diamond smuggling, night-clubbing and the gossiping of her slightly seedy social set who hover on the fringes of the literary world.

In 1960 Muriel Spark said: 'Of course, after finishing a

novel I am always exhausted, and life seems unbearable for a week or two. But the actual writing is more like play than work.[1] In the context of *The Comforters* (1951) and *Loitering With Intent* (1981) the complicated and busy lives of the two girls would leave their author exhausted. The high-spiritedness of the plots and the youth of the central characters do have a playtime atmosphere. But the writing of her first novel, though comparable with Caroline's retreat, was in a calmer situation than either of the girls:

> I took a lonely cottage in the country and started writing *The Comforters*. I wrote the first sentence on the day I moved in, while the rooms were still a jumble of packing-paper and saucepans and books.

Up to that time Muriel Spark's life had had much in common with Fleur and Caroline. It was fairly typical of the intelligent young woman trying to make her way in a literary career. Picking up jobs in literary associations (Mrs. Spark worked for the Poetry Society); getting poems and pieces of criticism published in journals and books; talking endlessly with friends in the same world; bringing out her first full-scale critical biography[2]; making do in a bed-sit. In her essay 'My Conversion'[3] she describes herself in the period before *The Comforters*:

> I was going about, but I was ready for a breakdown. I think it was the religious upheaval and the fact I had been trying to write and couldn't manage it. I was living in very poor circumstances and I was a bit undernourished as well.

She stresses her mental state during this phase: 'The oddest, most peculiar variety of themes and ideas of all sorts teemed in my head. I have never known such mental activity.'[4] That teeming mental state finds its expression in the concrete events of *The Comforters* and *Loitering With Intent* with the intricate and confused comings and goings of the plots themselves. The frustration in Mrs. Spark's remark 'I couldn't sort them out'[5] is evinced in the telegram episode of *The Comforters*:

> I sent Caroline a wire, and apparently Caroline has sent one to me. But they must have got the messages mixed up somehow. This is the message I sent to Caroline . . .

and after enquiring at the post office, 'Laurence cleared off before the question could become any more confused and public.'[6]

Few young writers would find it hard to identify with the Muriel Spark of the 1950s. Sitting among the book-filled cartons in my newly moved-into home, I too feel a sense of common ground. But in reading and criticizing Mrs. Spark's work I am not simply identifying with the writer and her background. I notice these superficial similarities of situation as part of the genuine reaction to seek perceivable truth in reading. A germ in a book is what each individual reader will assimilate as the truth for him of the work. The reader searches for the point in the book which applies to him, which he can recognize as being true for him.

A critic also assimilates when reading but, in order to form one sort of judgement of a book, he quite often suspends his reaction as purely a reader. Therefore the search and the recognition of truth becomes subconscious. A reader can say with outright and happily unconsidered bluntness: 'I don't like this novel. It is a bad book.' Reflecting, he might even add: 'It's just not credible—I can't see any truth in it.' He is comprehensively justified in these remarks because he is perfectly right—for him there is no truth in the particular book. He has that super 'throw it across the room' response! If he likes the book he can take it on board, consciously; with cries of delight pressing his friends to buy it—because he has recognized it as being true.

These purely personal reactions are not sufficient justifications for a critic's judgements. Not only must he find a more elaborate reason for his opinions, but these days he must find that reason not in himself—but in the author. The critic looks to the author's writing of the book to explain his like or dislike. Since the critic can only know the author through what he betrays in his style, his use of techniques, his chosen forms and his biography, these become the stuff of criticism.

So the convention has arisen of supporting opinion by reference to a range of stylistic and formal elements no longer based on assessment of personal response. This convention assumes the critic to be an unsusceptible 'control' and the author to be subject to as many half-recognized personal motivations as any reader. He may be, we are all readers, but so is the critic. The author has just as much claim to the throne of objectivity as his critic.

As a reader I did not enjoy *The Prime of Miss Jean Brodie* because, reminding me of my schooldays in a provincial girls' school, it was not for me a true recollection of those days. Coming to the book as a critic I should put aside the question of enjoyment. Having decided I did not like the book I should justify my dislike on formal grounds in a way which would tend to put Mrs. Spark in a bad light. A reader would say, without embarrassment, 'rotten book' and simply pick up something else. By comparison a critic is a reader looking for someone to blame for a bad read!

As a critic Muriel Spark has never blamed. Remembering she is a reader she has always sought to discover a personal truth through her criticism. In her introduction to the Brontë letters she advocates an imaginative, personal, perception of the subject:

> For where outstanding figures of literature are concerned, surely the greatest benefit to be derived from a study of their lives is that which penetrates the operation of the creative mind, interpreting the spirit which motivated it.[7]

Her writing on Mary Shelley and Emily Brontë gives a sense of her close identification with them. Discussing Emily's poems, she writes:

> Few poets can be said to have experienced the physical or psychological events portrayed during the precise month or year in which a particular poem was composed. . . . Such complete absorption in work is what most poets would describe as happiness, whether it lasts a whole afternoon, several days, or half-an-hour.[8]

Her description of the poet's sensations assumes such communality of experience between herself and Emily that the two become part of the same literary set. We can imagine Emily and Muriel discussing writing together in a pub's lounge bar or the kitchen at Haworth.

Muriel Spark said: 'Fiction to me is a kind of parable. You have got to make up your mind it's not true. Some kind of truth emerges from it, but it's not fact.'[9] This suggests her

seeing truth as not immutable but varying according to the
disposition of the reader. Mrs. Spark's imaginative identification in her criticism of Emily Brontë and Mary Shelley is of a
similar predisposed kind. Her criticism is creative not so much
in how she grows from and responds to the subjects as in what
she brings to them and what they reveal in her.

The working of this creative criticism is most apparent in
the close similarities between those facts of Brontë and Shelley
life which Muriel Spark highlights in her criticism and the
non-facts of the situations depicted in her novels. In the
introduction to *Child of Light*[10] Mrs. Spark draws a prophetic
parallel between the way of life around Mary Shelley, which
she rejected, and its 1950s incarnation:

> We all know (no loss to those who do not) the dilapidated
> Bright Young Things, phantoms from the 'twenties, who haunt
> the pubs of Soho as if seeking in those localities of earlier
> promise, some indistinct token of fulfilment like a glove
> inadvertently left behind them.

As Mary Shelley separates herself from this set of Shelley's
friends Muriel Spark relates their reaction: ' "Conventional
slave." Trelawney vituperated not before he had made good
use of her. "Bourgeois!" we can hear his present-day counterpart's outworn echo.' The scene is re-enacted in *The Comforters*
when Caroline discusses Baron Stock with an acquaintance
during the course of a long and rather unsatisfactory pub-
crawl. The girl announces Willi Stock is a satanist:

> 'Probably that's why Eleanor left him. She's so awfully
> bourgeois.'
> Caroline suddenly felt oppressed by the pub and the people.
> That word 'bourgeois' had a dispiriting effect on her evening—
> it was part of the dreary imprecise language of this half-world
> she had left behind her more than two years since.[11]

The function of Muriel Spark's comparison is not to see her
own times reflecting Mary Shelley's situation, nor to put it
forward as a prefigurement of the '50s. Mrs. Spark's critical
grasp of that element of Mary Shelley's society has enabled
her to recognize a true reaction to a 'half-world' she knows
well. So that some six years later Caroline is able to turn away,
realizing its every connotation.

Mrs. Spark often portrays Mary Shelley's life in terms of the 'half-world' which has a close resemblance to that depicted later in her novels. The poorness and disorder of the Shelleys' life together has much in common not simply with life in *The Girls of Slender Means* or *Loitering With Intent* but also with what we hear of Muriel Spark's early career. It may be too that Mrs. Spark was particularly drawn to Mary Shelley's description of the considerable time she spent in Scotland.

The repeated blackmailing attempts made against Mary towards the end of her life are all recounted. First Mary's protégé, Alexander Knox, has to deal with Gatteschi; then a 'G. Byron' has letters to sell; next a damaging memoir is threatened; and then a cousin of Shelley is writing a life! The same parasitism is portrayed in the servants of *Not To Disturb* with their memoirs already written and sold—even film rights under offer, against the expected deaths of their infamous employers. Then there is Alec Warner in *Memento Mori* with his card indexes of case histories. There are the farcical toings and froings of the Autobiographical Association when Fleur ransoms the manipulated memoirs against her own stolen novel *Warrender Chase.*

Shelley and Mary Shelley's friends 'all engaged in a certain amount of back-biting about her in later years' we are told. Images at once arise of the gossiping little intrigues among the old folk of *Memento Mori*, the bachelors, and also the Brodie set. 'Set' is the word Muriel Spark uses when describing the 'Letter to Edmund Burke' written by Mary Shelley's mother, Mary Wollstonecraft: 'It served to confirm Mary as one of the set.'[12]

So many of Muriel Spark's novels are about sets, groups of people easily recognized and even given a name. The theme is first apparent in her criticism as she moves from the decadent post-Romantic 'set' to a group defined by its very isolation: the Brontës of Haworth parsonage. Muriel Spark describes the 'harsh isolated northern parish' in *Emily Brontë: Her Life and Work*:

> In this gaunt house with a graveyard at the bottom of the garden, all but one of the Brontës died. Facing the broad unchanged moorland prospect, the parsonage and graveyard still stand isolated. Their characteristics seem inseparably

blended; the gravestones leaning awry like so many disused outhouses; and the house itself, a slab-like oblong memorial.

Here are the Brontës within their environment: an isolated group defined by situation, claustrophobic in communal death, and identified by affinity with the very buildings. This accurate and emotive description so closely pre-figures the novel themes one might conceive of the facts being twisted to fit a pre-formed idea but, of course, the Yorkshire moors and the Yorkshire stone are unalterable.

These magnetic elements of the Brontës' situation have drawn Mrs. Spark into critical work which will influence her profoundly. She recently said of her novel characters: 'It's a potentiality rather than oneself one recognizes in them, but they have to be a bit of you or you wouldn't know what you were talking about',[13] and the comment applies to her relationship with her critical subjects. Her criticism helped her to realize a potentiality in herself in much the way a novelist's creation affects the novelist. In this way, too, suggests Mrs. Spark, was Emily Brontë's whole life and awareness altered by writing *Wuthering Heights*.

The legend which grew up around Emily Brontë almost immediately after the publication of *Wuthering Heights* was a narration of her life determined by the book's existence, postulates Mrs. Spark. Moreover the legend is no less true because it has little bearing on Emily's life before the book. So *Wuthering Heights* may have created Emily Brontë just as much as Emily wrote *Wuthering Heights*.

After 1846 the family's attitude towards Emily changed and 'Emily took on the aspect of a legendary being', writes Muriel Spark[14]: 'Charlotte began, now, to see her sister as a dramatic being. . . . Charlotte was ever more taken up with this new image of her younger sister as a creature of concealed and terrible powers.' There is a suggestion in Mrs. Spark's language that Charlotte is romanticizing her sister. She is portrayed seeing Emily as 'dramatic', with 'powers' which are 'concealed and terrible'. The view, if not fictive, certainly has a narrative aspect, and Mrs. Spark enquires after its validity: 'Had this larger-looming Emily, in fact, existed all along?' Looking at Brontë family letters she answers: 'Casual comments reveal nothing of the passionate lonely genius who, it seems, was revealed to her family in the last three years of her life.' She speculates: 'It may be that Emily herself did not realize her own nature until she had produced *Wuthering Heights*. Her verbs 'revealed' and 'realize' carry the sense of making visible and making real. Something new has been brought into the field of Emily's concrete awareness and that of her family and associates. A new element has come to life—*Wuthering Heights* is the agent which has brought it to life.

Just as Muriel Spark talks of that 'potentiality . . . one recognizes' and uses the phrase 'potential experience' of Emily's poetry,[14] so upon the writing of *Wuthering Heights* a potential is realized in the Brontë life. Mrs. Spark brings the process sharply into focus by comparison with anyone's experience of meeting unknowingly a famous person, asking:

> Which is the more accurate portrayal, that of the real man whom we chanced to meet, or that of our reconstruction—the legendary figure in other words: The second impression is the more real. The first merely prefigured the legend.

So, she concludes, the effect of the fame is concrete. The implications of having written *Wuthering Heights* become an absolute reality for Emily Brontë.

'As soon as she had said these words Caroline knew that she had hit on the truth', and the truth of her situation, which Caroline has just hit upon, is an embodiment of Muriel Spark's critical discoveries. Caroline Rose explains: 'The typewriter and the voices—it is as if a writer on another plane of existence was writing a story about us.'[15] She and Fleur Talbot at opposite ends of Mrs. Spark's *oeuvre* find their lives narrated by the novels they are writing and about to write.

Even before her novel establishes itself Caroline already has the capacity for third-person living common to many writers: 'She told herself "I'm good at packing a suitcase," forming these words in her mind . . .' and the next time she packs her suitcase we are again reminded of 'her customary habit of self-observation'. Muriel Spark also makes this point of John Masefield: 'Those parts of his life story which the poet himself has written about never fail to give the impression that life has always presented itself to him, as it were in the narrative form.'[16]

Gaining confidence Caroline even goes so far as to make a running commentary on her novel as well as herself. Of Mrs. Hogg: ' "Not a real-life character", she commented at last, "only a gargoyle" ', for her existence is purely functional. Like Dermot Trellis in Flann O'Brien's novel *At Swim-Two-Birds*:[17] when Mrs. Hogg ceases to influence she ceases to be.

Dermot Trellis does not disappear when he falls asleep but he loses control over the characters in the novel he (like everyone else!) happens to be writing. At liberty they behave with as much wilfulness as Caroline exhibits: ' "This interlude in my life is not part of the book in consequence." It was by making exasperating remarks like this that Caroline Rose continued to interfere with the book.' O'Brien's narrator, the narrator of Trellis, explains that Trellis's creation:

> The villain Furriskey . . . hatched a plot for putting sleeping-draughts in Trellis's porter. . . . this meant Trellis was nearly always asleep and awoke only at predeterminable hours, when everything would be temporarily in order. . . . they had to dash back to their respective situations, of course, when the great man was due to be stirring in his sleep. They hired a girl to mind the shop. . . .[18]

This delightful conceit of characters who know they are narrated and respond by setting about their narrator is shared by Muriel Spark and O'Brien in common with writers like Beckett and Italo Calvino. Caroline has the dual rôle of being not only a creation within her novel but eventually the writer of that novel. Trellis, similarly, is not only the narrator of obstreperous characters but is narrated himself. The action of these pseudo-novels upon the actual novel is a formal reflection of Muriel Spark's analysis of the effect of Emily Brontë's novel upon her being.

'We know Emily had been theorizing—delivering herself of ideas which, to Charlotte, were daring and original, but not practical',[19] writes Mrs. Spark. Supposing Emily to have evolved a philosophy from her own work, she adds: 'If it were put into practice, in fact, it would be highly dangerous, for its principles were destructive.' She continues by suggesting that 'Emily had begun to dramatize, in her own person, the aspirations expressed in her work.' This experience finds an equivalent expression in the mechanical effects of Caroline's novel. '. . . next day by car, though Laurence's MG was due for repair, instead of going by train . . .' the voices tell Caroline, whose response is:

> 'We must go by train. You see that, don't you, Laurence? It's a matter of asserting free will.'
> He quite saw. He thought, 'Why the hell should we be enslaved by her secret fantasy?'

Train or car, their actions will have been determined by the pseudo-novel, just as eventually Emily Brontë 'did not speak of delusions, she enacted them'.[21]

Muriel Spark describes Emily 'defining in terms of action, the principles which . . . she came to recognize in her work'. She attempts to place this response: 'The Romantic poets expressed in their personal conduct the hypotheses underlying their creative writings.'

Her later novel *Loitering With Intent* presents a more analytical expression of the process than the reactive *The Comforters*. The novel operates on the same convention: 'The story of "Warrender Chase" was in reality already formed',[22] explains Fleur, but it seems to be influencing the happenings at the Autobiographical Association: 'I saw before my eyes how Sir Quentin was revealing himself chapter by chapter to be a type and consummation of Warrender Chase, my character.'

Less intuitive and more rational than Caroline Rose, Fleur Talbot sets out to find some answers. The novel points towards Muriel Spark's personal understanding of the narrative effect. Fleur replies to Dottie: 'I said I would be able to explain when I had written a few more chapters of my novel *Warrender Chase*. . . . I have to work it out through my own creativity.'

Fleur and Caroline work out real events through their creativity; Muriel Spark works out personal realization, first through her criticism, then in her created works. Her criticism of Emily Brontë and Mary Shelley reveals her latent sense of such facets as the group, isolation and claustrophobia. In realizing these concerns she is converted from critic into novelist, she might say from agnostic to believer.

Mrs. Spark's creative criticism is an inversion of ordinary 'blaming' criticism. Where criticism studies the effect of a writer upon his work, she constantly observes the effect of his work upon the writer. Both in her criticism and her novels we see her abiding interest in people who are being affected. Her people are changed and disturbed either by novels they have written or are writing or by other people's novels and revelations. This at times clinical preoccupation causes some to see Muriel Spark as detached—in the way Dottie tells Fleur 'your head rules your heart'. In a recent interview Mrs. Spark recalls 'My mother's criticism of me was that my head ruled my heart' and her novels are impelled by analytic rather than emotional necessity.[23]

A measure of this is that Muriel Spark is inspired by criticism of her subjects, rather than influenced by reading their work. In her introduction to the Brontë letters she stresses the organic importance of storms: 'Time and again the sisters described some cataclysmic event of nature as a sympathetic manifestation of some inner personal tempest.'[24] Yet in *Not to Disturb* she deliberately deflates the Gothic storm motif. She contrives for the storm to rid the plot with ridiculous convenience of two unwanted 'extras', 'killed instantly without pain'. The storm is further deprived of any possibility of genuine function by the practical response to it: 'He gets drenched almost immediately for at that moment the storm descends with full concentration.'[25] The storm's crescendo is out of phase with the story's dramatic climax, and by the time we learn it has not even managed to bring the lines down, I feel quite sorry for that sad little shadow of the great 'wuthering' tempests.

Derek Stanford comments on the lack of organic elements in Muriel Spark's writing, especially in her portrayal of groups: 'There are plenty of studies of collective existence in her fictions, but none of a community as a positive enriching thing.'[26] Many of her novels concern one particular group, rarely stepping outside the unit, and titles like *The Bachelors* and *The Girls of Slender Means* delineate from the outset the situation to be explored. In *Memento Mori* the group is both defined and identified by situation. The situation is that of being old and being reminded of death.

The technique is even more pronounced in the opening lines of *The Bachelors*:

> Daylight was appearing over London, the great city of bachelors. Half-pint bottles of milk began to be stood on the doorsteps of houses containing single apartments from Hampstead Heath to Greenwich Park, and from Wanstead Flats to Putney Heath; but especially in Hampstead, especially in Kensington.[27]

There we have them, the eponymous bachelors: where they live and how they live—by half-pint measures. That is really all there is to be said, and by the end of the book, when Ronald counts the 'seventeen point one bachelors to a street—lying awake, twisting and murmuring, or agitated with their bedfellows, or breathing in deep repose between their sheets, all over London, the metropolitan city', that is really all that has been said. One particular redolent facet of London life has been encapsulated, like an insect in a killing-bottle. But it is only one section of London life, isolated from the rest for the purposes of observation. None of the bachelors have ordinary married friends. They are out of contact with the rest of life to such an extent that, when the court-room brings them into it, a sharp perspective lifts the novel's language to new energy and dynamism.

As Mrs. Spark cuts off alternative avenues for her group members they tend to be trapped by their definitive situations: 'trapped in the groove of habit'.[28] This is expressed concretely in *The Girls of Slender Means* when the defining measure—in this case a precise 36¼ inches—becomes all too real a trap as 'they assisted the three slim girls through the window.' As Sir Quentin Oliver draws members into his Autobiographical Association they too are trapped by their own folly and weakness.

In *The Hothouse by the East River* the intense, stuffy, eye-blinking heat pervading the novel epitomizes the trap's depressing claustrophobia: 'It is winter time in Elsa Hazlett's apartment; the rushing summer purr of the air-conditioner has ceased; the air quivers with central heating that cannot be turned off very far.'[29]

All the plot's efforts at development seem to return,

frustrated, to that constant, oppressive, fact of heat. The characters are torpid. Bemused, their conversation oscillates and collapses, words occluded by heat like the semi-dormant silk worms in Princess Xavier's breast: 'The apartment on the East River is empty and hot. Paul tries to turn the handles of the radiators in the drawing-room, but they are all swivelled as far to the right as they will go.'

Although the apartment has a vast outlook on the East River, and though characters mention shopping trips and visit night-clubs, there is no sense of an external perspective. There is no raucous New York scene as a context for the apartment and its occupants. Though Elsa may stare out over the East River, we have no impression of the river as having been seen. It is unsurprising, therefore, to learn that Paul and Elsa are cut off by the ultimate isolation of being dead. The apartment is demolished whose oppressive heat they only intended to endure. Just as her situation became clear to Caroline at the end of a fruitless pub-crawl, so the Hazletts' deadness becomes clear at the end of a vacuous evening of night-clubbing. The experience of these dreary fun-pursuits seems revelatory to Muriel Spark. By the end of them alternatives have been cut off more completely than before—for the Hazletts most completely.

Yet even when a group is placed in an external context it often serves only to make their isolation more apparent. In *Not To Disturb* we get a sudden brief glimpse of the house as we would see it, perhaps from the small, green, parked car—'The large windowed wall of the servants' hall looks out on a gravelled courtyard and beyond that, the cold mountains, already lost in the early darkening of autumn'—but, disturbingly, this only increases our apprehension of how lonely and apart is the house. That the servants' hall windows are not in fact looking out in this sentence but being looked at promotes our sense of the house's enclosedness.

The Prime of Miss Jean Brodie provides one of the most fully realized contexts for a 'group'. There is a lively sense of Edinburgh granite as the Brodie set swing their golf clubs or shudder at the slums. Yet is not Edinburgh, along with Dublin, an insular capital? Muriel Spark has written: 'I think the puritanical strain of the Edinburgh ethos is inescapable, but this is not necessarily a bad thing. . . . We were definitely given to understand that we were citizens of no mean city.'[30] In novels which could loosely be termed 'organic' or 'natural' novels, exemplified by *Wuthering Heights*, environment is assumed to affect emotions. Emotions in turn determine motivation and motives are what lead the characters in and out of traps. Muriel Spark's characters are not trapped by their motives. They are trapped by their situation—situations picked for them by their narrator in order to define their group identity. Environment in this case loses its catalytic function and becomes synonymous with situation. Mrs. Spark associates the environment of Edinburgh life closely with the situation of Edinburgh people: 'But the physical features of the place surely had an effect as special as themselves on the outlook of the people.' Her use of the general term 'outlook' rather than 'ideas', 'thoughts' or 'feelings' conveys no sense of people deriving specific motives from their surroundings other than an innate appreciation of the area. The Brodie set's environment and their situation are one and the same. They are Brodie girls and Brodie girls are Edinburgh's own 'crème de la crème.'

Ronald Bridges, one of the bachelors, is trapped by his situation of being an epileptic. His parallel, Alice Dawes, is also seen in terms of her state of health—she is both pregnant and a diabetic. The two characters, epileptic and diabetic, both learn special methods of emotional control. Ronald 'knew how to compose himself for a fit. He cultivated his secret method of retaining some self-awareness during his convulsions.'

Alice's method of determining emotion is superficially more artificial: 'Though she was not an insincere girl, she sometimes remembered to express those emotions which she wished to reveal, by certain miming movements of the head, hands, shoulders, feet, eyes and eyelids.'[31] Suffering under the imposed constraints of their alien situations, emotions are for them deceptive and unreliable. In defusing them a source of natural motivation in the novel is lost.

Derek Stanford points out a distrust of nature and the natural in much of Muriel Spark's work. Nature itself she had found less than pleasant in Africa: 'However mild and sweet nature seemed in Sussex Muriel could never forget what it had been in South Africa.' She may extend this to deposing the workings of nature upon life, he suggests: 'the notion that nature is never quite enough—that man cannot live by its laws alone'.

The function of drugs in *The Bachelors* is symptomatic of the non-organic attributes of Muriel Spark's writing. Ronald undergoes 'two years clinical trial of a new drug', in an effort to control his epilepsy, while the medium, Patrick, takes a

> new drug which had been employed, for experimental pur-
> poses, to induce epileptic convulsions in rats, and which, taken
> in certain minor quantities, greatly improved both the spec-
> tacular quality of Patrick's trances and his actual psychic
> powers.

Despite their seemingly diametrically opposed purposes Mrs. Spark's language and attitude towards them (coupled with Ronald's response to his) makes us suspect the two drugs of being one and the same. The parallel not only criticizes how arbitrary is modern medicine but draws Ronald and Patrick closer to a mutual identity. Asked what goes on in Patrick Seyton's mind, Ronald's reply 'described his own symptoms when a fit was approaching'.

In these terms Ronald and Patrick are not differentiated; within the novel, simply their moves are different. For Mrs. Spark manipulates her characters like a chess player—schematically. As the characters plot amongst themselves their actions are prompted by Muriel Spark's greater scheme. No organic forces surge into the novel to stir the characters' internal motivations. No random chaos of the irrational or the un-suspected emerges to undermine the plot's development. The bachelors and their friends perpetually scheme amongst them-selves, changing sides constantly from plot to counter-plot. Leaving his confederate, Marlene Cooper, Ewart Thornton 'departed to his rooms at Campden Hill where, from the depths of his leather arm-chair, he telephoned Freda Flower', but his betrayal of Marlene is unimportant and undisturbing, a matter simply of words and actions, not emotion.

Derek Stanford defines Muriel Spark's technique: 'A certain Byzantine-like elongation of personality, and behaviour pat-terns is her usual device for creating character.' When Muriel

Spark develops a deliberately contrived effect for her manipulations her writing is often delightfully energetic. From her opening words of *The Comforters* she declares her convention: 'On the first day of his holiday Laurence Manders woke to hear his grandmother's voice below.' At once we are in Famous Five territory and we know we are in for an adventure! The children's story preoccupation with good country cooking takes up the next few lines: 'Laurence shouted from the window, "Grandmother, I adore white bread and I have no fads." She puckered and beamed up at him.' The first day of the summer holidays, eight weeks before the school term begins in September . . . and who knows if there is any hidden significance about the bread? Of course there is; we quickly discover there are diamonds in the bread and Laurence finds out his grandmother runs a gang! As we expect a series of contrivances are to follow, just like the unbelievable Enid Blyton coincidences recently parodied by Adrian Edmonson of the 'Comic Strip' team.

Clues are dropped everywhere: 'Certainly she did not possess her blue hat at that time', puzzles Caroline. Intricate relationships of the he said-she said, but-his-cousin-was-her-first-husband variety add a pacy seasoning of West End farce.

Muriel Spark challenges us with her obvious artifice. Denied the opportunity to luxuriate in the narrative action by taking her plot seriously we must respond to her themes. With *The Comforters* we find ourselves wondering about the relationship between miracle and coincidence or questioning what really determines our actions; but where the theme is insufficient, it is dangerous to attempt such constructive artifice. When Mrs. Spark's use of device becomes merely mechanical she takes on the aspect of a scientific experimenter. The emotions of her characters are controlled. They are placed in an isolated situation, cut off from external and natural influences. They experience contrived events and their movements are manipulated. Her groups, especially, begin to resemble laboratory animals in their tanks and cages, ready for experimentation or inspection. The author becomes a scientist, providing a controlled set of circumstances in order to observe and draw conclusions. The eyes of the white-coated peer in at the three-sided glass window of the apartment by the East River.

Derek Stanford suggests a 'gimmicky' element in her writing, defining it as 'a formal device disproportionate to the meaning'. In keeping with her artificial plot-development Muriel Spark's use of symbol and motif has an obviousness very close to being gimmicky. Sometimes she explodes her motif into laughter: who could possibly talk about Muriel Spark and the herring-roe? Yet the roes are diamond-bearing in *The Comforters* and hoarded by Fleur to eat on toast with Lady Edwina. Then, too, an interest in canning, bottling and jamming pops up more than once, with Sir Edwina Manders and Sir Eric Findlay, Lady Edwina's son, just two of its proponents. Muriel Spark pokes fun at these minor formulae, while ritualizing her important metaphors so that we are aware of 'something highly formal and deftly mimetic'. Derek Stanford goes on to think of 'a puppet theatre' as a possible description.

The theatre of the courtroom works to such a formula in *The Bachelors*. Here Muriel Spark's formal use of directly pre-defined terms and situations has a compelling dramatic necessity. The court scene is technically indispensable to the plot: 'I may not be sent for trial; if it comes to court; the case may not come off.' This constant refrain among the bachelors reiterates the preoccupation of their enclosed little world. But when we enter the court we realize its action is not simply a device. It is not wholly part of the bachelors' pre-determined situation.

Under the hard brilliance of functional lighting, appraised by the bench's indifferent stare, the characters stand in dramatic perspective. The contrast is a contrived device, prepared for throughout the plot. Yet how so convincing: why do these petty happenings suddenly become important? The contrast might be expected to denigrate the bachelors, making trivia of the trial: a solemn fuss over a widow's nothing. In fact the conventions of the court's drama, the last-minute witness, the defendant's evidence—'the answers came without hesitation, clear and strong'—are genuinely, not artificially compelling. Here, at this final moment, the reader engages for the first time in the invented lives of these puppet-bachelors. Nor is this just because, ironically, Alice's life depends on the trial's outcome, since Mrs. Spark's use of device has always prompted an awareness of Alice as fictional.

The answer lies in Muriel Spark's very formalism. The courtroom scene is a formula in two senses. Not solely a technical device within the novel, it is an obvious symbol and as such provides a context independent of the novel. The judge is the judge. Within the novel he is appointed to assess the other characters, which he does very accurately:

> 'Mr. Bowles,' said the judge, 'are you wanting to put in actual evidence at this stage?'
> 'I was about to ask. . . .'
> The judge looked at his watch. Then he looked hard at Father Socket.

He is also a judge, a symbol of judgeness. He says: 'I only want to get our definitions clear so that the jury can see what it is dealing with. There has been a great deal of mystification in this case.' His is not just a court-scene. It is a court: an obvious metaphor of courtness, of the court's one fixed quality which is to discover the truth. If we get our 'definitions clear' as Mrs. Spark's judge advises, we can penetrate the 'mystifications' of her novels, and disclose a repeated search for what is true.

Derek Stanford recalls Muriel Spark wondering

> Had I, she asked, ever thought of becoming a Catholic? Sometimes she felt like setting out on a search in order to discover the truth. She would visit the Reference Rooms of out-of-the-way Public Libraries in case it had got deposited on the shelves in some ponderous or unlikely book. And she would see—quite literally—that no stone was left unturned; she would roll aside every boulder under which the truth might conceivably lie hidden.

That is just how the search for truth is expressed in her work, by very direct, obvious methods. Her truth seekers are exact metaphors for their functions. They are courts, judges, amateur sleuths, school girls, psychiatrists, even the police are called in to discover the source of the memento mori.

This concrete view of the truth as an actuality explains much of the artifice in Muriel Spark's work. If truth is so literal, so absolutely present as an object, then pure experiment should discover it. If you pick up enough stones it must be there, somewhere among the woodlice. Mrs. Spark's characters are turned over like the stones; her plots experiment to find the answer. Can the fictional manipulation of ciphers hold any real answers?

As a critic Muriel Spark had discovered the novel to be a constant agent of perception. Her work on Emily Brontë, especially, showed her a life deeply affected not just by notoriety but by what had been written down in a novel. Her criticism points out how fiction is more than a straightforward mirror to life. The process of narration demands a representation of fundamental human conditions. The novelist must not photograph, but re-create in a parallel world, the precepts and even the unconscious operations of his own world. As he writes in this at once intuitive and deeply conscious state his own perception is altered. As his perception changes and develops, all life around him is changing and mutable. The written affects the writer; the affected writer has an effect upon his environment. The critic detects these alterations and tracks them to source.

So Muriel Spark came to see narration as revelation. As she developed from critic to novelist, her novels frequently came to act as devices by which to search out this effect. In her writing we see Muriel Spark as a seeker of truth, but we also find her rejecting it, even where it means most. Derek Stanford has gone so far as to say: 'Truth for Muriel Spark implies rejection.'

In *Loitering With Intent* a type of rejection is at work when Fleur gives the loathed Beryl (a gemstone) her best brooch:

> I hated Beryl Tims . . . [who] simpered about my lovely brooch. I hated her so much I took it off and gave it to her really to absolve my own hatred. . . .
> 'Don't you like it?'
> 'Yes I do.'
> 'Then why are you giving it away?'

By rejecting the thing she loves Fleur is embracing what she hates and so defusing it. Thus she has rid herself of emotion— and she is even 'rewarded' by the glint in Beryl's eyes. Fleur imagines she is absolving her hatred, she is simply escaping from suffering; absolution here is a rejection of emotional hardship. Protestants might well criticise Catholic absolution in these terms.

As a Catholic Mrs. Spark is in a position to receive

absolution; but as a writer how is she to respond to the truth of her narrative? Derek Stanford writes of Muriel Spark's fiction as 'a kind of imaginative denial of her roots. With such a subtle artist, this denial is nothing so simple as a straightforward rejection or obliteration.' Organic novelists, like Emily Brontë, must live by the truth of what they have written. Because their work is derived from nature, its novelistic truth is the natural truth. Muriel Spark's novels are devices for discovering truths, but they do not compel the discoverer to absorb that truth. Muriel Spark describes how her writing was blocked before she became a Catholic 'because I was never sure what I was'.[32] When she became a Catholic she was able to write. Perhaps because her Catholicism would absolve her, enabling her to reject whatever her novels might reveal she was?

NOTES

References to Muriel Spark's novels give the date of first publication and the page number of the paperback version.

1. 'How I became a novelist', *John O'London's*, 1 December 1960.
2. *Child of Light: A Reassessment of Mary Wollstonecraft Shelley* was published by Tower Bridge in 1951. Previously she had edited a *Tribute to Wordsworth* with Derek Stanford.
3. 'My Conversion', *Twentieth Century*, 170 (Autumn 1961), p. 59.
4. Ibid., 60.
5. Ibid., 61.
6. *The Comforters* (London, 1957), her first novel.
7. *The Brontë Letters* (London, 1953), p. 11.
8. *Emily Brontë: Her Life and Work*, with Derek Stanford (London, 1953), p. 40.
9. 'My Conversion', 63.
10. *Child of Light*, p. 4.
11. *The Comforters*, p. 80.
12. *Child of Light*, p. 11.
13. Interviewed by Nicholas Shakespeare in *The Times*, Monday, 21 November 1983, p. 8.
14. *Emily Brontë*, pp. 13, 50.
15. *The Comforters*, p. 63.
16. *John Masefield* (London, 1953), Introduction, p. x.
17. Flann O'Brien, *At Swim-Two-Birds* (London, 1939).
18. Ibid., pp. 100, 101.

19. *Emily Brontë*, p. 81.
20. *The Comforters*, pp. 93, 97.
21. *Emily Brontë*, p. 88.
22. *Loitering With Intent* (London, 1981).
23. Interview with Nicholas Shakespeare.
24. *The Brontë Letters*, p. 13.
25. *Not To Disturb* (London, 1971), p. 86.
26. Derek Stanford, *Muriel Spark* (Fontwell, 1963), p. 134.
27. *The Bachelors* (London, 1960).
28. Derek Stanford in *Muriel Spark* of her poem 'The Fanfarlo'.
29. *The Hothouse by the East River* (London, 1973).
30. 'What Images Return' in *Memoirs of a Modern Scotland*, ed. Karl Miller (London, 1970), pp. 151—53.
31. *The Bachelors*, p. 22.
32. 'My Conversion', 61.

6

Muriel Spark and Satire

by JENNIFER L. RANDISI

Much of the difficulty critics have found in dealing with Muriel Spark's work stems, it seems to me, from a desire to fit external moral and literary assumptions into the text rather than to work from the inside of the text out toward Spark's intention. This desire may have led Patricia Stubbs to praise *The Mandelbaum Gate* for exemplifying 'external truths and values' and to fault *The Public Image, The Driver's Seat* and *Not To Disturb* for lacking a 'moral point'.[1] It is useful to remind ourselves that Muriel Spark is a self-proclaimed satirist. As early as 1961 she remarked that her conversion to Catholicism gave her 'something to work on as a satirist',[2] and in her description of the 'curious adventure' in the summer of 1944 that led her to become a writer, Spark reflected that 'I had even then a satirical cast of mind'.[3] She has further observed, in a speech to the American Academy of Arts and Letters, that 'ridicule is the only honourable weapon we have left'.[4] It should be clear that satire is the informing principle of Spark's work, and that any temptation we might feel to read her work otherwise may obscure to us her intention as a writer.

In 1934, Wyndham Lewis proclaimed that 'the greatest satire *cannot* be moralistic at all',[5] and more recently Northrop Frye has told us that the satirist's moral act is actually an act of selection from among various absurdities.[6] There is no moral centre in a satire; neither are there partial satires. If we accept Sheldon Sacks's notion of 'coherent satire', then we must accept that 'all parts of the work . . . have been selected to facilitate ridicule of the external objects of the satire, not to create fictional examples of ethical truths'.[7] Satire is largely a matter of consistent point of view, and Muriel Spark's satiric vision is contingent upon her theology; the position of the perceiver (the novelist) relative to the object perceived (society) is Catholicism once removed.

The distance Muriel Spark maintains from her art is the result of a clear-sightedness about what she is up to as a writer. In the much quoted essay 'The House of Fiction', Spark explained to Frank Kermode her distinction between truth and fiction.

> I don't claim that my novels are truth—I claim that they are fiction, out of which a kind of truth emerges. And I keep in my mind specifically that what I am writing is fiction because I am interested in truth—absolute truth—and I don't pretend that what I'm writing is more than an imaginative extension of the truth—something inventive.[8]

Spark's ability to distance herself from her work (an ability essential to the satirist) stems from a certainty of proportion and order.[9] Catholicism (absolute truth) puts fiction ('a pack of lies')[10] into perspective. As Spark explains in 'My Conversion',

> I didn't get my style until I became a Catholic because you just haven't got to care, and you need security for that. That's the whole secret of style in a way. It's simply not caring too much, it's caring only a little.[11]

Proportion and distance allow proper vision. And with proper vision the satirist can, as Frye puts it, 'pass a dead centre, and finally see the gentlemanly Prince of Darkness bottom side up'.[12]

As W. O. S. Sutherland has noted, the satirist is concerned with falsehood, but paradoxically the basis of that falsehood is truth.[13] In *Memento Mori*, Charmian tells us that 'the art of fiction is very like the practice of deception',[14] and indeed Spark's works are constructed out of lies that are parables and lies that are myths. In 'My Conversion', Spark explains that 'fiction to me is a kind of parable. You have got to make up your mind it's not true. Some kind of truth emerges from it, but it's not fact.'[15] Abdul's orange groves of *The Mandelbaum Gate* are this kind of fiction.

'How are Abdul's orange groves thriving?' He puzzled for a few moments, then smiled. The displaced poor were already being urged to recall the extent of the lands and possessions from which they had fled before the Israelis' onslaught. More and more, the bewildered homeless souls, in thousands and tens of thousands, agreed and then convinced themselves, and were to hold for long years to come, that they had, every man of them, been driven from vast holdings in their bit of Palestine, from green hilly pastures, and so many acres of lush orange groves as would have covered Arabia.[16]

Abdul's orange groves are not factual, but they are true in the sense that they illustrate a psychological reality. The truth emerges out of the falsehood.

Lies that are myths, on the other hand, substitute falsehood for truth. In 'The House of Fiction', Spark asserts that 'to me the plot is the basic myth'[17] and in *Loitering With Intent*, novelist Fleur Talbot agrees with her.

The true novelist, one who understands the work as a continuous poem, is a myth-maker, and the wonder of the art resides in the endless different ways of telling a story, and the methods are mythological by nature.[18]

Nowhere is the connection between methodology and mythology clearer than in *The Takeover* and *The Abbess of Crewe*. Populated by myth-makers of all kinds, *The Takeover* postulates with Hubert that

. . . in the world of symbol and the worlds of magic, allegory and mysticism, deceit has no meaning. Lies do not exist, fraud is impossible. These concepts are impossible because the materialist standards of conduct from which they arise are non-existent.[19]

Within his self-created mythology, Hubert smuggles Maggie's original artwork to Switzerland (replacing it with elaborate fakes) and Coco de Renault manipulates Maggie's fortune by way of a 'global plan . . . so intricate that it might have been devised primordially by the angels as a mathematical blueprint to guide God in the creation of the world'.[20] Myth rewrites history, so that what is viable as truth is the self-created past. Like it or not, we must agree with Hubert that 'appearances *are* reality.'[21]

The appearance of spiritualism replaces the political reality in *The Abbess of Crewe* in the same way that Hubert's fakes replace Maggie's originals.[22] The Abbess tells us early in the novel that 'history doesn't work. Here, in the Abbey of Crewe, we have discarded history. We have entered the sphere, dear sisters, of mythology.'[23] She further defines the mythology they have entered as 'history garbled', and explains to Sister Winifrede that 'a good scenario is a garble. A bad one is a bungle. They need not be plausible, only hypnotic, like all good art.'[24] Good art is a good lie, whether parable or myth. And satirists are the greatest of hypnotists and deceivers for, as Yeats reminds us in the section of '1919' that Spark uses as her epigraph to *The Abbess of Crewe*, they 'Traffic in mockery'.

In 'A Theory of Satire', Alvin P. Kernan defines the picture drawn by the satirist as the 'scene', and says that such pictures are always both disorderly and crowded.[25] Malcolm Bradbury distinguishes Spark's more recent novels (*The Public Image, The Driver's Seat, Not To Disturb*) from her previous work by defining them as 'novels of ending' or 'endings'.[26] Taken together, the two comments provide a useful way of looking at the social landscape of a Muriel Spark novel. Like a painting, her scenes are static; we are presented with the whole picture at the outset, so that the process of reading is largely a process of assimilating detail as it emerges to us. *Memento Mori* ends with its epigraph; *The Mandelbaum Gate* begins and ends at the gate; *Not To Disturb* takes place only in the house of Baron and Baronness Klopstock; *Robinson* takes place on an island; *Doctors of Philosophy* occupies one room; *The Prime of Miss Jean Brodie* opens with 'the Brodie set' and there our vision is focused for the remainder of the novel. The scene, then, is fixed. Robert C. Elliott has observed in 'The Satirist and Society', that in 'mythico-linguistic thought—to use Cassirer's phrase—the part does not merely represent the whole, it *is* the whole'.[27] Spark's canvases are small, crowded, and often unfinished, but they are 'the whole'.

What happens within the novel's scene is traditionally referred to as its plot. Yet the 'most striking quality of satire', according to Kernan, 'is the absence of plot'.[28] In a Muriel Spark novel, plot is another word for fate.[29] That is, the relationship between the reader and the novel's plot is analogous to the relationship between the Christian and providence. In 'My Conversion', Spark expresses herself 'a great believer in providence' and defines her relationship to it as 'not quite fatalism, but watching until you see the whole pattern emerge'.[30] And this is precisely what we do as readers. I don't mean to imply that this is an easy process; anyone who has read Spark knows that it can be quite difficult, and that the difficulty arises from Spark's refusal to give in to our expectations of what plot in a novel should be. Here the development of plot has more to do with the development of a photograph. The longer we look, the sharper, but not necessarily the clearer, the picture. For example, *The Hothouse by the East River* begins with the line 'If it were only true that all's well that ends well, if only it were true.' Who is speaking and why all is not well are questions whose answers emerge only by the end of the novel, and they emerge by a fleshing out of fate rather than by a traditional plot line. Fate is not a straight line; it is as full of turns as a serpentine. Fleur Talbot confides in *Loitering With Intent*, 'I do dearly love a turn of events.'[31] And so does Muriel Spark.

The turns of event we experience as readers result from the way time and place are treated in the novels. If scene is fixed then surely plot is fluid. Characters are obsessed with points in time and place, and these points emerge to us through a convolution of narrative sequence. Elsa and Paul (*The Hothouse by the East River*) are haunted by World War Two and in turn haunt New York City; the servants of the Baron and Baronness (*Not To Disturb*) are obsessed with the murder about to take place; Lise (*The Driver's Seat*) monomaniacally searches for her murderer; Miss Jean Brodie (*The Prime of Miss Jean Brodie*) is preoccupied with the duration of her prime and the identity of the girl who betrays her. Even Spark sees through the restricted focus that obsession requires. In 'The House of Fiction', she tells Frank Kermode that the people she is studying become 'the centre of the world, and everyone else is on the periphery. It is an obsession until I've finished writing about them.'[32] The difference between Spark and her characters is that for the latter, the obsession is never 'finished'. Rather, it extends either before the action begins or after the final page.

136

Set within the fluidity of time and place is the disruption of violent action. Where obsessions recur, violent actions occur once and are over. They are as intrusive and startling as a pinprick on a balloon. Ronald Paulson has argued in *The Fictions of Satire* that violent actions are 'symbolic actions that convey the central meaning of the satire'.[33] The message of violent action in Spark's work is that one cannot control one's fate (even Lise does not know where or when her murderer will appear). Like 'the thud of the V-1's near or far' Spark recalls hearing in the summer of 1944,[34] violent action is unpredictable and irrevocable. It is not a moral issue, but rather as much a matter of chance in the fictional world as it is in the factual.

Violent action is most often violent death. Nearly all the novels record the violent death of one of the characters, and those that don't (*The Abbess of Crewe, The Bachelors, The Takeover, The Ballad of Peckham Rye*) contain characters capable of murder who, for one reason or another, are not able to commit the crime within the narrative frame. Lise of *The Driver's Seat* self-consciously arranges her own stab-wound homicide, and Lister of *Not to Disturb* choreographs the crime of passion involving the Baron, the Baronness and Victor Passerat. It is by clutching Caroline's throat in *The Comforters* that Georgina Hogg drowns, just as it is his innocence that allows Freddy Hamilton to cross and recross the place of violence that is the Mandelbaum Gate. Both Mary Macgregor of *The Prime of Miss Jean Brodie* and Joanna Childe of *The Girls of Slender Means* burn to death in building fires, and of those in *Memento Mori* who receive the imperative 'Remember you must die' it is significantly only Dame Lettie who suffers a violent death. Convinced someone is after her, Dame Lettie's fiction (the story of her fears) is responsible for her death (is heard by thieves who rob and murder her). Where violent death might, in tragedy, result from a character's attempt to rise above the common, in satire it is the product of pettiness, evil and accident.

In Spark's fiction, the institutions of education (*The Prime of Miss Jean Brodie*), marriage (*Territorial Rights, The Takeover, The Bachelors, The Hothouse by the East River*, and many of the stories in *The Go-Away Bird*), and the church (*The Abbess of Crewe* is

137

the most notable example) are presented as mean-spirited, wrong-minded and destructive. Derek Stanford has said that Spark's work is a 'polemic against togetherness'[35] and his remark seems particularly true of her attitude toward organized society. Institutional agencies of all kinds are ridiculed by Spark's characters. The Marcia Blaine School for Girls is, in the opinion of Miss Jean Brodie, an 'education factory',[36] Anthea Leaver of *Territorial Rights* regrets relinquishing her money and trust to Mr. B. of G.E.S.S. (Global-Equip Security Services), and Grace Gregory complains, in the same novel, that she doesn't 'know why the RC church doesn't stick to politics and keep its nose out of morals'.[37] Matthew, one of *The Bachelors*, asserts that 'there are only two callings, Holy Orders and Holy Matrimony, and one must choose',[38] while the following conversation takes place between Nancy and Emilio in *The Takeover*:

> 'How do you know when you're in love?' she said.
> 'The traffic improves and the cost of living seems very low.'[39]

What is eerily ironic in her ridicule, however, is that in an odd way what her characters say is true; schools often are education factories, and the traffic does seem to improve when we are in love. Spark's ridicule is close to low burlesque which, as David Worcester defines in *The Art of Satire*, 'creates a standard below its victim and makes us measure him against the standard'.[40] Spark's characters are only 'victims' within the context of her satire.

What makes Spark's social criticism work so well is her insistence on placing all of her characters squarely within it. The characters, individually, are not above the scene they inhabit collectively. The great social leveller is blackmail. Joe Ramdez and Miss Rickward of *The Mandelbaum Gate* attempt to blackmail Barbara Vaughan by producing a fake of Harry Clegg's birth certificate, Sir Quentin of *Loitering With Intent* blackmails the members of the Autobiographical Association, and Robert Leaver of *Territorial Rights* implicates several characters in a murder by way of his blackmailing letters. We might well agree with Pierre's assertion in *The Hothouse by the East River* that 'everything is blackmail'.[41] Blackmail is effective because it is based on the social reality that, as Mary

Tiller observes in *Territorial Rights*, 'we all have something to hide.'[42] The fact that all Spark's characters *do* have something to hide is what fixes them in a social world composed of pettiness and accident. The blackmailers are thus important components of the social world, and they are Spark's ambassadors of evil.

In at least ten of Spark's novels one character recognizes in another the presence of absolute evil. Lise recognizes Richard for the murderer he is,

> 'I stabbed her but she didn't die. I never killed a woman. . . .'
> 'No, but you'd like to. I knew it this morning. . . .'[43]

Caroline knows that Georgina is, as her name suggests, 'a beast',[44] and both Patrick Seton and Miss Jean Brodie echo the words of the devil himself:

> She is mine, he is thinking. The others were not mine but this one is mine.
>
> 'Give me a girl at an impressionable age, and she is mine for life. . . .'[45]

Sally Stranger finds Miss Jean Brodie guilty of believing herself 'the God of Calvin',[46] and Fleur Talbot recognizes in Sir Quentin 'pure evil'[47] just as Jean Taylor sees the danger in Mrs. Pettigrew.[48] Lister and the Abbess of Crewe construct evil worlds around them. These people are happy. As Grace Gregory tells Anthea in *Territorial Rights*,

> 'The really professional evil-doers love it. . . . The unhappy ones are only the guilty amateurs and the neurotics,' said Grace. 'The pros are in their element.'[49]

The evil character most 'in his element' is Dougal Douglas of *The Ballad of Peckham Rye*. Described as a beast, a grotesque, a chameleon and a succubus, Douglas tells Humphrey that he's 'one of the wicked spirits that wander through the world for the ruin of souls'.[50] Like Alec Warner of *Memento Mori*, Douglas is interested in 'human research' and, like Georgina Hogg, he has no private life, literally disappearing when without social context.[51]

Lesser ambassadors are recognized by their bestial names and mannerisms. In *The Ballad of Peckham Rye*, Trevor Lomas's girlfriend is named Beauty but Trevor calls her 'snake',[52] and Dottie of *Loitering With Intent* complains of her husband's lover—' "he's so pathetic, that Gray Mauser!" '[53]—as if he were a cat. Percy Mannering grins 'like an elated wolf . . . as if he were half-beast, half-man, instead of half-poet, half-man',[54] and the name of Victor Passerat, the illicit lover in *Not To Disturb*, sounds like the successful rodent he is.

The ambassador of evil is a catalyst, and responses to him are what constitute plot (fate) and define identity. The disembodied telephone message 'Remember you must die' determines behaviour in *Memento Mori*, just as Robinson's death hoax occupies much of that novel and causes January to 'come to think of the island as a place of the mind'.[55] Our final image of Sally Stranger is after her evolution into Sister Helena, clutching the bars of her grille and trying to sort out the mystery of Miss Jean Brodie's influence on her. And Lise, lost in the city that holds her murderer, knows that 'the one I'm looking for will recognize me right away for the woman I am, have no fear of that.'[56] Although it is only by chance that they are on the same aeroplane, as soon as she sees him Lise recognizes Richard and forces him in turn to recognize himself. And it is only after her betrayal of Miss Jean Brodie that Sally Stranger can become Sister Helena and write 'The Transfiguration of the Commonplace'.

Recognition can be epiphanic. In 'A Catholic Quartet', Josephine Jacobsen writes,

> The commonplace is stifling; the fabrications of the ego are cruel and basically stupid; but by transfiguration, the materials of the commonplace come into their proper radiance.[57]

It is by a process of transfiguration that Jean Taylor of *Memento Mori* recognizes the telephone caller as 'Death himself', an epiphany that enables her in dying to meditate 'confidingly upon Death, the first of the Four Last Things to be ever remembered'.[58] The agent of transfiguration is ultimately language itself or, more precisely, the power of language.

The voices having the most transfiguring power are those belonging to the satirists.[59] Spark's heroines, as critics have noted,[60] tend to be difficult, neurotic and egotistical, but they are often possessors of the satiric transfiguring voice. Caroline Rose of *The Comforters* refers to this voice as 'the mocker', a voice of 'cynical lucidity' that would 'overtake part of her mind',[61] and Paul of *The Hothouse by the East River* observes that Elsa, too, has become 'a mocker'.[62] But it is Fleur Talbot of *Loitering With Intent* who understands this voice most clearly:

> In fact, I was aware of a *demon* inside me that rejoiced in seeing people as they were, and not only that, but more than ever as they were, and more, and more.[63]

The power of the artist is the power of transfiguration. Yet because the artist is a liar, the process is daemonic. It transforms life into art. The creation of fiction is thus an inversion of God's power. It is the flesh made word rather than the Word made flesh.[64]

Fiction is largely the manipulation of character by author. In Spark's fiction, however, the boundaries separating who is 'inside' from who is 'outside' have been traced with invisible ink. In her first novel, one of Spark's characters overhears passages of the novel as they are typed. Once she becomes aware of herself as a character in a fiction she becomes critical of its author.

> The Typing Ghost has not recorded any lively details about this hospital ward. The reason is that the author doesn't know how to describe a hospital ward. This interlude in my life is not part of the book in consequence.[65]

In the following line, however, it is the novelist who complains about the character: 'It was by making exasperating remarks like this that Caroline Rose continued to interfere with the book.' Caroline controls and is controlled by an agency both outside and inside the story. Both character and novelist are satirists, and the novel itself is a fictive hall of mirrors where illusion is reflected endlessly.

By her second novel, Spark has given us a first-person narrator, but in the opening paragraph of *Robinson* January Marlow tells us that her memory (the text) is based on sources external to it.

> If you ask me how I remember the island, what it was like to be stranded there by misadventure for nearly three months, I

would answer that it was a time and landscape of the mind if I did not have the visible signs to summon its materiality: my journal, the cat, the newspaper cuttings, the curiosity of my friends; and my sisters—how they always look at me, I think, as one returned from the dead.

The internal landscape is only recreated by the external 'visible signs'; the internal is only visible through the external. In *Memento Mori*, Spark's next novel, the relationship is reversed; it is the invisible sign (the telephone message) that creates the internal landscape. The caller has many voices but his message is always the same: Remember you must die. Henry Mortimer and Jean Taylor come to regard him as a prompter and understand his message to mean that 'if you don't remember Death, Death reminds you to do so'.[66] Death, then, becomes an invisible mocker.

In Spark's latest novel, the book itself becomes a satirist. Form and content are inextricably bound when Fleur Talbot's *Warrender Chase* is set into motion by the evil Sir Quentin. As Fleur confides to Solly, 'I think he's putting my *Warrender Chase* into practice. He's trying to live out my story.'[67] The inversion makes Fleur a creator of life as well as art. As she explains to Dottie, 'I could have invented all of them—the lot.'[68] Fleur is both character ('I was falling into the same trap as Marjorie in my novel'[69]) and author, for even while Sir Quentin is stealing her first novel, she is filing the experience for use in her second.

> I felt quite excited. It was like writing the pages of a novel, and I consciously kept these plans fixed in part of my brain to transform into the last chapters of *All Soul's Day*, as I eventually did in my own shadowy way.[70]

Which is the lie, art or reality? Late in the novel, Fleur feels

> it was almost as if Sir Quentin was unreal and I had merely invented him, Warrender Chase being a man, a real man on whom I had partly based Sir Quentin.[71]

By substituting art for reality and then reminding us that art is a lie, the satirist stands us on a carpet only to pull it out from under us. *The Girls of Slender Means* and *The Ballad of Peckham Rye* draw upon folk song and poem, forms of cultural and literary history, to develop their fictions. Yet when form (for example, the poetry Joanna Childe uses in her elocution lessons) is removed, content disappears with it (Joanna Childe only gains meaning through her elocution lessons). The relationship between form and content is paradoxical. Form is made possible by content, just as content takes shape through form. But in Spark's fiction form and content come dangerously close to cancelling each other. Her novels are curiously like Picasso's neon paintings; as soon as the picture is complete, it has vanished. After her novel is finished, Fleur says of her central character, 'Warrender Chase never existed, he is only some hundreds of words, some punctuation, sentences, paragraphs, marks on the page.'[72]

When he sees her in the Kensington graveyard, a policeman suspects Fleur of 'desecrating and violating', of 'obstructing and hindering without due regard', of 'loitering with intent'.[73] But it is the satirist who is most guilty of these crimes, for the satirist is the supreme illusionist. Once the mockery has been stripped away, we are left with nothing but marks on the page and the suspicion that someone has been hindering and violating. By the end of a Muriel Spark novel we realize that we, too, have been loitering with intent. We have been participating in fiction. And this is the final mockery: if we are looking for absolute truth, we must look elsewhere.

NOTES

1. Patricia Stubbs, *Muriel Spark* (London: F. Mildner & Sons, 1973), pp. 11 and 26 respectively.
2. Muriel Spark, 'My Conversion', *Twentieth Century*, 170 (Autumn 1961), 60.
3. Muriel Spark, 'The Poet's House', *Encounter*, 30 (May 1968), 48.
4. Quoted by Peter Kemp, *Muriel Spark* (London: Paul Elek, 1974), p. 113.
5. Wyndham Lewis, 'The Greatest Satire is Nonmoral', in *Satire: Modern Essays in Criticism*, ed. Ronald Paulson (Englewood Cliffs, N.J.: Prentice-Hall, Inc., 1971), p. 70.
6. Northrop Frye, *Anatomy of Criticism: Four Essays* (Princeton: Princeton University Press, 1957), p. 224.
7. Sheldon Sacks, *Fiction and the Shape of Belief: A Study of Henry Fielding With*

Glances at Swift, Johnson and Richardson (Chicago: University of Chicago Press, 1964), p. 11.

8. Frank Kermode, 'The House of Fiction: Interviews with Seven English Novelists', *Partisan Review*, 30 (Spring 1963), 80.
9. In 'My Conversion' Spark writes: 'I used to worry until I got a sense of order, a sense of proportion' (63).
10. Kermode, p. 80
11. Spark, 'My Conversion', 63.
12. Frye, p. 239.
13. W. O. S. Sutherland, Jr., *The Art of the Satirist: Essays on the Satire of Augustan England* (Austin: University of Texas Press, 1965), p. 10.
14. Muriel Spark, *Memento Mori*, in *A Muriel Spark Trio* (Philadelphia: J. B. Lippincott Company, 1962), p. 576.
15. Spark, 'My Conversion', 63.
16. Muriel Spark, *The Mandelbaum Gate* (New York: Alfred A. Knopf, 1965), pp. 103–4.
17. Kermode, p. 79.
18. Muriel Spark, *Loitering With Intent* (New York: G. P. Putnam's Sons, 1981), p. 139.
19. Muriel Spark, *The Takeover* (New York: Viking Press, 1976), p. 138.
20. Spark, *The Takeover*, p. 140.
21. Spark, *The Takeover*, p. 102.
22. For a detailed analysis of politics in *The Abbess of Crewe* see Barbara Y. Keyser, 'Muriel Spark, Watergate, and the Mass Media', *Arizona Quarterly*, 32, 146–53.
23. Muriel Spark, *The Abbess of Crewe* (New York: Viking Press, 1974), p. 12.
24. Spark, *The Abbess of Crewe*, pp. 92 and 95 respectively.
25. Alvin P. Kernan, 'A Theory of Satire', in *Satire: Modern Essays in Criticism*, ed. Ronald Paulson (Englewood Cliffs, N.J.: Prentice-Hall, Inc., 1971), p. 253.
26. Malcolm Bradbury, 'Muriel Spark's Fingernails', *Critical Quarterly*, 14, 244.
27. Robert C. Elliott, 'The Satirist and Society', in *Satire: Modern Essays in Criticism*, ed. Ronald Paulson (Englewood Cliffs, N.J.: Prentice-Hall, Inc., 1971), p. 214.
28. Kernan, p. 270.
29. Malcolm Bradbury makes this point when he observes that 'plot is destiny' ('Muriel Spark's Fingernails', p. 244).
30. Spark, 'My Conversion', 63.
31. Spark, *Loitering With Intent*, p. 199.
32. Kermode, p. 80. Spark also refers to the process of writing as 'a sort of obsession' in 'The Poet's House' (p. 48).
33. Ronald Paulson, from *The Fictions of Satire*, in *Satire: Modern Essays in Criticism*, ed. Ronald Paulson (Englewood Cliffs, N.J.: Prentice-Hall, Inc., 1971), p. 341.
34. Spark, 'The Poet's House', p. 49.
35. Derek Stanford, *Muriel Spark: A Biographical and Critical Study* (Fontwell: Centaur Press Ltd., 1963), p. 110.

36. Muriel Spark, *The Prime of Miss Jean Brodie* (Philadelphia: J. B. Lippincott Company, 1962), p. 115.
37. Muriel Spark, *Territorial Rights* (New York: Coward, McCann & Geoghegan, Inc., 1979), p. 236.
38. Muriel Spark, *The Bachelors* (Philadelphia: J. B. Lippincott Company, 1961), p. 79.
39. Spark, *The Takeover*, p. 47.
40. David Worcester, from *The Art of Satire*, in *Satire: Modern Essays in Criticism*, ed. Ronald Paulson (Englewood Cliffs, N.J.: Prentice-Hall, Inc., 1971), p. 123.
41. Muriel Spark, *The Hothouse by the East River* (New York: Penguin Books, 1977), p. 65.
42. Spark, *Territorial Rights*, p. 176.
43. Muriel Spark, *The Driver's Seat* (London: Macmillan and Co. Ltd., 1970), p. 153.
44. Muriel Spark, *The Comforters*, in *A Muriel Spark Trio* (Philadelphia: J. B. Lippincott Company, 1962), p. 204.
45. Spark, *The Bachelors*, p. 161, and Spark, *The Prime of Miss Jean Brodie*, p. 16.
46. Spark, *The Prime of Miss Jean Brodie*, p. 176.
47. Spark, *Loitering With Intent*, p. 167.
48. Spark, *Memento Mori*, pp. 420–21.
49. Spark, *Territorial Rights*, p. 235.
50. Muriel Spark, *The Ballad of Peckham Rye*, in *A Muriel Spark Trio* (Philadelphia: J. B. Lippincott Company, 1962), pp. 233, 250–51, 242–43, 256–57, and 313 respectively.
51. Spark, *The Ballad of Peckham Rye*, pp. 296 and 299.
52. Spark, *The Ballad of Peckham Rye*, p. 291.
53. Spark, *Loitering With Intent*, p. 103.
54. Spark, *Memento Mori*, p. 406.
55. Muriel Spark, *Robinson, A Novel* (Philadelphia: J. B. Lippincott Company, 1958), p. 185.
56. Spark, *The Driver's Seat*, p. 95.
57. Josephine Jacobsen, 'A Catholic Quartet', *Christian Scholar* XLVII (1964), p. 142.
58. Spark, *Memento Mori*, pp. 563 and 608.
59. I am here using Alvin P. Kernan's definition of the satirist as 'but one poetic device used by the author to express his satiric vision, a device which can be dispensed with or varied to suit his purpose' ('A Theory of Satire', p. 259).
60. See, for example, Stanford p. 116 and Stubbs p. 5.
61. Spark, *The Comforters*, p. 43.
62. Spark, *The Hothouse by the East River*, p. 8.
63. Spark, *Loitering With Intent*, pp. 10–11.
64. Stanford makes this point in his analysis of Spark's poem 'Against The Transcendentalists', p. 89.
65. Spark, *The Comforters*, p. 180.
66. Spark, *Memento Mori*, p. 563.

67. Spark, *Loitering With Intent*, p. 176.
68. Ibid., p. 105.
69. Ibid., p. 178.
70. Ibid., p. 151.
71. Ibid., p. 181.
72. Ibid., p. 83.
73. Ibid., p. 197.

7

Spark and Scotland

by TREVOR ROYLE

In 1956, shortly after publishing his first novel, *Tunes of Glory*, the novelist James Kennaway (1928–68) wrote a letter to his mother in which he attempted to discern the course that his life appeared to be taking:

> There is nothing to worry about but there are facts to be faced. I have changed quite a lot. I've remained a child, more of a child than before, even, in some directions; and in others I've outstripped my contemporaries. I suppose I'm what is called an outsider now. No team spirit, no society in the accepted sense. A lot of amusing acquaintances, a handful of friends who are becoming less not more close, neither English nor Scottish, nor richer nor poorer, uneasy.[1]

It was an accurate enough assessment of his position. Kennaway had been born a Scot, in Perthshire, the county where his father had been a lawyer and factor to the landed gentry of Strathearn, his childhood had been spent in middle-class comfort; and yet, he had chosen to leave it all behind him, to live in exile in London where he pursued a successful career as a commissioning editor with the publishers, Longmans Green. In the following year he was to abandon that calling to become a full-time writer; until his death in 1968 he earned a rich living from writing film scripts in London and Hollywood. His other novels are *Household Ghosts* (1961), *The Bells of Shoreditch* (1963), *The Mindbenders* (1963), *Some Gorgeous Accident* (1967), *The Cost of Living Like This* (1969) and *Silence* (1972).

For someone from Kennaway's background, his letter was not an unusual or inaccurate statement of his circumstances. He had been educated at Trinity College, Glenalmond, a Scottish boarding school established during the Victorian period to provide the Scottish upper middle classes with an English-style education that led inevitably to Cambridge or Oxford (where Kennaway attended Trinity College between 1948 and 1951). To have chosen a Scottish university, in the opinions of masters and boys, was to plump for the second best; to have stayed in Scotland, if the boy was ambitious, was to admit to a terrible personal failing, to a belief that the heights had never been attempted. It never crossed Kennaway's mind that he should ever live in Scotland. As a Scot, he was sentimentally attached to a romantic version of the country's past and its traditions, and he was proud of its scenery, but he had no interest in the everyday concerns of contemporary Scotland and its society which he disliked for its 'touchy patriotism and conservatism of an unbelievably fast hue'. It is a common enough paradox for the exile that he should both love and hate the place of his birth. On the one hand, Scotland existed for Kennaway as a never-never land of whimsy and charm; on the other, the harsh reality of a people denied an identity by the forces of historical and political change, subject to caution and blighted by physical and spiritual poverty, prevented the possibility of a return. It is also in the nature of things that the conundrum can never be ignored by the exile, and that in the case of the writer that it should find its way into his or her work, as, indeed, it did into Kennaway's.

Although two of his novels are set in Scotland—*Tunes of Glory* and *Household Ghosts*—and two others have Scottish elements within their structures—*The Bells of Shoreditch* and *The Cost of Living Like This*—Kennaway was not concerned with the creation of a distinctly Scottish form of fiction. (As we shall see, it is illuminating to note that while Kennaway and Spark were writing in the 1960s, other Scottish writers, Gordon Williams, Alan Sharp, Archie Hind, William McIlvanney, amongst others, were engaged in what Alan Bold, in *Modern Scottish Literature*, described as the school of 'proletarian romanticism'— novels springing from their working-class childhoods in the industrialized west of Scotland.) Neither was Kennaway concerned with novels that mirrored reality (whatever that reality might be); rather he stood at an oblique angle to it and created a stylized version of what he had perceived. Thus, what emerges is very different from those Scottish novels of the same period which portrayed, almost in documentary style, the grim actualities of day-to-day life, say, in a post-war housing estate with all its negation of moral and spiritual growth. Instead, the design of Kennaway's fiction brings into focus a world perceived through the sensations of its participants. David Dow, a Scottish school-master's son in *Household Ghosts*, a neurophysiologist with a successful career in London, returns to the Perthshire of his childhood in an attempt to free a beautiful girl, Mary Ferguson, daughter of a batty landed family, from an unsatisfactory marriage and from the mould in which she is trapped by family circumstance. He offers himself to her, both as the interpreter of her dilemma and as a lover (Mary's husband, Stephen, is impotent), but although he takes her with him to London, where she enjoys a precarious freedom, he evades the responsibility of loving her and forces her to break her trust in him. Through his servile lack of commit-ment, Mary returns to the ghosts of her past, leaving David with the understanding that he is a destroyer, that however much he might think he is in love with her he must also betray her, that however much he understands her predica-ment he also despises it. At the novel's end, David Dow characterizes his position in terms of the paradox of the Scot who is at once in love with his country and who yet chooses to reject it:

> For many years, usually when drunkish, I have bored my friends with the suggestion that the Scots, of all people, are misunderstood. A glance at their history or literature (and especially if you count Byron as a Scot, which after dinner, at least, is permissible) reveals what lies underneath the slow accent, the respectability and the solid flesh. Under the cake lies Bonny Dundee. But even as I put forward these theories with enthusiasm I am doing everything in my power to suppress the one contemporary sign of that splendid vitality which I had ever come across. They christened her Mary. I cast myself, perversely, as Knox.[2]

That sense of betrayal by the man (or woman) who wants to protect his (or her) love and yet who must destroy it, who loves and hates the object of his (or her) affection is implicit in the theme of *Household Ghosts*. It is also integral to the plot of another Scottish novel that was published that same year, Muriel Spark's *The Prime of Miss Jean Brodie*.

Muriel Spark was born ten years before Kennaway and came from a Scottish-Jewish background in an Edinburgh that was not very different from the small-town respectability that he had enjoyed as a child. She was educated at James Gillespie's School for Girls, one of Edinburgh's principal schools, founded by an eighteenth-century snuff merchant, which served as a model for the Edinburgh school in *The Prime of Miss Jean Brodie*. After leaving school she married and left Edinburgh to spend some time in Central Africa. During World War Two she worked in the Political Intelligence Department of the Foreign Office and settled in London; between 1947 and 1949 she edited *Poetry Review* and was also General Secretary to the Poetry Society. Her early publications included literary biographies of Mary Shelley, John Masefield and (with Derek Stanford) Emily Brontë and her first poems were published in 1952. In 1957 she published her first novel, *The Comforters*; and in recent years she has lived in New York and in Rome. Thus, like Kennaway, she was an early exile from Scotland and, like him, her subsequent relationship to the country and to its literature has been questioned by some critics, almost as if nationality and literary identity were commodities to be bought or sold.

About her own relationship to Scotland, Muriel Spark has been remarkably frank. In an essay first published in the *New Statesman* and subsequently collected in Karl Miller's anthology of essays in honour of Hector MacIver, *Memoirs of a Modern Scotland*, she gave expression to her 'cautious, affectionate, critical' appreciation of Edinburgh, a recognition that was heightened by her sense of acceptance by it and its people:

> Nevertheless, it [Edinburgh] is the place where I was first understood. James Gillespie's Girls' School, set in solid state among the green meadows, showed an energetic faith in my literary life. I was the school's Poet and Dreamer, with appropriate perquisites and concessions. I took this for granted,

150

and have never since quite accustomed myself to the world's indifference to art and the process of art, and to the special needs of the artist.[3]

Edinburgh also impressed itself on her imagination by its ancient beauty and unexpected city-scapes, by the sheer perpendicularity of it all. In spite of its drawbacks—which she characterized as the 'nevertheless' principle, the careful balancing of opposites—she, like her father before her, 'breathed the informed air of the place, its haughty and remote anarchism'. To use her own 'nevertheless' principle, Muriel Spark enjoyed a mixed Scottish and Jewish inheritance; nevertheless she is a novelist with a peculiarly Scottish frame of mind. When pressed on the subject she has been prepared to confirm the influence that a Scottish childhood has had on her writing:

> I am certainly a writer of Scottish formation and of course think of myself as such. I think to describe myself as a 'Scottish Writer' might be ambiguous as one wouldn't know if 'Scottish' applied to the writer or the writing. Then there is the complicated question of whether people of mixed inheritance, like myself, can call themselves Scottish. Some Scots deny it. But Edinburgh where I was born and my father was born has definitely had an effect on my mind, my prose style and my ways of thought.[4]

That questioning of the validity of one's national identity is peculiar to the peoples of small nations, especially when they themselves are unsure who they really are, or who they might become. The English, with several centuries of Empire-building behind them, tend to assume that anyone writing in the English language can be considered one of them, that English-ness can be conferred on them by a process of assimilation. Not so the Scots, who take a greater degree of interest in the claims of nationality; as a result Scottish writers, especially novelists, are tested more thoroughly in the incontrovertible Scottish-ness of their work. Partly, that lack of confidence has been created by the limbo in which Scotland finds itself; it is part of the United Kingdom and yet its separate identity, history, customs, traditions and literature— all of which it is rightly proud—have declined since the seventeenth century when King James VI galloped south to become King James I of England. There is an identifiable and strong Scottish literary tradition, exemplified at its best by the writings, after 1603, of Ramsay, Fergusson, Burns, Scott, Stevenson and MacDiarmid, and also by the work of a variety of poets, novelists, dramatists, historians, diarists and essayists; but it is a tradition beset by self-doubts and questionings about whether it is indeed still a tradition.

Another reason is linguistic. In which language should a Scottish writer choose to write, archaic Scots, English or Gaelic? Given the fact that the latter is now only a minority language, albeit with a healthy modern literature, the selection is narrowed, by usage and tradition to Scots and English. 'Every genuine literature,' wrote Edwin Muir,

> requires as its condition a means of expression capable of dealing with everything the mind can think or the imagination conceive. It must be a language for criticism as well as poetry, for abstract speculation as well as fact, and since we live in a scientific age, it must be a language for science as well. A language which can serve for one or two of those purposes but not for the others is, considered as a vehicle for literature, merely an anachronism. Scots has survived to our time as a language for simple poetry and the simpler kind of short story, such as *Thrawn Janet*; all its other uses have lapsed, and it expresses therefore only a fragment of the Scottish mind. One can go further than this, however, and assert that its very use is a proof that the Scottish consciousness is divided. For, reduced to its simplest terms, this linguistic division means that Scotsmen feel in one language and think in another; that their emotions turn to the Scottish tongue, with all its associations of local sentiment, and their minds to a standard English which for them is almost bare of associations other than those of the classroom.[5]

Muir's statement that Scots think in one language and write in another has grown in notoriety since he first argued it some fifty years ago, and the debate it provoked with his friend and contemporary, the poet Hugh MacDiarmid, still rumbles on today. (MacDiarmid had set out earlier to dissociate Scottish poetry from the sentimentality of the nineteenth century and to bring it into line with contemporary European literature.

He had also evolved for his own early lyrics a 'synthetic Scots' based on current idioms and obsolete words in dictionaries 'to adapt an essentially rural tongue to the very much more complex requirements of our urban civilisation',[6] an 'experiment' in which Muir claimed 'he [MacDiarmid] has written some remarkable poetry; but he has left Scottish verse very much where it was before'.[7])

Muir's somewhat laboured attempt to reach the conclusion that Scotland could only create a national literature by writing in English was a cause of much bitter discussion, but it did help to polarize the language problem in Scotland and its relationship to the country's literature. What Muir did not take into account was that writers are not so chained to the language of their childhood as he supposed, and that writers in Scotland have felt free to express themselves in standard English, American English and in the various dialects and shades of Scots that continue to exist, mainly as spoken language. But if Muir's statement is taken a stage further to include identity, then the argument still holds good; Scots writers continue to feel orphaned at home from their traditions, but if they move away from them, or deny them, then they find themselves in exile. Hence James Kennaway's feeling that he was 'neither English nor Scottish, uneasy', and Muriel Spark's questioning 'whether people of mixed inheritance, like myself, can call themselves Scottish'. Both writers are linked inalienably to the country of their birth and early education, yet both have felt themselves to be in exile from it. (A third reason for Scotland's lack of confidence is political. It is a nation without statehood, a country without a centre with meagre means of communication, and with a group of writers unsure who might be their audiences and how they might relate to them.)

For all those reasons—here only briefly sketched in— Scottish writers and critics have shown a tendency to be touchy on the one hand and hidebound on the other. A statement like the following will bring forth the prickly rejoinder that Spark is in fact a Scottish writer: 'Muriel Spark was born in Edinburgh in 1918. Her father Jewish, her mother Presbyterian, she was educated in the latter faith, an unlikely beginning for one of England's more important contemporary writers.'[8] The observation that 'Mrs. Spark's later novels ornament the literature of England rather than Scottish literature'[9] produced the rebuke that

> nationality is not after all one of the most important of a writer's characteristics; the concept of it is in many ways a piece of rather jaded nineteenth-century parochialism. And it is only in a small country, conscious of a sense of inferiority that the question can be asked. Not all small countries either; do the Irish feel a need to disown Beckett?[10]

Given the lack of certainty and the plethora of doubts that surround contemporary Scotland and its literature, where do writers like Kennaway and Spark stand in relation to them?[11] Kennaway's novels are perhaps easier to assess, both because he rarely strayed from Scottish themes (and wrote less) and because his life has been made more public, with Scotland occupying an uneasy position in his consciousness.[12] Muriel Spark, on the other hand, has led a more private life, and although she has stated her indebtedness to Scotland, her most familiar appearance has been in the long-disappeared world of literary London during the immediate post-war years.[13] However, since she has claimed that Edinburgh has had a noticeable effect on her mind, prose style and ways of thought, it is fruitful to examine that comment in relationship to her Edinburgh novel, *The Prime of Miss Jean Brodie*. (Here I am agreeing that Spark is a 'writer of Scottish formation'; I am not applying a nationality test.)

The Prime of Miss Jean Brodie is set in Edinburgh during the 1930s and on one level it contains one of the best portraits drawn of the city during that period, a picture devoid of false romanticism, the trap into which so many Scottish writers have fallen:

> They approached the Old Town which none of the girls had properly seen before, because none of their parents was so historically minded as to be moved to conduct their young into the reeking network of slums which the Old Town constituted in those years. The Canongate, The Grassmarket, Lawn-market, were names which betokened a misty region of crime and desperation: 'Lawnmarket Man Jailed.' (p. 39)

Edinburgh is also seen as a city of contrasts, at once 'a European capital, the city of Hume and Boswell' (p. 53), and yet, 'a foreign country which intimates itself by its new smells and shapes and its new poor' (p. 39). But it is the delineation of Edinburgh as a dark and sombre place that is such a telling counterpoint to the creation of its main character, Miss Jean Brodie, the monstrous teacher of susceptible young girls at the Marcia Blaine School. (Edinburgh is seen through 'the haunted November twilight' (p. 23); 'outside light rain began to fall' (p. 123).) Jean Brodie, herself, has a suitably dark lineage:

> I am a descendant, do not forget, of Willie Brodie, a man of substance, a cabinet maker and designer of gibbets, a member of the Town Council of Edinburgh and a keeper of two mistresses who bore him five children between them. Blood tells. He played much dice and fighting cocks. Eventually he was a wanted man for having robbed the Excise Office—not that he needed the money, he was a night burglar only for the sake of the danger in it. Of course, he was arrested abroad and brought back to the Tolbooth prison, but that was mere chance. He died cheerfully on a gibbet of his own devising in seventeen-eighty-eight. However all this may be, it is the stuff I am made of. . . . (p. 117)

Deacon William Brodie is one of Edinburgh's most famous historical characters, a man whose exploits have become part of the city's mythology. By placing her heroine within his family lineage, Muriel Spark was doing more than just adding a touch of local colour. Brodie was everything that his descendant described; a town councillor who held the post of Deacon of Wrights and Masons, he led a double life as head of a gang of burglars by night and thereby held the city within a reign of terror. His come-uppance was due to over-reaching. He bungled a robbery in the General Excise Office in Chessel's Court in the Canongate and was forced to flee to Holland. Through a series of accidents and betrayals he was arrested, returned to Scotland and hanged on a gallows which he himself had designed in happier times. Edinburgh had been scandalized by his actions, but the myth lived on and the story of Deacon Brodie became one of the city's most potent legends: a man who led a life full of contradictions. He was an upright leader of the community by day, a man who commanded the respect of his fellow citizens, wealthy, church-going and conformist. At night, he changed his complexion to become an enemy of society, an outsider who used his inside knowledge to rob his compatriots, a felon, womanizer and lover of drink and gambling. (Edinburgh abounds with such dichotomous characters. In the previous century, Major Weir, covenanting upholder of public morality, admitted to a second life of sorcery and incest, and was burned at the stake.)

That sense of secret alienation from society while at the same time claiming public allegiance to its morality is a recognizable feature of Scottish fiction. Robert Louis Stevenson used the Deacon Brodie story as a partial source for his novel *The Strange Case of Dr. Jekyll and Mr. Hyde* (1886), in which the central character, Dr. Henry Jekyll, haunted by his consciousness of a double identity within himself, experiments with a drug that will separate his personality into good and evil. The evil aspect is a hideous physical manifestation whom he calls Mr. Edward Hyde. In that guise evil is allowed to rule and Hyde begins to commit a number of crimes, culminating in a murder. Increasingly unable to control his metamorphoses Jekyll finds Hyde becoming the dominant character, and to save himself from public exposure is forced to take his own life. James Hogg's *Private Memoirs and Confessions of a Justified Sinner*, a novel of diabolic possession, theological satire and local legend, is a more complete enunciation of the same theme. The story, which is set in the years immediately prior to the Act of Union of 1707, is told in three parts, the 'Editor's Narrative', the 'Private Memoirs and Confessions of a Sinner' and the 'Editor's Comments' at the end. Each part is designed so that it forms an overall pattern of objective, set against subjective, experience. The 'Editor's Narrative' concerns two brothers, George Colwan, the son of a laird, and Robert, who is supposed to be the illegitimate son of his mother's spiritual adviser, the Rev. Robert Wringhim. The brothers, who grow up apart, are always in conflict when they meet, and when George is murdered Robert is suspected of fratricide and disappears.

In the 'Private Memoirs and Confessions' the same story is told from Robert's point of view. This section is also an account of the antinomian obsession that sins committed by an 'elect and justified person' cannot imperil the hope of salvation. Robert has reached this conclusion from the narrowly Calvinistic teachings of the Rev. Wringhim and, aided and abetted by Gil-Martin, a shadowy figure of evil who is the personification of the Devil, he commits a number of crimes, including the murder of his brother George. At the end of the novel, still believing himself to be justified in his actions, but haunted by the diabolic Gil-Martin, he finally takes his life. Finally, the 'Editor' tells the reader how he came into possession of the manuscript and he describes Robert's death. The figure of Gil-Martin exists on two levels. He is the living impersonation of the Devil in the folk tradition and therefore a figure to be feared; he is also the agent of evil, capable of taking possession of Robert's mind and causing him to turn to evil. This dualism between inner and outer reality leads Robert to believe himself to be two people, and the concept of a divided personality is the dominant theme of the novel.

A similar dichotomy is present in Miss Brodie and this leads her to espouse an absurd combination of ideals. She admires Mussolini's fascist Italy yet berates the team spirit fostered by the Girl Guides: 'Perhaps the Guides were too much a rival fascisti, and Miss Brodie could not bear it' (p. 38). She encourages a sense of individuality amongst the girls she teaches but will not allow them to speak their minds: ' "Who is the greatest Italian painter?" "Leonardo da Vinci, Miss Brodie." "That is incorrect. The answer is Giotto, he is my favourite" ' (pp. 9–10). She is a lover of things Mediterranean, especially Italian, yet she fears the Roman Catholic church.

> Her disapproval of the Church of Rome was based on her assertions that it was a church of superstition, and that only people who did not want to think for themselves were Roman Catholics. (p. 112)

She denies herself the love of the romantic artist Teddy Lloyd but sees nothing wrong in sharing the bed of Gordon Lowther, the music master:

> She was not in any doubt, she let everyone know she was in no doubt, that God was on her side whatever her course, and so she experienced no difficulty or sense of hypocrisy in worship while at the same time she went to bed with the singing master. Just as an excessive sense of guilt can drive people to excessive

action, so was Miss Brodie driven to it by an excessive lack of guilt. (p. 113)

Given so many contradictions and a style of teaching that bordered on the philosophy of the *fascisti* she so admired, Jean Brodie is disliked by her fellow teachers, a grim crew of middle-aged ladies who resent her advanced methods. But as Spark makes clear, Miss Brodie is only set apart from the school by her ideas; she is still a respectable lady by day:

> It is not to be supposed that Miss Brodie was unique at this point of her prime; or that (since such things are relative) she was in any way off her head. She was alone, merely, in that she taught in a school like Marcia Blaine's. There were legions of her kind during the nineteen-thirties, women from the age of thirty and upward, who crowded their war-bereaved spinster-hood with voyages of discovery into new ideas and energetic practices in art or social welfare, education or religion. The progressive spinsters of Edinburgh did not teach in schools, especially in schools of traditional character like Marcia Blaine's School for Girls. It was in this that Miss Brodie was, as the rest of the staff spinsterhood put it, a trifle out of place. But she was not out of place amongst her own kind, the vigorous daughters of dead or enfeebled merchants, of ministers of religion, University professors, doctors, big warehouse owners of the past, or the owners of fisheries who had endowed these daughters with shrewd wits, high-coloured cheeks, constitu-tions like horses, logical educations, hearty spirits and private means. (pp. 52–3)

Unable to act out her own philosophy—prevented both by convention and by the passing of her prime—she encourages her group of schoolgirls, the '*crème de la crème*', to become her surrogates. She inspires Joyce Emily to go to Spain to fight for Franco (where she loses her life). She attempts (but fails) to ease Rose Stanley, who is 'famous for sex', into Teddy Lloyd's bed. The remaining girls in the Brodie set fulfil other functions and it is one of them, Sandy Stranger, who most resembles Jean Brodie, who becomes her mentor's eyes and ears. Sandy Stranger becomes, in effect, the other half of Miss Brodie: 'Sandy was never bored, but she had to lead a double life of her own in order never to be bored' (p. 24).

And just as Miss Brodie's world is one of make-believe—her

educational radicalism is a petty enough revolt against
Edinburgh bourgeois society—so also does Sandy Stranger
manufacture her own form of fantasy. With Jenny Gray, one of
the Brodie set and later destined to be a second-rate actress
(significantly none of the '*crème de la crème*' reach their own
prime), she composes 'The Mountain Eyrie', a soppy romantic
story about Hugh Carruthers, Jean Brodie's fiancé who was
killed in World War One. She has imaginary conversations
with literary figures like the Lady of Shalott, Mr. Rochester
from *Jane Eyre* and Alan Breck, the romantic hero of Robert
Louis Stevenson's novel, *Kidnapped*. She also casts herself in
the rôle of one of Pavlova's pupils after Miss Brodie has taken
them to the ballet, but try as she may, it is her teacher who
intrudes in the persona of the famous ballerina:

> 'Sandy,' said Anna Pavlova, 'you are the only truly dedicated
> dancer, next to me. Your dying Swan is perfect, such a
> sensitive, final tap of the claw upon the floor of the stage. . . .' 'I
> know it,' said Sandy (in considered preference to 'Oh, I do my
> best'), as she relaxed in the wings.
> Pavlova nodded sagely and gazed into the middle distance
> with the eyes of tragic exile and of art. 'Every artist knows,' said
> Pavlova, 'is it not so?' Then, with a voice desperate with the
> menace of hysteria, and a charming accent, she declared, 'I
> have never been understood. Never. Never.' (p. 81)

Sandy Stranger uses the fantasies as a buffer between her and
Miss Brodie, and as the novel unfolds—as Sandy matures—so
does reality break into her perception of that relationship.
Early on, Miss Spark gives a clue, both to Jean Brodie's dual
personality, and to Sandy's understanding of it (this while
they are in the junior school):

> Some days it seemed to Sandy that Miss Brodie's chest was flat,
> no bulges at all, but straight as her back. On other days her
> chest was breast-shaped and large, very noticeable, something
> for Sandy to sit and peer at through her tiny eyes while Miss
> Brodie on a day of lessons indoors stood erect, with her brown
> head held high, staring out of the window like Joan of Arc as
> she spoke. (p. 10)

The realization that Jean Brodie can be two people, radical
teacher with the best interests of her pupils at heart, and

immoral leader willing to sacrifice them in her own interests, becomes the novel's main theme, and it is through Sandy that we perceive it. Having become Miss Brodie's closest confidante and a sounding board for her ambitions, Sandy finds that she has become the one member of the set who can use her authority for good or for evil. She has learned well from her teacher and can now make her or break her.

She chooses the latter course, the path of betrayal, for two reasons. Firstly, she becomes Teddy Lloyd's lover, thereby taking Miss Brodie's place in his bed and thwarting the ambition that it should be Rose, but having done so, she finds that he can only reproduce the likeness of Jean Brodie in all his portraits of the 'set'. While caught up in the position of go-between and sex surrogate, Sandy attempts both to discover what sparks Lloyd's interest in such a ridiculous woman, and also to try to understand Miss Brodie's fear of having an affair with a Roman Catholic married man; and as her occupation runs its course she stumbles on Miss Brodie's politics as the means of her destruction (it is 1939 and Miss Brodie is a silly fascist). 'I am not really interested in world affairs,' says Sandy to the headmistress 'only in putting a stop to Miss Brodie' (p. 167). Secondly, Sandy's decision to betray her teacher may owe its surface reasons to politics but her real argument is based on Miss Brodie's corruption of morality. ('But you won't be able to pin her down on sex', she lies to the headmistress.) Sandy destroys Miss Brodie because she knows that she believes too firmly in the doctrine of Calvinism, the belief that she (and her set) is (are) of the Elect and that the rest of the school are of the Damned. ('She thinks she is Providence, thought Sandy, she thinks she is the god of Calvin, she sees the beginning and the end' (p. 161).) This is the ultimate heresy for the Catholicism that Sandy is later to adopt, but it is one which she has come to understand at an early age and through the teachings of Miss Brodie:

> Fully to savour her position, Sandy would go and stand outside St. Giles Cathedral or the Tolbooth, and contemplate these emblems of a dark and terrible salvation which made the fires of the damned seem very merry to the imagination by contrast, and much preferable. Nobody in her life, at home or at school had ever spoke of Calvinism except as a joke that had once been

taken seriously. She did not at the time understand that her environment had not been on the surface peculiar to the place, as was the environment of the Edinburgh social classes just above or, even more, just below her own. She had no experience of social class at all. In its outward forms her fifteen years might have been spent in any suburb of any city in the British Isles; her school with its alien house system, might have been in Ealing. All she was conscious of now was that some quality of life peculiar to Edinburgh and nowhere else had been going on unbeknown to her all the time, and however undesirable it might be she felt deprived of it; however undesirable, she desired to know what it was, and to cease to be protected from it by enlightened people.

In fact, it was the religion of Calvin of which Sandy felt deprived, or rather a specified recognition of it. She desired this birthright; something definite to reject. It pervaded the place in proportion as it was unacknowledged. (pp. 143–44)

Edinburgh, as we have seen, is, at a certain level, imbued with a sense of Calvinism, a city wherein Deacon Brodie can be respectable citizen by day and notorious robber by night, believing all the while that his sins can be justified. It is Miss Brodie, heir to that legendary man and his beliefs, who shows that side of Edinburgh to her pupils and having imparted that knowledge also sows the seeds of her own destruction. (It is pertinent to note that part of the Deacon Brodie myth embraces a belief that he was betrayed by an associate.) Sandy Stranger recognizes the awesome power of Calvinism and as she prophesies rejects it in the most potent way possible; in later years she becomes a Roman Catholic and enters a convent under the name of Sister Helena of the Transfiguration (as well as its religious allusion to Christ on the mountain, transfiguration can also mean metamorphosis, her conventional name also being an apt description of her actions). Nevertheless (the Spark/Edinburgh dichotomy), Sandy is no longer at ease in her new world. Having written a best-selling book on psychology, called 'The Transfiguration of the Commonplace', she can only place its main influence as 'a Miss Jean Brodie in her prime'. There is no escape for her in the convent and the ambiguity of her position is made clear by the references to her clutching

the bars of the grille as if she wanted to escape from the dim parlour beyond, for she was not composed like the other nuns

161

who sat, when they received their rare visitors, well back in the
darkness with folded hands. (p. 43)

Has she confined herself within the Catholic Church in
reparation for betraying her teacher? Did Miss Brodie's crime
amount to setting herself up as God or was she just a ridiculous woman who tried, and failed, to set herself up against
middle-class conventions? Was she the manipulator or was she
just a victim? To these questions Mrs. Spark does offer an
answer. When Miss Brodie writes to Sandy to ask which of the
set betrayed her, she receives the enigmatic answer: 'If you did
not betray us it is impossible that you could have been
betrayed by us. The word betrayed does not apply . . .'
(p. 169). But it does. Miss Brodie may have betrayed her girls
by acting as God over their lives, but Sandy also played the
Judas when she came to give her evidence to the headmistress.
That sense of duality within a fictional hero or heroine—the
destroyer who both loves and hates the object of obliteration,
the sinner who is justified—is a recurring theme in Scottish
fiction. Through her employment of it in *The Prime of Miss Jean
Brodie*, Muriel Spark wrote a novel whose 'Scottishness' can be
proved; it is even set in a Scottish city and the description of
Edinburgh is vividly realized. But what price nationality when
similar themes are brought to bear in her other novels set in
London or New York? In a sense the creation of Miss Brodie
and her awful Edinburgh school exorcized her Scottish childhood in much the same way that *The Girls of Slender Means*
helped her to lay aside the ghosts of post-war London. Thereafter her novels became less concerned with time and place,
less rooted in identifiable localities. The countryside of *Not To
Disturb* is scarcely Switzerland, New York is a mere symbol of
monstrous wealth and absence of life in *The Hothouse by the East
River*, 'home of the vivisectors of the mind', and the Rome of
The Public Image is a private city; only in her most recent novel,
Loitering With Intent, has she returned to an identifiable locale,
the London of past years. But however much the sense of place
becomes blurred, the themes remain—the genesis of evil, for
example, in *The Mandelbaum Gate* and *The Abbess of Crewe*; and
the moral ambiguities of characters like Dougal Douglas in *The
Ballad of Peckham Rye*, Mrs. Pettigrew in *Memento Mori* and

162

Patrick Seton in *The Bachelors*. These are the themes of 'a writer of Scottish formation', as Mrs. Spark has so candidly described herself.

The publication of *The Prime of Miss Jean Brodie*, with its several obtrusive Scottish themes, allowed Muriel Spark to be identified in Scotland as a 'Scottish writer'. In 1970, nine years later, Karl Miller described her position as being 'on any serious estimate the foremost living Scottish novelist, she has yet to be admitted to the Northern pantheon',[14] which was an accurate way of saying that although she was a Scottish writer in the widest interpretation of that category, narrow parochialism required that she was less of a Scottish writer than some of her contemporaries. (Hitherto, her friend, Derek Stanford, had listed the Scottish influences on her work, and her rejection of them, in the first major study of her novels.[15]) If her Edinburgh novel provided Scottish critics with the opportunity of claiming Mrs. Spark as their own, its publication gave her substantial financial success; it was later made into a stage play, a memorable film with Maggie Smith giving a definitive interpretation of the title rôle, and, more recently, a television serial. During the period of those public successes Mrs. Spark's own fiction was changing and becoming more private and more concerned with style and form, even though, as I have noted, many of the themes recurred in one novel to the next.

In Scotland, during the same period, the novel of childhood or youth spent in the industrial west of Scotland enjoyed a literary vogue, the most substantial being Alan Sharp's *A Green Tree in Gedde* (1965), Archie Hind's *The Dear Green Place* (1966), William McIlvanney's *Remedy is None* (1966) and Gordon Williams's *From Scenes Like These* (1968). Of these novelists, only McIlvanney continued to live and work in Scotland (as a novelist Hind has been silent since the publication of *The Dear Green Place*), and in 1975 he produced *Docherty*, a powerful and moving evocation of Graithnock, a fictional representation of his native Kilmarnock during the first quarter of this century. McIlvanney's chosen instrument of interpretation is the young, all-seeing, all-knowing boy, Conn Docherty; through his eyes we see the strengths and weaknesses of the small, claustrophobic mining community and

163

become aware of its own inner sense of rhythm. Striding through the novel like a colossus is the figure of Tam Docherty, Conn's father, a man possessed of his own sense of virtue and yet alive to a knowledge of the working man's degraded place in society. *Docherty* won for McIlvanney the Whitbread Award for Fiction and established him as a major writer. He alone of his near-contemporaries seems to have been able to transform the material and experiences of his own past into a fiction that has all the perspective of an altered consciousness. Alan Sharp never completed the trilogy begun with *A Green Tree in Gedde* and now lives in California where he is a successful script-writer for the cinema. Gordon Williams lives in London where he writes mainly for television, leaving the poet and critic Alexander Scott to lament in both cases:

> Too many of our novelists, after producing studies of childhood and adolescence in their native environment, depart to fresh woods and pastures new and thereby deny themselves the opportunity of looking at the Scottish scene through more mature eyes with the understanding which only residential experience can bring.[16]

Can it be, one asks, that Scotland is so bereft of experience that it can only be viewed through the kind of disengagement from reality that the childhood vision allows?

McIlvanney, Sharp and Williams are all identifiably Scottish writers in that their early novels were engaged with the backgrounds from which they sprung—'For me', wrote McIlvanney,[17] 'self-fulfilment in isolation is meaningless; you are what you are in relation to the society you live in.' Hence *Docherty*, but while a novelist must have that solid picture of the society he writes about, lest his characters become detached or mere cardboard cut-outs, society is ever-changing, the values of one age become the taboos of another, judgements alter, views of the past become distorted, and so on. The writer, too, changes, becomes an exile from his past—whether that past be the working class of the West of Scotland or the middle-class gentility of Edinburgh or Perthshire—and finds it difficult to reconcile that past with the writing.

> Of course all writers are in a sense expatriates, from class or nation, if only because they reflect on, and make use of,

experience which to others is simply the natural way of living. The very act of trying to extract significance from the moment, to evaluate action and feeling, to give a shape to experience, necessarily separates you from the way most people live their lives.[18]

As described by the Scottish novelist Allan Massie, that sense of separation affects most novelists, and it is little wonder that, with the exception of McIlvanney, who evinces a strong sense of integration with his society in all his novels, most Scottish writers of the post-war years have escaped from the confines of their pasts and have used at least one novel as a means of bringing about that disengagement. But it is precisely because those novelists wrote on Scottish themes, or lived in Scotland, that their novels are considered to be Scottish, while the national identities of those written by Muriel Spark, James Kennaway and others are still pondered upon.

Nationalism is a poor way of judging a writer and his or her work. It leads to touchy patriotism, jingoistic argumentativeness and to the kind of critical parochialism that praises a work simply because it is Scottish, fates that have not escaped Scottish literature over the years. As a result, the concept of Scottishness as interpreted by the country's literature this century has been, and remains, in a state of confusion. On the one hand that lack of critical orderliness leads to the exclusion of writers like William Drummond of Hawthornden (1585–1649), James Thomson (1700–48) and even John Buchan (1875–1940), either because they chose English as a means of literary communication, or because they wanted to live outwith Scotland; on the other it will give grudging acceptance to Scottish-born writers who live elsewhere, provided that their books touch on things Scottish. Muriel Spark and James Kennaway, linked in their fiction by a fastidiousness of prose style and themes which inspect betrayal and the strange dichotomy of love and hate, fall into both categories. Half English, half Scottish yet entirely writers of Scottish formation, both became constitutional exiles (to use Muriel Spark's phrase) and, paradoxically, both can never escape the consequences of having spent their formative years in Scotland. Their fiction has been made stronger by that condition, and so too has Scottish literature.

165

Muriel Spark: An Odd Capacity for Vision

NOTES

1. James and Susan Kennaway, *The Kennaway Papers* (London, 1981), p. 72.
2. James Kennaway, *Household Ghosts* (London, 1961), p. 174.
3. Muriel Spark, 'What Images Return', in Karl Miller (ed.), *Memoirs of a Modern Scotland* (London, 1970), p. 152.
4. Quoted in Alan Bold, *Modern Scottish Literature* (London, 1983), p. 221.
5. Edwin Muir, *Scott and Scotland* (London, 1936), p. 8.
6. *Scottish Chapbook*, Vol. I, No. 3, October 1922.
7. Muir, op. cit., p. 9.
8. Karl Malkoff, *Muriel Spark* (New York, 1968), p. 4.
9. Maurice Lindsay, *The History of Scottish Literature* (London, 1977), p. 435.
10. Allan Massie, *Muriel Spark* (Edinburgh, 1979), pp. 95–6.
11. For a fuller, and more recent, discussion on the relationship of the Scottish writer to his or her national identity, see *Chapman*, 34 (Summer 1983).
12. At moments of extreme anguish and marital breakdown Kennaway would describe the dark side of his character, the 'Jim side', as 'the horrid little Scot'. 'In other words a familiar James is becoming an unfamiliar, unpredictable and unlovable Jim.' For a fuller discussion of his life and work, see Trevor Royle, *James and Jim: A Biography of James Kennaway* (Edinburgh, 1983).
13. Derek Stanford, *Inside the Forties* (London, 1977) contains an admirable description of literary life in post-war London.
14. Karl Miller, 'Romantic Town', in Miller, (ed.), op. cit., p. 118.
15. Derek Stanford, *Muriel Spark* (Fontwell, 1963), pp. 25–6, 37–40, 45.
16. Alexander Scott, 'Literature', in Duncan Glen (ed.), *Whither Scotland? A Prejudiced Look at the Future of a Nation* (London, 1971), p. 218.
17. William McIlvanney, 'Growing up in the West', in Miller (ed.), op. cit., p. 171.
18. Allan Massie, 'The Artful Art of James Kennaway', in James Campbell (ed.), *New Edinburgh Review Anthology* (Edinburgh, 1982), pp. 128–29.

8

The Liberated Instant: Muriel Spark and the Short Story

by TOM HUBBARD

1

We profess to admire Muriel Spark; we vigorously defend her from the charge of elegant trifling; we tend to falter, though, when we try to account for her steady output of short stories. Mrs. Spark is not of course unique in having such work played down or even ignored; we have not yet learned to accord the short story equal status with the novel. We still assume that only big is beautiful, or at least important, and are apparently content to regard these pieces as mere *jeux d'esprit*, tossed off in a twinkling for the *New Yorker* or *Winter's Tales*.

Even so, there is something odd about this neglect. If I may resort to parodied cliché—a manner relished by the authoress herself—Muriel Spark and the short story were meant for one another. She has produced many novels but only one of them, *The Mandelbaum Gate*, can be described as 'full-length'. That book is not one of her favourites and she has stated that she will never again write a long one.[1] Like Sandy Stranger, Mrs. Spark prefers to act on the principle of economy; she is reluctant to fill 'a little glass with a pint of beer'.[2] She's a distiller rather than a brewer; the little glass contains a fine malt. She has sound Scottish antecedents: Stevenson, one of

167

her early loves, both preached and practised concision; going further back, there are the border ballads which Mrs. Spark admires for the 'sequence of events stated in such a way that they have the power to suggest what is left unsaid'.[3] As a poet, long before she turned to fiction, she was well trained in compression; the next step, logically enough, was the short story, a half-way house between the poem and the novel. It is not surprising to find that many of her stories, for example 'The Ormolu Clock',[4] rely less on a resolvable plot than on the evocation of an atmosphere; they are poems in prose. On the other hand, she can handle a clear plot mechanism with considerable narrative skill; during her period of transition from poetry to fiction she wrote a study of the then Poet Laureate, John Masefield, and concentrated on his flair for telling a good story.

The short story is appropriate to her unremitting irony. There are two reasons for this. First, irony is most effective when it uses economical means; it must cut quickly and cleanly. Its temper is utterly opposed to the rhetorical and the overblown; indeed these tend to be its targets. Second, irony and the short story derive power from the setting of a situation and its consequent reversal. Muriel Spark thrives on such contradiction.

> I approve of the ceremonious accumulation of weather forecasts and barometer-readings that pronounce for a fine day, before letting rip on the statement: 'Nevertheless, it's raining.' . . . To have a great primitive crag [Edinburgh Castle Rock] rising up in the middle of populated streets of commerce, stately squares and winding closes, is like the statement of an unmitigated fact preceded by 'nevertheless'.[5]

The 'nevertheless' principle had intrigued Scottish writers long before its particular expression by Muriel Spark. Burns mused on the best-laid schemes which 'gang aft agley'. In his analysis of irony, John Davidson wrote: 'By it our enterprises are whirled away from our most resolved intentions.'[6] Perhaps the most familiar example in Mrs. Spark's longer fiction is the frustration of Jean Brodie's schemes by her most trusted disciple. More readily than the shortest novel, however, the short story can be perceived as a totality. It can achieve a more concentrated power; expectations and illusions can be steadily but not too elaborately built up, and the effect of collapse, when it comes, is accordingly maximized. Raymond and Lou Parker in 'The Black Madonna'[7] pride themselves on a liberal, enlightened outlook which supposedly marks them off from their neighbours; *nevertheless*, when events take an unforeseen turn, they display their latent prejudices more dramatically than most. In 'The Fathers' Daughters',[8] Henry Castlemaine is a literary has-been; like his books, his devoted middle-aged daughter, Dora, is stuck on the shelf. The ambitious young critic Ben Donadieu is initially more interested in working on Kenneth Hope, a novelist who is as in fashion as Castlemaine is out of it. Hope's daughter, the 20-year-old Carmelita, is in her own way working on Ben. *Nevertheless*, at the end of the tale Ben undertakes to lead a Castlemaine revival and conveniently takes Dora on board as well.

In her short stories Muriel Spark can most trenchantly exploit her talent for surreal juxtaposition, which, far from being clever-clever gimmickry, is an essential part of her ironic method, her preoccupation with the 'nevertheless'. In 'The Curtain Blown by the Breeze',[9] the boerish Sonia Van der Merwe, encouraged to get-sophisticated-quick, surpasses the expectations of her female admirers who have only wanted a bit of bitchy fun at her expense. Her household in the middle of the African wilds is incongruously transformed into an island of pseudo-European vogue: 'It was less than a year before she got round to adding the Beardsley reproductions.'[10] The juxtaposition is not in fact as bizarre as it seems; only a thin curtain separates the primitive from 'civilisation'; it can be blown at any time. Daphne du Toit in 'The Go-Away Bird'[11] duly departs for England and is initially taken by its twee charm; before long she learns that, no less than the veldt, it has its predators, and she herself is being stalked.[12]

Mrs. Spark once remarked 'how sharp and lucid fantasy can be when it is deliberately intagliated on the surface of realism.'[13] This applies to many of her short stories. She is perhaps at her most surreal when, by resorting without warning to the supernatural and the extra-terrestrial, she upsets the complacencies of the everyday. Samuel Cramer, the over-ripe romantic protagonist of a Baudelaire short story, is resurrected, in 'The Seraph and the Zambezi',[14] as a white settler going to seed in Rhodesia. Grotesque as this seems, it is all made plain in a matter-of-fact manner and, with convincing naturalism, Mrs. Spark builds up an atmosphere of tawdry and pretentious banality. Cramer is still pathetically and absurdly devoted to self-aggrandizement; having written a Nativity Masque, he prepares to mount it on a makeshift stage. Assuming that he has a right to exploit the celestial in the cause of the egotistical, he takes the part of the First Seraph; the performance has hardly begun when he is suddenly confronted by the real thing. Cramer protests that this is his show.

> 'Since when?' the Seraph said.
> 'Right from the start,' Cramer breathed at him.
> 'Well, it's been mine from the Beginning,' said the Seraph, 'and the Beginning began first.'[15]

The Moon people, in 'The Playhouse Called Remarkable',[16] are more benevolently inclined to the earthlings, who in turn give them rougher treatment than Cramer is able to inflict on the Seraph. Thematically related to *The Ballad of Peckham Rye*, the story tells of events just after Noah's Flood, when the Six Brothers of the Moon attempt to bring vision to the people of Hampstead. After initial successes they are eventually routed by the forces of populist philistinism—the 'tum tum ya movement'—as led by Johnnie Heath, assistant editor of the local rag and later Mayor. However, the Moon people's influence persists in the long run, as they have introduced literature, art and music to the world. A more recent story, 'The Executor'[17] concerns a Scotswoman on the make. Susan Kyle is a brisk Edinburgh bourgeoise who has always frowned on the irregular life-style of her uncle, a writer. She takes up her responsibilities for his literary remains—'archive as they called it'—with an enthusiasm that is something other than disinterestedly literary. During his lifetime she has already inventoried and sorted his papers, pleased with herself for having imposed order on his chaos.

> You didn't catch me filing away a letter from Angus Wilson or Saul Bellow in the same place as an ordinary "W" or "B", a Miss Mary Whitelaw or a Mrs. Jonathan Brown. I knew the

170

value of these letters, they went into a famous-persons file, bulging, and of value.[18]

The uncle dies and the archive is sold to a Foundation, but Susan keeps back the manuscript of ten chapters of an unfinished novel; she resolves to complete and publish it. Whenever she takes it up, however, and turns to the page headed 'Chapter Eleven', she finds it freshly inscribed in her uncle's hand. By this means the late writer tells her that he knows what she's up to. Terrified, she asks God to make her as 'strong and sensible' in a crisis as her heroine Margaret Thatcher. But the uncle persists in his supernatural needling; the Foundation rings up and queries Susan about the novel, to which many of the letters have referred. (In her efficient, philistine way, she had merely *filed* the letters; unconcerned with their content, she had not bothered to read them.) Susan's game is up and before she parts with the novel she notices her uncle's last inscription, a particularly cutting farewell.

'There are trap-doors and spring-guns in these two volumes, there are gins and pitfalls; and the precipitate reader may stumble unawares upon some nightmare not easily to be forgotten.'[19] Stevenson's comment on Poe is equally applicable to Mrs. Spark. But the supernatural is not essential for her to create an atmosphere of menace. Her characters (and her readers) may be unnerved by some eccentric or misfit who turns out to be rather more sinister than quaint. Examples are Selwyn Macgregor, in ' "A Sad Tale's Best for Winter" ', and Hamilton in 'Alice Long's Dachshunds'.[20] 'The Ormolu Clock' may well be Mrs. Spark's most disturbing short story, and not just because of Herr Stroh, a despised outcast. It describes the confident ascendancy of a hotelier, Frau Lublonitsch, and the accompanying decline of her business rival, the feckless Stroh. The narrator (who is not necessarily Mrs. Spark's mouthpiece) offers a sympathetic evocation of Frau Lublonitsch and her achievements. True, she works her girls fourteen hours a day, but they do the work 'cheerfully', and she mucks in more than anyone else. However, a note of unease is sounded at an early stage.

> Just as she turned to attack the day's work, I saw that she glanced at the sorry Hotel Stroh across the path. I saw her mouth

171

turn down at the corners with the amusement of one who has a certain foreknowledge; I saw a landowner's recognition in her little black eyes.[21]

It's all too smug and assured for our comfort. The tension rises, but doesn't snap, when Stroh's menacing quality becomes clear. The Lublonitsch and Stroh establishments face each other; the path which separates them leads to the Austro–Yugoslav border. Mrs. Spark, however, is not concerned with any iron curtain in the usual sense; in this story the frontier tension is between the domains of the two hoteliers. From his window Stroh stares into the narrator's room; he uses field-glasses—as much the equipment of the border guard as of the peeping Tom. The narrator trusts that Frau Lublonitsch or one of her sons will go across 'to deliver a protest'; the violation is territorial as much as personal and calls for a response at the highest diplomatic level.

There is no need for anything so explicit. In Frau Lublonitsch's opulent room there is a magnificently wrought clock, formerly in the possession of Stroh's grandfather 'when things were different' and which Stroh was forced to sell to her. She perches this clock on a ledge of her roof, and Stroh is accordingly warned. Time is running out for him, and this is an effective if cold and merciless way of reminding him. Offended as she has been by Stroh, the narrator does not join in the townspeople's gossiping at his expense; she wonders if he can live another winter. As for Frau Lublonitsch, the consensus view of her seems too cosy; the adoring community does not realize that she may be a more subtle menace than Stroh.

> She would take the Hotel Stroh. She would march on the bridge, and beyond it. The café would be hers, the swimming pool, the cinema. All the market place would be hers before she died in the scarlet bed under the gold-fringed canopy, facing her ormolu clock, her deed-boxes, and her ineffectual bottle of medicine.

Stroh loses his remaining guests and the story concludes thus:

> Everyone likes to be on the winning side. I saw the two new arrivals from the Hotel Stroh sitting secure under the Lublonitsch chestnut tree, taking breakfast, next morning. Herr

Stroh, more sober than before, stood watching the scene from his doorway. I thought, why doesn't he spit on us, he's got nothing to lose? I saw again, in my mind's eye the ormolu clock set high in the sunset splendour. But I had not yet got over my fury with him for spying into my room, and was moved, all in one stroke, with high contempt and deep pity, feverish triumph and chilly fear.[22]

This unresolved, ambiguous air prompts us to wonder where the real threat comes from—from an *individual*, Lublonitsch or Stroh—or from the *situation*, an international incident in microcosm.

Incidentally, 'The Ormolu Clock' is evidence that the 'nevertheless' principle need not rely on an unexpected, sudden reversal. The unsettling effect is developed steadily throughout the piece; the appearance of the ormolu clock on the roof, and Stroh's reaction to it, may be considered a climax, but we have been prepared for it. Towards the end of 'The Pawnbroker's Wife'[23] Mrs. Jan Cloote spins her fantasy about a compass having been presented by a film star to her daughter. The narrator then reveals (to the reader, but not to Mrs. Cloote) that the compass had actually belonged to herself, and that she had been given it when she was 14. The attentive reader will recall that, earlier in the tale, the narrator had casually mentioned a compass which she had pawned and had never seen again. Such a reader enjoys the neatness with which the tale is constructed, but he will not be startled or shocked. This does not prevent the application of the 'nevertheless' principle to Mrs. Cloote, although she herself remains complacently ignorant of it.

2

Using various means, including the supernatural, the symbolic, and the subtle, Muriel Spark transfigures the commonplace and jolts us into seeing it in a new light. In this respect the 'nevertheless' can be related to Brecht's *Verfremdungseffekte*, usually translated as the 'estrangement' or (less satisfactorily) 'alienation' effect:

If empathy makes something ordinary of a special event, alienation makes something special of an ordinary one. The

173

most hackneyed everyday incidents are stripped of their monotony when represented as quite special.[24]

Let us take a reader who unquestioningly accepts a stereotype of 'rebellious' working class and 'conservative' middle class. Much of what happens in actual experience will not register with this reader, either because it does not correspond to his preconceptions or is so familiar that he simply doesn't notice it. In the story 'You Should Have Seen the Mess'[25] the narrator, a young working-class girl, obsessed with respectability and cleanliness, is shocked by the free-and-easy behaviour of the middle-class people with whom she comes into contact. From her naïve point of view, such behaviour is worthy of notice. Perhaps our hypothetical reader would pass it by in real life; presented in this fictional form, and through eyes to which the familiar is unfamiliar, the phenomenon is brought to his attention. Our reader is admittedly an extreme case, himself a crude stereotype, but I think we can take the point that in this story Mrs. Spark is challenging certain expectations, and her 'nevertheless' principle is once again eloquently sustained.

Not the least of the reasons for this is that, like Brecht, Mrs. Spark eschews empathy; we do not 'identify' with the narrator of 'You Should Have Seen the Mess', nor with anyone else in the story. If the girl sheds light on other people's lifestyles, they in turn shed light on her own lifestyle, and it too is rescued from being taken for granted. Here is her response to Willy Morley, a well-off artist and bohemian, and his response to her.

> I could not deny that I liked Willy, in a way. There was something about him, I will say that. Mavis said, 'I hope he hasn't been making a pass at you, Lorna.' I said he had not done so, which was almost true, because he did not attempt to go to the full extent. It was always unhygienic when I went to Willy's place, and I told him so once, but he said, 'Lorna, you are a joy.'[26]

We are made aware of implications missed by the girl, although ironically we receive the information only by means of her own reportage. Unable to accept a single point of view at its face value, we are freed from the limitations of the partial; we can respond to the situation in its totality and thus be capable of cool, objective criticism.

In consequence we can acquire an 'overview'. For both the Christian Spark and the Marxist Brecht, the 'overview' would seem to be the necessary alternative to a narrow, egoistic perspective. It can of course be argued that Christianity and Marxism are themselves subject to falli- bility. Neither writer is a church- or party-hack, and one might prefer to relate Mrs. Spark's 'nevertheless' and Brecht's 'estrangement' to the practice of any artist of integrity and vision; he or she upsets existing relationships in order to create new ones, and reality can therefore be apprehended in ways previously unknown.

Even so, the faiths of Mrs. Spark and Brecht enable them to extract a phenomenon from its immediate context and to measure it against eternity or history. Both writers refuse to be satisfied by any notion that time can only be experienced while it is passing, that it is merely linear, one-dimensional.

It was her reading of Proust which revealed to Mrs. Spark just how the 'commonplace' could be 'estranged' from its normal setting and thus 'transfigured' into something 'special'. The Christian sacraments are based on 'the idea that the visible world is an active economy of outward signs embodying each an inward grace'.[27] There is nothing new about that, writes Mrs. Spark, but the implications have been overlooked. With a mistaken dualism Christians have been too ready to see matter and spirit in conflict, assuming that spirit 'triumphs by virtue of disembodiment'. It is necessary to correct this by accepting 'that deep irony in which we are presented with the most unlikely people, places and things as repositories of invisible grace'; in other words, such people, places and things may appear trivial or irrelevant, 'nevertheless' they can lead us to spirituality. The taste of madeleine cake and tea may seem commonplace and therefore unworthy of mention, but for Proust's Marcel it always evokes his past 'in a special and meaningful way'; during his childhood, on Sunday mornings, his aunt would give him such refreshments, and the sensation has proved unexpectedly powerful, even 'sacramental'.

A mere tea-soaked crumb, then, can disrupt chronology and reveal eternity. Mrs. Spark quotes Proust's explanation:

Let a sound, a scent already heard and breathed in the past
be heard and breathed anew, simultaneously in the present and
the past, real without being actual, ideal without being
abstract, then instantly the permanent and characteristic
essence hidden in things is freed and our true being which has
for so long seemed dead but was not so in other ways awakens
and revives, thanks to this celestial nourishment. An instant
liberated from the order of time has recreated in us man
liberated from the same order, so that he should be conscious of
it.[28]

In her own art Mrs. Spark makes use of the 'active economy
of outward signs', transfiguring them in her own actively
economical way. Each of her short stories is itself a liberated
instant—an encapsulation of what is significant and authentic,
rescued from the prevailing obscurity and mystification.

A wild bird whose call is 'go'way, go'way', a curtain blown
by a breeze or a storm—such an 'outward sign' or symbol
affords not only a neat title, but gives a short story a taut unity
more subtle than can be achieved by the most ingeniously
structured plot. As with Proust, however, these motifs are
invaluable for reasons of content as much as those of form. The
go-away bird is Daphne's link with the eternal; its cry unites
her present and her past and transcends them. Try as she will
to find some niche in this world, her exile is a calling, and it is
the bird which calls. She leaves South Africa, but cannot leave
the bird behind; in England he is grotesquely echoed and
parodied by the budgerigar which is the unwelcome 'gift' to
Daphne from her devious landlady. If the go-away bird gives
Daphne an awareness that 'The fundamental things apply/ As
time goes by',[29] the full significance of its cry is lost on such
shallow, self-centred people as Ralph Mercer, popular novelist
and Daphne's lover, who finds her a useful source of material
then drops her. When she tells him about the bird, he is not
interested; visiting South Africa after her death, he hears it
first behind her grave, then more frequently in other places. It
gives him the creeps and he scuttles back to England.
Daphne—who is one of Mrs. Spark's few 'sympathetic'
characters—has tended to *listen* to the bird; everyone else has

explained her interest in terms of ornithology rather than eternity. We are told at the beginning of the story that 'It was possible to hear the bird, but very few did, for it was part of the background to everything.'[30] Daphne is one of the very few, and can extract the essential from the clamour of the actual and the temporal.

An eternal—or, alternatively, historical—dimension is of particular advantage to the short story; it is enriched by the dialectical tension between such boundlessness and its own formal brevity. Mrs. Spark uses history to this effect in the autobiographical piece 'The First Year of My Life'.[31] Political and military events of the last year of World War I are juxtaposed with the simultaneous growth of an individual baby. The consequences are ironical as well as multi-dimensional; the infant's antics deflate the pomposities and pretensions of the public figures of the time. The curious result is that although the historical details provide such a broad sweep, they are also, paradoxically, belittled. The child may be tiny in comparison with 1918; may not 1918 appear even tinier in a larger scheme of things?

In the Proustian tradition, Mrs. Spark makes much of timeshifts and flashbacks. Again, this helps to achieve amplitude of content despite economy of form; a whole lifetime can be conveyed within thirty-odd pages, as in 'Bang-bang You're Dead'.[32] In this story the flashbacks are related whenever Sybil shows her friends another film of her life in Southern Africa. This juxtaposition of past and present results in the ironic contrast of grotesquely differing points of view; Sybil's friends interpret what they see in a naïvely optimistic manner, charmed by the apparent glamour and exoticism of it all. For Sybil, however, the camera has captured only the superficial appearance of a reality which she actually experienced and which was extremely ugly.

Another timeshift device is the initial presentation of a sequence of events, say a conversation, and its repetition later on in a different context. This enables the same material to be viewed from different perspectives; the second appearance might be more illuminating than the first—even ironically so. The device is familiar to readers of *The Prime of Miss Jean Brodie*. In a short story any repetition might, on first thoughts, seem to jeopardize the ideal of economy, but this apparent contradiction did not mar the border ballads, as Mrs. Spark has pointed out.[33] This position is vindicated in her own 'A Member of the Family'.[34] The story opens with a chunk of dialogue between Richard and Trudy, in which he invites her to meet his mother. We are plunged straight into the situation; no words are wasted on introducing the pair. Then we are whisked back in time; the tale unfolds, we learn more about the characters, and a portion of that conversation is eventually repeated in its proper chronological sequence. This time, because of what we now know, and because the conversation is fresh in our memory, the repeated passage has acquired a tension absent at the beginning of the tale. What *will* happen when she meets his mother?

Tense—and also terse. The effect has been achieved subtly and suggestively. It would have been impossible if the events had been spelled out according to the clock, which shows time passing at only a single pace in a single direction.

3

Muriel Spark is not an escapist. Her work cannot be dismissed on the grounds of irresponsible frivolity or pseudomysticism. She believes in a dimension beyond the human, yet that impels her not to deny human life but to criticize it. The 'nevertheless' principle is not to be confused with negativity, which is the easier option preferred by lesser writers.

'An instant liberated from the order of time has recreated in us man liberated from the same order, so that he should be conscious of it.' An apparent fragment, such as a short story, contains the possibility of wholeness. Liberated itself, it attempts to liberate us; like all art, it asserts our freedom to confront seeming chaos with a totally integrated consciousness and our consequent ability to detect and create order. As I have tried to show, because of its form the short story has a particular responsibility to extract the essential from the non-essential.

I have just used the words 'freedom' and 'responsibility'; Muriel Spark is very much concerned with their interdependence. Self-fulfilment is not to be confused with self-indulgence. Proust explored the decadence of the late nineteenth century; Mrs. Spark has explored the rather less charming decadence of the middle and late years of the present century. In 'The Portobello Road'[35] the murdered Needle makes her posthumous way

> among the solemn crowds with their aimless purposes, their eternal life not far away, who push past the counters and stalls, who handle, buy, steal, touch, desire and ogle the merchandise. I hear the tinkling tills, I hear the jangle of loose change and tongues and children wanting to hold and have.[36]

Mrs. Spark posits the individualism of being and becoming against the egoism of holding and having. The latter prefers contentment to challenge; it is not genuinely individualistic because it is happy to take the line of least resistance and conform to the false values, the bad faith of a mindless collective. Like the narrator of 'Come Along, Marjorie',[37] Mrs. Spark prefers 'different from' to 'same as'. 'Different from' is a particularly important instance of the 'nevertheless' principle. Sybil in 'Bang-bang You're Dead' finds that 'different from' is not a comfortable position. She reads the *Journals* of Kierkegaard, the founder of existentialism. In her own life she faces the existential challenge of being a genuine individual and not compromising with the conventional lie: 'the price of allowing false opinions was the gradual loss of one's capacity for forming true ones.'[38]

Kierkegaard conceived that his task was 'to create difficulties everywhere'.[39] Muriel Spark does likewise. Her 'nevertheless' principle is a constant threat to complacency. She does not disturb for disturbance's sake; her faith implies a commitment to positive moral values. Even the most coolly critical of her fictional protagonists is herself subject to criticism, even self-criticism; Sybil, for example, cannot be taken as embodying an ideal standard of human behaviour, and she knows it.

That point merits explanation. 'Bang-bang You're Dead' has a discernibly Scottish flavour in its treatment of 'doubles'. Sybil and Désirée are extreme opposites in personality and outlook, but they resemble one another physically; are they the split parts of a possible unity? Sybil may be a person of 'integrity', insofar as that word is related to 'honesty', but not in the sense of 'wholeness'. Certainly Désirée lacks depth and disinterestedness, but there is a want of sexuality, and even humanity, about Sybil. She herself recognizes this, and is troubled by self-questioning: 'Am I a woman . . . or an intellectual monster?'[40]

The freedom to achieve integrity—in both senses of honesty and wholeness—is a challenge to any writer. If such freedom can be successfully exercised in art, there is encouragement for its exercise in real life. The reader of a Spark short story may wish to judge for himself if it aspires to MacDiarmid's 'multeity in unity', the ability to be 'at once infinitely great and infinitely small'[41]; he may consider how far, indeed, such a liberated instant can recreate liberated man himself.

NOTES

The texts are taken from *The Go-Away Bird with Other Stories* (London, 1958; the first edition, published by Macmillan) and *Bang-bang You're Dead and Other Stories* (London, 1982; a Granada Paperback Original). Between them these two collections include most of Mrs. Spark's short stories to date; there is no repetition, that is to say no single story in one collection appears in the other. I should also point out that the two collections contain all stories appearing in *Voices at Play* (London, 1961) and *Collected Stories I* (London, 1967; reprinted 1975). *The Go-Away Bird with Other Stories* has also appeared in Penguin.

For an earlier discussion of the short stories see Derek Stanford, *Muriel Spark: A Biographical and Critical Study* (Fontwell, 1963), pp. 107–20.

In the following references, all items are by Muriel Spark unless otherwise indicated.

1. 'Keeping It Short', *Listener* (24 September 1970), p. 412. It is ironic, therefore, that critics of her short stories have tacitly or openly considered that the longer they are, the better; see Charles Alva Hoyt, 'Muriel Spark: the Surrealist Jane Austen', in *Contemporary British Novelists*, ed. Charles Shapiro (Carbondale, 1965; reprinted 1976), p. 137.
2. 'The House of Fiction', *Partisan Review* (Spring 1963), p. 80.
3. *John Masefield* (London, 1953), p. 104.
4. *Bang-bang You're Dead and Other Stories*, pp. 81–92.
5. 'What Images Return', in *Memoirs of a Modern Scotland*, ed. Karl Miller (London, 1970), pp. 152, 153.
6. John Davidson, *The Man Forbid and Other Essays* (Boston, 1910), p. 134.

7. *The Go-Away Bird with Other Stories*, pp. 1–27.
8. *Bang-bang You're Dead and Other Stories*, pp. 155–68.
9. Ibid., pp. 50–67.
10. Ibid., p. 57.
11. *The Go-Away Bird with Other Stories*, pp. 74–137.
12. 'Daisy Overend', from the same collection, pp. 138–49, is an excellent example of a story characterized both by ironic reversal and the revelation of savagery beneath the civilized veneer. It is an acid study of a socio-intellectual climber. The narrator enters Daisy's brittle world and cannot resist helping to foil her cool intrigues.
13. *John Masefield*, p. 174.
14. *The Go-Away Bird with Other Stories*, pp. 174–84. 'The Seraph and the Zambezi' won an *Observer* competition in 1951 and marked Mrs. Spark's debut as a writer of short stories.
15. Ibid., p. 181.
16. *Bang-bang You're Dead and Other Stories*, pp. 68–80.
17. *New Edinburgh Review* (Summer 1983), pp. 2–4. This story first appeared in the *New Yorker*.
18. Ibid., p. 3.
19. R. L. Stevenson, 'The Works of Edgar Allan Poe', in *Essays Literary and Critical* (Tusitala Edition: London, n.d.), p. 184.
20. *The Go-Away Bird with Other Stories*, pp. 66–73; *Bang-bang You're Dead and Other Stories*, pp. 142–54.
21. *Bang-bang You're Dead and Other Stories*, p. 83.
22. Ibid., pp. 91–2.
23. *The Go-Away Bird with Other Stories*, pp. 28–43.
24. Bertolt Brecht, *The Messingkauf Dialogues*, translated by John Willett (London, 1965; reprinted 1977), p. 76.
25. *The Go-Away Bird with Other Stories*, pp. 150–58.
26. Ibid., p. 157.
27. 'The Religion of an Agnostic: a Sacramental View of the World in the Writings of Proust', *Church of England Newspaper* (27 November 1953), p. 1.
28. Ibid.
29. *The Go-Away Bird with Other Stories*, p. 99.
30. Ibid., p. 74.
31. *Bang-bang You're Dead and Other Stories*, pp. 169–76.
32. Ibid., pp. 7–40.
33. 'The Border Ballads are concerned with the lyrical winding in and out of a situation; for all their repetitiveness and length, they are models of narrative economy' (*John Masefield*, p. 104).
34. *Bang-bang You're Dead and Other Stories*, pp. 127–41. This story actually has a ballad-like, legendary flavour; it may be read as a modern version of Bluebeard and his wives.
35. *The Go-Away Bird with Other Stories*, pp. 185–215.
36. Ibid., p. 189.
37. *The Go-Away Bird with Other Stories*, pp. 159–73.
38. *Bang-bang You're Dead and Other Stories*, p. 26.

39. *A Kierkegaard Anthology*, ed. Robert Bretall (Princeton, 1946; paperback edition, 1973), p. 194.
40. *Bang-bang You're Dead and Other Stories*, p. 40.
41. Hugh MacDiarmid, *Complete Poems 1920–1976*, ed. Michael Grieve and W. R. Aitken (London, 1978), Vol. 2, pp. 1016, 874.

9

Mrs. Spark's Verse

by WALTER PERRIE

Critics writing about Muriel Spark's novels generally refer to the fact that she began her literary career as a poet. How she came to be a novelist is left unexplained or is understood to have been a matter of mere circumstance: that Mrs. Spark won a short-story competition and was thereafter invited by Macmillan's to write a novel. What precisely the poet and novelist have in common is generally left vague. In fact, apart from Derek Stanford's remarks, written more than twenty years ago now,[1] there has been nothing of substance on Mrs. Spark's poetry, though that has not deterred some critics from sweeping and unsupported generalizations on the subject. That she is (somehow) essentially a poet is a view which Mrs. Spark has encouraged, tracing the evidence of her poetic talents to, at least, her Edinburgh schooldays:

> I was the school's Poet and Dreamer, with appropriate perquisites and concessions. I took this for granted, and have never since quite accustomed myself to the world's indifference to art, and to the special needs of the artist.[2]

Some critics have been quicker than others to take up Mrs. Spark's hints and cues. Karl Malkoff, for example, writes of her

> Approaching the novel with all the suspicion of a poet accosting an alien, and perhaps inferior, medium. Miss Spark [sic] uses a dazzling assortment of techniques to accomplish in prose what she had first attempted in verse: to create by cutting through the barriers of overused language and situation a sense of

183

reality true to experience, an imaginative extension of the world, a lie that shows us things as they are—a supreme fiction.[3]

In less egregiously fulsome vein Patricia Stubbs writes

> nor has she, I think, ever quite escaped as a novelist from her early affection for the tight, economic form of poetry as against the looser genre of fiction. Indeed, all her ideas on the novel reflect her quite profound mistrust of it, which provides again an ironic and ambiguous comment on a writer who has spent twenty years on a form which she regards as 'second rate'.[4]

Such views originate with Mrs. Spark who, discussing her career with Frank Kermode, explained the shift from poetry to fiction thus: 'I was asked to write a novel, and I didn't think much of novels—I thought it was an inferior way of writing.'[5]

The fact is, of course, that critics are interested in Mrs. Spark's fiction and not in her poetry, of which there is very little, none of it recent and much of it undistinguished. Her poetic achievement consists of one pamphlet of verse[6] and the *Collected Poems I*,[7] the latter being in large measure a reprint of the former. For a collected edition it is a slim volume indeed, containing only forty-five poems and five short translations from Latin. Of those forty-five, the majority are of page-length or less. Moreover, most of the poems were written in a relatively short period between the late '40s and early '50s since when she has concentrated almost entirely on prose. From 1947–49 she was secretary to the Poetry Society and editor of its journal, the *Poetry Review*. In the course of her editorship she published and was supported by 'the band of poets who acted as her special body of house-carls'[8] and who, needless to say, proclaimed her literary virtues. The poems of her own which she published in the *Poetry Review* and other small magazines of the period constitute the great bulk of her output.

One of the first things to strike a reader of the *Collected Poems* will be the highly cerebral, argumentative quality of the work which aims for the kind of neo-classical tone achieved by Eliot. Mrs. Spark much admired Eliot's example, so much so that before she became a Roman Catholic (1954) and during her brief interest in Anglicanism, she attended Eliot's church. Eliot was a crucial figure for her and seems, too, to have figured in some of her delusions during a period of break-down between about 1953 and 1956.[9] The formal, detached-observer tone of Eliot's verse is deceptive inasmuch as it is the surface of work essentially symbolist and emotive in character. Despite the mock-Augustan poise, Eliot's real masters were the symbolists and late-Romantics. While the syntactic surface of his verse may be conventional and well-ordered, the content of imagery and rhythm embedded in that syntax is symbolist in intent and sensory in content. Eliot's metrics strongly suggest the control—not the absence—of great intensities of feeling, and it was by his virtuoso control of such techniques that Eliot achieved his by now characteristic effect of lucidity, musicality and detachment overlaying a symbolist content of great depth and emotive power. It has been worth dwelling on these characteristics to highlight their exclusion from Mrs. Spark's verse, in which feeling, for example, is absent rather than controlled. Mrs. Spark's fundamental techniques are narrative and didactic rather than symbolist. That being so, her poems could be effective only if they displayed genuinely Augustan qualities: wit, concision, humour, elegance, all of which call for great formal dexterity. What we have intead of these, however, is obscurity and even technical ineptitude. It is as though what had really appealed to Mrs. Spark in Eliot's example was the impression of a detached superiority but without a complete grasp of the real nature of Eliot's enterprise. One or two examples will illustrate the point.

'The Fall'

The European Bison fell from grace.
So did the white-tailed Gnu.
Likewise the Blesbok, as also the Mountain Zebra.
The Giant Tortoise must have sinned too.

Everyone knows about the Dodo;
The same goes for the Great Auk.
The inoffensive Okapi's crime
Was trying to be other beasts at the same time.
And there is the case of the Blue-Buck.

They all came to a halt and are dissolved in mystery.
Who remembers, now, Steller's cullionly Sea-Cow?
It, too, through its innocent fault
Failed the finals in history.

'The Fall' depends for its effect on the intellectual *frisson* afforded by the inappropriate application of the concepts of sin and moral responsibility to the realm of biological or natural causation. The idea might sustain a witty poem if carried off with sufficient verve and skill, but where, as here, these qualities are absent, it seems merely inflated and whimsical. Metrically the poem is confused, lacking in coherent rhythmic form or development. The rhymes are a mixture of perfect, imperfect and non-rhyme without apparent artistic motive. What limited interest derives from the use of unusual words such as 'cullionly' is lost in the banality of such flat constructions as 'They all came to a halt'. The paradox is *merely* stated. The tensions which might have brought it to life are lacking, and so the poem lacks emotive as well as intellectual force. Without music, passion, sensory detail or effective wit, it is difficult to imagine *any* poem holding one's attention.

I find 'The Fall' fairly representative both of the level of Mrs. Spark's technical ability and of her poetic concerns. The first poem in *Collected Poems I* displays just the same combination of overly cerebral manner and flawed performance:

'Elementary'

Night, the wet, the onyx-faced
Over the street was shining where
I saw an object all displaced
In black water and black air.

Was it myself? If so I found
An odd capacity for vision.
Capacity, I understand
Is limited by fixed precision.

Being the measure of displacement:
The void exists as bulk defined it,
The cat subsiding down a basement
Leaves a catlessness behind it.

That vision then, shall I concede is
Proved by a void capacity?
What's good enough for Archimedes
Ought to be good enough for me.

But knowing little of natural law
I can't describe what happens after
You weigh a body such as I saw,
First in air and then in water.

Whatever one might make of this obscure piece—and one is not provided with enough information to arrive at any very secure interpretation—its manner is clearly argumentative and rationalistic. Feeling and sense words are largely absent. Like 'The Fall' it deals in generalities in an emotionally neutral manner. Formally it is, again, unsatisfactory. In the first stanza an *abab* rhyme scheme with perfect rhyme is established only to be abandoned in the second stanza where two perfect rhymes clash with two very weak half-rhymes. Particularly irritating is the shift in tense in line two of the third stanza, the only evident justification for which is the need to rhyme 'defined' with 'behind' and the metrical absurdity which would result if the tenses were consistent. Such a procedure does nothing to inspire confidence in an author's poetic gifts. Metrically the poem opens with the jerky rhythms generated by the requirements of a rhyme-determined syntax. By half way through the second stanza these have given way to the relative fluency of

Capacity, I understand
Is limited by fixed precision,

with its echo of the Eliot of the *Sweeney* poems and 'The Hippopotamus'.

At no point is the very abstract vocabulary and argument tightened into wit or effective paradox. The lines just quoted, for example, make little sense. Capacity, as usually understood, is potential force or volume. It is clear from stanza three that Mrs. Spark means volume, so that all that these three lines say is that volume is a finite displacement. So what? The sophistical manner does not disguise the feebleness of content and that impression is reinforced by the banality of:

187

What's good enough for Archimedes
Ought to be good enough for me.

The whole poem seems contrived and to little purpose. It is not just that Mrs. Spark has not the poetic resources to achieve a neo-classical detachment, but that her whole approach—in which form seems contrived around a cerebral content remarkable only for its exclusion of empirical subject-matter—is one in which effective poetry could hardly be written.

In a few cases, such as 'Bluebell among the Sables', Mrs. Spark does succeed in combining a relatively straightforward content with a competent enough control of form, but these are also precisely the poems in which she has been less ambitious and has produced, at best, very minor pieces. It is in the two long pieces in *Collected Poems I* that a more curious content surfaces; these are 'The Ballad of the Fanfarlo'—inspired by a short story by Baudelaire—and 'The Nativity', which make up about a third of the volume. In them the complex of ideas which underlies many of the short poems—in particular, such poems as 'Against the Transcendentalists' and 'The Rout'—is much more overt. There is in fact a fairly consistent range of theme and idea underlying Mrs. Spark's poetry but, in most cases, as a background of reference rather than as a content directly expressed, and it is that fact which explains at least some of their obscurity. Trying to make poems out of ideas rather than experience in a fuller sense, she has been driven to that allusive and condensed manner which makes the poems so obscure simply in order to produce anything which looks remotely like poetry rather than what it really is, versified argument and propositional statement.

The longest poem in the collection is 'The Ballad of the Fanfarlo': twenty pages of obscure narrative composed mainly in uncomfortable quatrains. Derek Stanford has made as much sense of it as anyone is likely to. As he says 'one felt there was a logic in it, but failed perhaps to grasp the imaginative premise.'[10] His summary is not likely to be bettered:

> The subject . . . is that the Romantic personality (symbolized by Samuel Cramer) is merely a mask, a *persona*, disguising an essential emptiness within. And because the inner ego is unreal,

the self is asserted all the more by the speaker. The *persona* becomes a character-ideal, and the pursuit and worship of this false self obscures from the man all knowledge of his true nature and its actual failings. It also precludes him from attendance upon, and submission to, God.[11]

If Cramer is modern man, then modern man is seen as egotistical, selfish, cruel and motivated wholly by self-interest. For Mrs. Spark 'Romanticism is equated with inflated egoism, and egoism versus egoism with the inevitable destruction of man.'[12] The text, however, is so rambling and obscure as to leave any more detailed interpretation open to question. What is clear is that Mrs. Spark held very firm views about the general nastiness of what she took to be Romanticism and the general desirability of what she understood to be the virtues of Classicism: chiefly order, control and detachment. Again, Eliot seems to have been an influence here. One thinks of the essays in *The Sacred Wood*. To give but one example, Stanford observes that 'Cramer's Romantic Ego is Byronic, as indeed is some of his rhetoric',[13] and one hears here an echo of Eliot's dismissive remarks on Byron as an essentially dishonest kind of writer.

What Mrs. Spark is driving at is most fully elaborated in 'The Nativity', if only because there its statement is so much more extreme. The poem dates from later than most of the others and seems to have been composed roughly at the time of her breakdown. The emotional cast of its contents is a disturbing one and it seems, in its way, to have been a decisive piece. While aesthetically it is quite unsatisfactory, it does I think occupy a central place in Mrs. Spark's development. After 'The Nativity' she seems to have concentrated almost exclusively on prose.

'The Nativity' is in four sections: 'The Conversation of the Three Wise Men'; 'The Conversion of the Shepherds'; 'The Conversation at the Inn', and 'The Conversation of the Angels'. Each section takes the form of reported conversation: I and II in irregular and loosely rhythmical free verse, III and IV in a mixture of free verse and quatrains. The reportage is heavy with 'said' and 'replied', devices more suited to prose. Indeed, there is little beyond the line divisions to indicate that this is anything other than an eccentric prose. The primary motive for this reportative and narrative style seems to have been to keep a very disturbing and unpleasant content at as great an emotional distance as possible.

In the first section we have a conversation between three odd beings called a Flate, a Droom and an Aspontal. They are quarrelling viciously, each claiming to have been deceived into a notion of kinship when, in fact, each is utterly unlike the others. Their motivations are based on egotism, hatred and isolation:

> The Droom said, 'You're a sly one:
> I was given to understand you were a Droom.
> Look at your lips hewn out of sallow amber.
> Look at your funny head all amethyst-encrusted,
> Cut square. I should have known there is
> No other Droom on earth. No one's to be trusted.'

as though distrust had an epistemological rather than experiential base. All that holds the three together is the command laid on them to follow the star.

Sections II and III rework the same theme. For the flavour of the piece here is II entire:

The Conversation of the Shepherds

> The Gladanka was saying, 'If a ewe gives
> A dead lamb and you kick her three times thrice
> In the face before sunset how many suns will
> Rise before her blood stinks?' And the
> Weezabaw laughed, rubbing his corns with a stone.
> And the Shorket said, 'Sod the riddle the same as
> You sodded the ewe.' The Gladanka was saying,
> 'I knew a ewe give a dead lamb every time
> Till the farmer slit her belly and stuffed it back.'
> And the Weezabaw laughed, 'Gladys', he said,
> 'Gladys Barker was that ewe's name.' 'Sod the name,'
> Said the Shorket, 'of the day I married the hollow-
> Bellied Gladys Barker. If she's a Shorket
> I'm a cherub with six eyes.' The Gladanka was
> Saying, 'Your teeth grow out of your chin, you
> No-Gladanka.' And the Weezabaw laughed;
> 'You two,' said the Weezabaw, 'you two will be
> The death of me. You ought to see yourselves.

Whatever you both are is far, far
Short of a Weezabaw. You with the vertical mouth,
Keep in your tongue or it will wash your ears; and
You with the nose on top of your head, smell out
The principalities of heaven for all of us.'

In this outpouring of hatred and cruelty I can find no aesthetic
purpose—only a relatively uncontrolled release of disturbing
materials. One cannot but recall that this was written not so
very long after the holocaust of European Jewry and that Mrs.
Spark came from a Jewish background. It is a theme to which
she returned more directly in *The Mandelbaum Gate*. The idea
that creatures hate and fear each other purely on the basis that
they are different is hardly one that the twentieth century can
claim to have outgrown. The third section reintroduces
characters from 'The Ballad of the Fanfarlo' and the matter of
that section is the same non-communicative, egotistical
quarrelling which figures in I and II.

Section IV attempts a resolution of I–III. 'The Conversation of the Angels' consists of eight quatrains, an odd couplet
and a twenty-four line free verse conclusion. Each quatrain
reports a proposition about the nature of man as viewed by the
angels. Thus, the first quatrain runs:

Before the jubilees of Angels
They said, 'What is that mess of meat and bone?'
Before the songs of Archangels
They answered, 'That is no one.'

The propositions asserted are that the essence of the person is
non-material; that 'Man is no one'; that 'Each man is one and
Man is none', that is, that there is no common essence of
humanity (man in general) because 'None is like another
man.' The fourth quatrain asserts that 'Each is known to no
man' and the fifth that 'Divine affection/ For them isn't easy'
but that, despite that, each individual is precious to God
because 'being all/ There is of his kind. He's irreplacable.' The
seventh and eighth quatrains assert that sin consists in 'The
consumption/ Of men by men. They've all got/ An ache to eat
what they are not', and that their individual value is knowable
only to the Holy Ghost. The conclusion—somewhat obscure—
asserts that the discrepancy between species (individuals) and

191

human incongruity, both between individuals and between God and man, can only be resolved by the mediation of Christ. The poem concludes:

> One said, 'What's common to men?'
> And one replied, 'Uncommonness alone.
> Fly for the grace
> Of common uncommonness
> Which is to be made known.
> Uncommon men become
> Common to men in Christ's face,
> Mediator of angels and of men.'

'The Nativity' seems to have been Mrs. Spark's first full literary avowal of a Christian resolution to what she saw as the problem of the human condition, though it must be observed that her theology as presented here is not shared by any Christian church. There are several extraordinary features to be observed of this poem. The most obvious is the extreme degree of dissociation between the tone and manner of sections I–III and that of their 'resolution'. It is not just that the opening sections display a cruel, selfish and violent world but that in the aesthetic disorder with which they do so, they carry a powerful charge of emotion. In extreme contrast section IV is abstract, cerebral and obscure to a degree which rigorously excludes sense, feeling and emotion. It is the *idea* of a resolution rather than an emotional or spiritual katharsis which is presented. The fact is, of course, that the final section thereby fails to go any way towards resolving the tensions generated in I–III, either aesthetically or morally. They remain dissociated with the resolution retaining that aura of frigid over-control so prevalent in her poetry and I–III seeming to revel in an hysteria of squalor and wickedness. It is as though Mrs. Spark had to believe, for whatever reasons, that a purely formalistic resolution to a difficulty, a sort of intellectual sleight of hand, was the same as the real thing. The second feature worth remarking is the oddity of the theology. Mrs. Spark accepts the basic (and non-Christian) premise so beloved of fascist ideologies that 'others are different' and carries it to an extreme conclusion which she grounds in the ontological claim that that is how men are. Even odder is the fact that the *proffered* motive for so doing is epistemological scepticism which, I would suggest, can only be a rationalisation of the real situation. What is disturbing about scepticism is that it does answer some element in our experience while seeming to be (unanswerably) based on pure rationality. Mrs. Spark's position is the polar opposite of all those which seek to account for human misery and cruelty by pointing to social or historical—and thereby, usually, contingent—factors. And yet, as some sort of Christian, Mrs. Spark would presumably wish to assert that an option was available; that is, that cruelty and misery can be overcome through submission to the mediation of Christ. But given that Mrs. Spark seems to ground her position in an ontological claim, how that submission is ever to come about is a matter left wholly unanswered. Her views as stated are self-contradictory.

'The Nativity' dates from a very disturbed period in Mrs. Spark's biography. Having quarrelled with her employers in the Poetry Society she was scraping a meagre living in London, working for various publishers and co-operating with Derek Stanford on several literary projects. In 1952–53 she had felt increasingly drawn to religion and, after a flirtation with Anglicanism, joined the Catholic Church in 1954. Shortly thereafter she underwent a severe mental breakdown. It is from this period—1953–56—that both 'The Nativity' and her first novel, *The Comforters* (1957), date. Of this period she has written 'My own conversion (to catholicism) was really an instinctive rather than an intellectual experience. . . . Anyway, I decided at last to become a Catholic, by which time I really became very ill. I was going about, but I was ready for a breakdown',[14] and:

> The first reaction I had when I became a Catholic was that my mind was far too crowded with ideas, all teeming in disorder. This was part of my breakdown. The oddest, most peculiar variety of themes and ideas of all sorts teemed in my head. I have never known such mental activity. It made me suffer a lot. But as I got better I was able to take them one at a time. . . .[15]

Derek Stanford, who knew her well at that time, has written that her 'deepest wish was for stability'[16] and of her 'inability to locate her own image'.[17] She was looked after for a time by a

Father O'Malley, an amateur Jungian therapist.[18]

Mrs. Spark's poems have little aesthetic merit, a fact not altered by the observation that her novels may do. Her verse seems to have been as much a response to a need for self-expression as of aesthetic concerns, an impression strongly supported by 'The Nativity'. Further comment on the poems is therefore not really a matter for the critic. In Mrs. Spark's case, however, the matter does not rest there for, as we have observed, interest in her poetry derives mainly from its relation to her fiction. What is important in that respect is that the themes and ideas, with which she dealt in her poetry and which seem to have been exaggerated rather than changed during her period of breakdown, seem also to be the dominant material of her novels and of her ideas about fiction and, indeed, to have been present from the beginning of her literary career.

Mrs. Spark has made it clear that, for her, 'The Catholic belief is a norm from which one can depart. It's not a fluctuating thing.'[19] What she found in it was essentially stability. As Barbara says, in *The Mandelbaum Gate*, 'Either the whole of life is unified under God or everything falls apart.'[20] The fact that her breakdown *followed* her conversion suggests that she needed that stability afforded by an external authority before she could 'let go' the disturbing psychic contents which figure in 'The Nativity', for example. Having, at least in part, resolved her personal difficulty in that way, there would be no need for a fundamental revision of her ideas.

Mrs. Spark's poetry states an extreme form of epistemological scepticism. Since that scepticism extends to other minds, it leads to one variety or other of solipsism. Mrs. Spark has taken to its extreme a view central to much modern writing, both literary and philosophical. Certainly since Descartes the problems of scepticism have formed the trunk from which the different branches of Western philosophy have sprouted. Mrs. Spark, however, is not a philosophical sceptic in the usual sense. By opting for a religious stance she makes particular claims about the nature both of the problem and its solution. To use a rather old-fashioned terminology, her scepticism about Appearance is met by her claims about Reality. Just how fully these views persist in her novels can be seen by looking at the sort of world she presents in *The Hothouse by the East River* (1973).

The Hothouse by the East River is in many respects the most characteristic of Mrs. Spark's works inasmuch as it contains in the space of a short novella all those features of technique and theme which figure with obsessive regularity in the other novels. Though some critics have thought highly of it, I find it a deeply unsatisfactory work. In it are portrayed a group of characters as crazed as any to be found in her fiction and who, as has often been observed, inhabit a characteristically closed world—one bounded by their own obsessions. Much of the action takes place in a New York flat overlooking the East River, though the text is seamed with flashback scenes to the England of 1944 and the final scenes are enacted on the streets of New York.

The protagonists are a husband and wife—Paul and Elsa—and their small circle of family, friends and associates. The narrative style is God's eye reportage but heavy, not to say turgid, with sarcasm and irony, evident both in the exchanges between characters and in the voice of the narrator. Its complex plot is not readily summarized, but its essentials are that Paul and Elsa are English emigrés. Elsa is very rich and, apparently, either deranged or possessed. Her shadow falls the wrong way. Whether this is some strategem of her husband's to have her certified, and so secure her money for himself, is left, initially at least, as a possibility. Paul is haunted by the conviction that he is being pursued by a figure from their wartime past. Conversation between the various characters is a fabric of misunderstanding and non-communication, sparking off endless verbal puzzles. Many of the incidents are thoroughly surreal and all of the characters are motivated by self-interest, greed, cruelty and vanity. Some are portrayed as merely stupid—Garven, Elsa's therapist, is simply a pasteboard target for the author's prejudices. It is just the same sort of world as was portrayed in 'The Ballad' and 'The Nativity'. It is a world peopled by shallow grotesques and only towards the end of the book do we learn that the pseudo-naturalistic style of reportage is itself a false trail and that the characters are either ghosts or are fantasized by ghosts. Paul and Elsa were killed in 1944 and what seems to resolve the book is

Elsa's acceptance of the fact that she is dead; she and Paul having intended to settle in New York after the war and having died in an emotionally disturbed condition generated by Paul's jealousy. The figure who haunts Paul is a character to whom both he and Elsa had some sort of emotional attachment.

In *The Hothouse by the East River* Mrs. Spark's distaste for the world is given substantial rein. What skill has gone into its composition is vitiated by the self-indulgence both of setting up pasteboard characters simply to mock them and by the endless and gratuitous playing with logical and verbal puzzles. A typical example is:

> . . . 'Try to recollect what you did yesterday.'
> 'I never do today the same as I did yesterday,' she says. 'Why should I remember?' . . .[21]

This sort of thing is done with much greater subtlety and depth by Beckett. The epistemological points are treated by Mrs. Spark simply as excuses to display her cleverness, since they are left unresolved and, beyond establishing the fact of non-communication, contribute nothing to the development of the text, merely side-tracking the reader to no purpose. Indeed, throughout the book she treats her readers with contempt: a fact which says more about Mrs. Spark than about her readers.

That Mrs. Spark's concerns have not fundamentally changed between 'The Nativity' and *The Hothouse* is very clear. Of the latter Peter Kemp has written:

> Variously, the novel has displayed the impossibility of attaining full knowledge of another person, and the subsequent difficulty that can be involved in coming to terms with the stubbornly residual 'cloud of unknowing', the opaque area of private history and personality-enigma, that, like Elsa, every individual trails around with him.[22]

Allan Massie writes of its 'central pre-occupation with the heresy of solipsism',[23] though that places a misleading emphasis on Mrs. Spark's views. Certainly, she is centrally concerned with the evils of egoism but she sees that as a product of a legitimate scepticism, and it is the fact that the scepticism is legitimate—rationally at any rate—which is the strength of her position. Solipsism is not in fact a common view if taken seriously. Egoism is all too common but refers properly to behaviour rather than belief. In fact, certain features of her position are very close to—and may, given her Scottish Presbyterian schooling and interest in philosophy, derive in part from—those of David Hume. Hume resolved his scepticism with the suggestion that our most common concepts and beliefs were grounded not in reason but in a kind of natural association of ideas. Mrs. Spark writes in *The Hothouse*:

> The East window behind Elsa which looks out on the dark daylight full of snow, a swirling grey spotted-muslin veil, beyond which, only by faith and experience can you know, stands the sky over the East River.[24]

Hume would query the 'faith' but it is by faith that, for Mrs. Spark, egoism can be overcome. In *The Hothouse* none of the characters attracts our sympathy or affection but the least condemned is Elsa and it is she who says 'You can be mistaken about anything.'[25]

The heart of the aesthetic problem about Mrs. Spark's approach to fiction is that she presents us with a view of the world so one-sided as to be a lie. The problem is two-fold: is the lie convincing on its own terms; does the lie serve some aesthetic, moral or empirical purpose? The idea that Mrs. Spark's work might simply be escapist entertainment hardly arises, so bleak are the worlds she presents.

There seems to be substantial critical concensus about the answer to the first of these questions, and that is that Mrs. Spark has a very mixed success. Where, as in *The Hothouse*, the characters are simply caricatures or targets for the author's hostilities, that constitutes a simple failure of seriousness. On such grounds one would have to consider her a minor novelist who has, hitherto at least, failed to produce a sustained body of serious work. This generation of unbelief within a text has to be sharply distinguished from the credibility or otherwise of the text in relation to the way we ordinarily go about our business in the world. In this respect J. R. R. Tolkien's remarks—and Tolkien took his Catholicism and story-telling very seriously indeed—are highly apposite:

What really happens is that the story-maker proves a successful 'sub-creator'. He makes a Secondary World which your mind can enter. Inside it, what he relates is 'true': it accords with the laws of that world. You therefore believe it, while you are, as it were, inside. The moment disbelief arises, the spell is broken; the magic, or rather art, has failed. You are then out in the Primary World again, looking at the little aborted Secondary World from outside.[26]

This is, in fact, the classic Coleridgean view. If the rule which Tolkien states is breached, then the text becomes a pseudo-text (rather like bad allegory), for it then requires continuous translation from one world to the other and that is aesthetically disruptive: a realization of that fact was the basis of Brechtian theatre. Mrs. Spark specifically denies that her work aims for that particular kind of disruption.

What has confused at least some discussions of Mrs. Spark's work is the fact that some critics have conflated the issues of internal and external credibility and have been aided and abetted in their confusion by Mrs. Spark. In terms of the Primary World the picture Mrs. Spark presents in her work is a travesty, but to say so begs the question at issue, which is whether it is any part of the novelist's business to present us with a picture of how things are. Mrs. Spark's views on fiction derive in large measure from the writings of Cardinal Newman: a fact she has acknowledged. The doctrine at issue is that of the economy of truth. Its basis, as Marc Shell points out, can be found in the Gospels:

> In the parable of the sower, for instance, Jesus suggests that the steward should match his ability to give with his students' ability to receive the truth. In order to dispense truth, it may be necessary to tell a kind of untruth. . . . a kind of lying.[27]

It is a doctrine sanctioned by St. Paul. Shell continues:

> The attempt to define the difference between falsehood and pious economy has given rise to theories of metaphor and fiction. Cardinal Newman, for example, compares economy with the *disciplina arcani*. Economy is 'setting (the truth) out to advantage', as when 'representing religion, for the purpose of conciliating the heathen, in the form most attractive to their prejudices', and the *disciplina arcani* is a 'withholding [of] the truth' in the form of allegory, by which the same text may

express the same truth at different levels to different people. . . .
All men are children blind to truth, and, as Newman argues,
every poet accommodates to (and sometimes even flatters) the
feelings and prejudices of the hearer.[28]

A more sophistical, pernicious and fanatical doctrine it would
be difficult to devise.

As a justification for lying the doctrine of the economy of
truth is entirely dependent on the absolutist view of truth and
on the assurance that one had access to it. That this is Mrs.
Spark's view, or is very close to it, is clear from her remarks on
the subject:

I don't claim that my novels are truth—I claim that they are
fiction, out of which a kind of truth emerges. And I keep in my
mind specifically that what I am writing is fiction because I am
interested in truth—absolute truth—and I don't pretend that
what I'm writing is more than an imaginative extension of the
truth—something inventive. . . . What I write is not true—it is
a pack of lies. There is a metaphorical truth and moral truth,
and what they call anagogical, you know, the different sorts of
truth; and there is absolute truth, in which I believe things
which are difficult to believe, but I believe them because they
are absolute. . . .[29]

Mrs. Spark is either deeply confused or deliberately evasive.
This becomes clear from the rest of the interview (with
Professor Kermode) where she, more or less immediately,
shifts her ground. Kermode asks whether she would invoke the
classic defence to the charge that poets are liars: that theirs is a
no-claim case about the world. At first she agrees with this—
in which case she would not be interested in non-artistic
truths—and then shifts her ground again to the claim that her
novels have a reportative truth about her own subjectivity:
'events occur in my mind, and I record them. Whether it fits in
with this theory, that theory, this myth, that myth, has
nothing to do with me.'[30] That would be an effective dis-
claimer on *any* artistic or moral responsibility and would
switch the basis of assessment from aesthetics to psychology.
Kermode accepts these remarks at face value and concludes
that 'For Mrs. Spark the novel is true because it happens in
the author's mind as he writes.'[31] By this stage confusion has
been overtaken by incoherence.

Bad though this situation is, worse is to come, for it is clear that Mrs. Spark has taken over Newman's notion of economy—which is about morality—and turned it into a notion about aesthetics. Derek Stanford made a similar observation about some of her early poetry:

> What is most remarkable about this poem ['Against the Transcendentalists'] is the way in which she reconciles an Art-for-Art's sake attitude with a Christian position. She does this by applying to morality the same near-to-hand standards as she applies to art.[32]

Allan Massie makes a similar point, though he attributes to the phenomenon a colouring of liberal relativism which seems quite alien to the tone of Mrs. Spark's concerns:

> It is precisely this sense of awareness and this awareness that one has, for the purposes of art, selected a particular truth, that is perhaps a truth only from that selected angle, that distinguishes Muriel Spark's work and gives it its peculiar elegance, held in its dandy pose.[33]

What Massie has seen is that there is a fundamental, albeit confused, aestheticism underlying all of Muriel Spark's writings. As Stanford remarks: 'She was much taken with Newman's remark that a Christian view of the universe being almost necessarily a poetic one.'[34] And that odd remark, already quoted, about the 'special needs' of the artist says as much.

The unfortunate truth seems to be that Mrs. Spark has no clear idea of what she is about and shifts her ground in relation to the promptings of her interlocutors. What she has created is a jungle of aesthetic and philosophical incoherence. She has written not out of a consistent world-view, or view of art, but from consistent obsessions and in Newman's doctrine of the economy of truth found a specious justification for what she was in any case already doing. The real test of her work, were we to take it absolutely seriously, would be that posed by George Steiner in his discussion of Flaubert:

> Flaubert does no less than assert . . . that artistic excellence, the high seriousness of the true artist, carries its own complete moral justification. Even as it comes to active being in a sphere strangely between truth and falsehood, the work of art lies

200

outside any code of current ethical convention. . . . its true morality is internal. The justification of a work of literature is, in the deep sense, technical; it resides in the wealth, difficulty, evocative force of the medium. Trashy prose, be it humanely purposive and moral in the utmost, merits censorship.[35]

Most of Mrs. Spark's work fails that test. The fact that human sympathy and kindness and affection are excluded from Mrs. Spark's worlds is not accidental. The guts of the Flaubertian approach is that, as Auden says, love is a peculiar intensity of attention. In literature the failure of such attention bespeaks a failure of seriousness which may, ultimately, be the same thing as a failure of imagination.

The alternative to treating Mrs. Spark's work as primarily aesthetic is to treat it as stating a kind of truth about the primary world. On that basis the strength of her position derives, as has already been noted, from the general force of scepticism which, however unsatisfactory it may be as an intellectual stance, has something deep in it about our experience of the world—or it would not have been such a central issue for such a very long time. Even so, though Mrs. Spark trades off the effectiveness of scepticism, her understanding of it seems shallow and is certainly internally incoherent. If it were really the case that individuals constituted species, communication *would* be impossible and there would be no call for fiction. Mrs. Spark seems to have given little thought to the nature of language or she would have realized that even lying has to be rule-governed. The position she states in 'The Nativity', and which is implicitly present in the novels, is very close to that argued by Leibniz in *The Monadology*.

More often than not the 'ten-thousand things' get done and the speech-acts required in their doing go unremarked. That intricate web of tacit conspiracy on which our worlds rest goes largely unremarked until something goes wrong, when attention is sharply drawn to the failure. Since the failures get all the attention, the exception is all too easily confused with the rule, and writers who take such failures as the starting point for explanations of the nature of language (or communication) generally end by asserting the impossibility of what they set out to explain and by asserting only the absurdity of their own procedure, for they have failed to account for the appearance which generated their interest.

In *The Monadology* Leibniz asserts that monads—the simple, ultimate, sensing constituents of reality—have no windows, by which he means that there can be no communication between them. In order therefore to account for the appearance of communication and interaction—and to avoid making God out to be a deceiver, an issue raised by Descartes—he had to develop the notion of a universal pre-established harmony between the perceptions of all the monads which comprise reality—pre-established by God. Thus, although no interactions actually take place, it appears to the monads, and the world goes on, as though they did. In fact, the sequence of perceptions which characterizes each individual monad and which is the substance of its individuality is wholly internal and pre-regulated by God. In Leibniz's case the need for this elaborate deception was generated by his need to make his extreme rationalism consistent. Mrs. Spark seems to occupy some sort of similar position but without the consistency.

Scepticism and reason, like Christianity and diabolism, are two sides of a much-worn coin. In recent years that ancient dichotomy has come in for some fatal criticism and clarification, resulting mainly from work in the philosophy of language. That there was something unsatisfactory about the sceptical position was acknowledged by Hume in his observation that his arguments seemed to lose their force when he left his study and involved himself in the world again. Reason and doubt have fought a 400-year battle in the efforts of various philosophers either to ground our experience in reason or, at least, to hold at bay the incursions of scepticism which threaten the fabric of knowledge. What has become evident is that the concepts of doubt and reason which have been at stake have been empty in the face of the complexities of our experience of the world, partly at least as a consequence of the fact that philosophers have generally held far too simplistic views about the nature of language and the ways in which expressions like 'doubt' and 'reason' are used. The notion of reason which figures, for example, in the writings of Kant is a simplistic and artificial one if we attempt to apply it to the ways in which we use words like 'reasonable' and 'reasoning' in practical life, for all that Kant was a genius. These observations would not affect our legitimate puzzlement about the world—only that particular rationalistic ground for puzzlement would be seen to be misplaced. The relevance of these points to Mrs. Spark's writings is that, intent on excluding feeling, sensation and emotion from much of her work, she has been caught up in the traditional confusions of epistemology and has failed in much of her work to move beyond them onto the ground of a more complete grasp of experience. Where she has succeeded in doing so is precisely where she has abandoned her rationalistic obsessions and looked with a less prejudiced eye at what actually happens; *The Prime of Miss Jean Brodie* is a case in point. One can only regret that she has not been able to do so more often or more consistently for, as Tolkien remarked, 'The right to freedom of the sub-creator is no guarantee among fallen men that it will not be used as wickedly as is Free Will.'[36]

NOTES

1. D. Stanford, *Muriel Spark* (London, 1963).
2. K. Miller (ed.), *Memoirs of a Modern Scotland* (London, 1970), p. 152.
3. K. Malkoff, *Muriel Spark* (New York, 1968), p. 3.
4. P. Stubbs, *Muriel Spark* (British Council, 1973), p. 4.
5. F. Kermode, *The House of Fiction* in *Partisan Review*, Spring 1963, 79.
6. M. Spark, *The Fanfarlo and Other Verse* (London, 1952).
7. M. Spark, *Collected Poems I* (London, 1967).
8. D. Stanford, *Inside the Forties* (London, 1977), p. 153.
9. D. Stanford, *Inside the Forties*: see especially pp. 189–92.
10. D. Stanford, *Muriel Spark*, p. 78.
11. Ibid., p. 94.
12. Ibid., p. 98.
13. Ibid., p. 97 (footnote).
14. M. Spark, *My Conversion* in *Twentieth Century*, Autumn 1961, 59.
15. Ibid., p. 60.
16. D. Stanford, *Inside the Forties*, p. 150.
17. Ibid., p. 151.
18. Ibid., p. 192.
19. M. Spark, *My Conversion*, 60.
20. Quoted by Stubbs, op. cit., p. 30.
21. M. Spark, *The Hothouse by the East River* (London, 1973), p. 86.
22. P. Kemp, *Muriel Spark* (London, 1974), p. 155.

23. A. Massie, *Muriel Spark* (Edinburgh, 1979), p. 80.
24. M. Spark, *The Hothouse by the East River*, p. 46.
25. Ibid., p. 114.
26. H. Carpenter, *J. R. R. Tolkien: A Biography* (London, 1977), p. 191. Quoted from his Andrew Lang lecture.
27. M. Shell, *The Economy of Literature* (Baltimore, 1978), p. 105.
28. Ibid., p. 106.
29. F. Kermode, op. cit., pp. 81–1.
30. Ibid., p. 81.
31. Ibid.
32. D. Stanford, *Muriel Spark*, p. 89.
33. A. Massie, op. cit., p. 11.
34. D. Stanford, *Muriel Spark*, p. 58.
35. G. Steiner, *On Difficulty and Other Essays* (Oxford, 1978), p. 110.
36. H. Carpenter (ed.), *The Letters of J. R. R. Tolkien* (London, 1981), p. 194.

Notes on Contributors

ALAN BOLD was born in 1943 in Edinburgh where he attended university and trained as a journalist. Since 1966 he has been a full-time writer and visual artist and since 1975 has lived in rural Fife writing books and contributing features regularly to *The Scotsman* and occasionally to the *New Statesman*, *T.L.S.*, *Glasgow Herald* and *Tribune*. He has published many books of poetry, including *To Find the New*, *The State of the Nation* and a selection in *Penguin Modern Poets 15*. His *In This Corner: Selected Poems 1963–83* represents his best work over the past two decades; with the artist John Bellany he has collaborated on *A Celtic Quintet* and *Haven*. He has edited many anthologies including *The Penguin Book of Socialist Verse*, *The Martial Muse*, the *Cambridge Book of English Verse 1939–75*, *Making Love*, *The Bawdy Beautiful*, *Mounts of Venus*, *Drink To Me Only*, *The Poetry of Motion*. He has also written critical books on *Thom Gunn & Ted Hughes*, *George Mackay Brown*, *The Ballad*, *Modern Scottish Literature* and *MacDiarmid: The Terrible Crystal*. He has edited *The Thistle Rises: a MacDiarmid Miscellany* and *The Letters of Hugh MacDiarmid*. He has exhibited his Illuminated Poems (pictures combining an original poetic manuscript with an illustrative composition) in venues as varied as Boston University and the National Library of Scotland.

Notes on Contributors

FRANCIS RUSSELL HART is Professor of English at the University of Massachusetts at Boston. His books include studies of Lockhart, Scott, the novel in Scotland, and (with J. B. Pick) a biography of Neil Gunn. His articles concern nineteenth-century fiction, the Gothic Novel, biography and autobiography, and Scottish fiction. He has recently completed *A Poetics of Adventure*, and is working on studies of literature and pedagogy.

TOM HUBBARD was born in Kirkcaldy in 1950. In recent years he has worked in Edinburgh University Library, where he sorted and listed the Christian Salvesen archive and catalogued a portion of the library of Hugh McDiarmid. He has taught literature to internal and extra-mural W.E.A. classes in Edinburgh and Fife and has contributed to a number of periodicals including *Cencrastus* and the *Scottish Review*. He was awarded a Ph.D (Aberdeen University) for a thesis on lower-class intellectuals in Mark Rutherford, George Gissing and H. G. Wells. He is currently pursuing post-doctoral research on Scottish fiction between 1880 and 1914, with financial assistance from the Carnegie Trust for the Universities of Scotland.

ALLAN MASSIE was born in Singapore in 1938 and was educated at Glenalmond and Trinity College Cambridge. He is the editor of the *New Edinburgh Review* and author of four novels—*Change and Decay in All Around I See*, *The Last Peacock*, *The Death of Men*, *One Night in Winter*—and a critical study of Muriel Spark.

JANET MENZIES, who was born in Liverpool in 1958, works for *Kentish Times* newspapers and lives in Kent. She is a graduate of Cambridge University where she read Anglo-Saxon, Norse and Celtic, and English. While she was at Cambridge the *Journal of Beckett Studies* published her article 'Beckett's Bicycles'. After Cambridge, she joined the *Daily Telegraph*, where she worked on the book page, reviewing. Her freelance writing has included articles for the *Evening Standard* on various aspects of London life. She recently contributed to *J. R. R. Tolkien: This Far Land*, edited by Robert Giddings.

WALTER PERRIE was born in 1949 in the Lanarkshire mining village of Quarter. Educated locally and at Hamilton Academy, he took an M.A. in philosophy at the University of Edinburgh. Full-time poet and essayist, his last two volume-length poems have attracted considerable attention. The recipient of various literary prizes and awards, he lives in Edinburgh. His first collection of essays on the philosophy of literature—*Out of Conflict*—was published in 1982.

FAITH PULLIN taught English and American literature at the University of Ibadan before taking up her present post at the University of Edinburgh. She is editor of *New Perspectives on Melville* (1978), has written on D. H. Lawrence and Afro-American literature, and is currently engaged on a critical study of three contemporary women novelists, Rosamund Lehman, Elizabeth Taylor and Barbara Pym.

JENNIFER L. RANDISI was born in San Mateo, California, in 1950 and received her Doctorate from the State University of New York at Stony Brook in 1979. Dr. Randisi has published articles on writers of the American south, British writers, and film. Her study of Eudora Welty's novels (*A Tissue of Lies*, University Press of America) was published in 1982. Dr. Randisi teaches American literature, and is currently working on a book treating the river as a metaphor in American literature. She resides in Southern California.

TREVOR ROYLE was born in Mysore, India, in 1945 and his childhood was spent in Malaya and Scotland. He was educated in St. Andrews and Aberdeen, and between 1971 and 1979 he was Literature Director of the Scottish Arts Council. A full-time writer, journalist and broadcaster, his previous books have ranged over football, military history and Scottish literature. His most recent publications are: *Death Before Dishonour: The True Story of Fighting Mac*; *James and Jim: A Biography of James Kennaway*; *The Macmillan Companion to Scottish Literature* and *The Kitchener Enigma*.

VALERIE SHAW was born in 1941 in Perth and educated in Edinburgh. She studied at the University of Edinburgh and at Yale University, and is currently a lecturer in the Department of English literature at the University of Edinburgh. She is the author of *The Short Story: A Critical Introduction*.

Index

Index

Muir, Edwin, 152–53
Mussolini, Benito, 157

Newman, John Henry, 25, 60–3, 66, 99, 198, 200

O'Brien, Flann, 119
O'Malley, Father, 194
Orwell, George, 95

Paulson, Ronald, 137
Pavlova, Anna, 88. 159
Penzoldt, Peter, 24
Picasso, Pablo, 46, 143
Proust, Marcel, 25, 45, 175, 176, 179

Radcliffe, Ann, 34
Ramsay, Allan, 152

Sacks, Sheldon, 132
Scholes, Robert, 76
Scott, Alexander, 164
Scott, Sir Gilbert, 57
Scott, Sir Walter, 152
Sharp, Alan, 148, 163, 164
Shell, Marc, 198
Shelley, Mary, 23, 114, 115, 116, 120, 150
Sheridan, Richard Brinsley, 41
Smith, Maggie, 163
Spark, Muriel, Works by: *The Abbess of Crewe*, 30, 35, 41, 134–35, 137, 162; *The Bachelors*, 25, 26, 28, 33, 35, 48, 54, 98, 100, 121, 122, 124–25, 127, 137, 138, 163, 193; *The Ballad of Peckham Rye*, 26, 33, 74, 137, 139, 142, 162, 170; *Bang-bang You're Dead and Other Stories*, 65, 168–79; *Child of Light*, 115; *Collected Poems 1*, 44–6, 184–203; *The Comforters*, 30, 32, 37, 49–50, 77–9, 84, 112, 115, 118, 126, 137, 140, 141, 150; *Doctors of Philosophy*, 135; *The Driver's Seat*, 30, 32, 36, 40, 75–7, 97, 132, 134, 136, 137; *Emily Brontë*, 116; *The*

Girls of Slender Means, 27, 30, 32, 35, 37, 47, 50–5, 57, 63, 102, 104–5, 116, 121, 122, 137, 142, 162; *The Go-Away Bird with Other Stories*, 137, 169–79; *The Hothouse by the East River*, 29, 30, 38, 97, 107, 122, 136, 137, 138, 141, 162, 195–97; *Loitering With Intent*, 24–5, 27–8, 35, 36, 37, 47–69, 79–84, 99, 102, 106, 112, 116, 120, 129, 136, 138–39, 140–41, 162; *The Mandelbaum Gate*, 25, 27, 30, 32–3, 98–9, 105, 132–33, 135, 162, 167, 190, 194; *Memento Mori*, 30, 31, 35, 36, 71, 77, 98, 101, 116, 135, 137, 138, 140, 142; *Not To Disturb*, 30, 32, 35, 37, 40, 97, 121, 123, 134, 136–37, 140, 162; *The Prime of Miss Jean Brodie*, 35–6, 39, 82–91, 96, 101–4, 114, 123, 135, 136, 137, 150, 154–63, 177; *The Public Image*, 29, 36, 37, 48, 71–4, 132, 135, 162; *Robinson*, 24, 36, 47, 63, 135, 141; *The Takeover*, 29, 31, 32, 35, 38, 40, 107, 134, 137, 138; *Territorial Rights*, 30, 35, 37, 38, 40, 137, 138, 139
Stanford, Derek, 36, 50, 53, 54, 57–8, 60, 121, 124, 125, 127, 128, 130, 138, 150, 163, 183, 188, 189, 193, 200
Steiner, George, 200
Stevenson, R. L., 152, 156, 159, 167, 171
Stubbs, Patricia, 26–7, 132, 184
Sutherland, W. O. S., 133

Thatcher, Margaret, 171
Thomas, Dylan, 54
Thomson, James, 165
Todorov, Tzvetan, 34, 39
Tolkien, J. R. R., 197, 198
Trilling, Lionel, 41

Walpole, Horace, 23, 38
Waugh, Evelyn, 77, 95, 104
Weir, Major, 156
Williams, Gordon, 148, 163, 164
Woolf, Virginia, 94
Worcester, David, 138